Robert Hutton is the UK political correspondent for Bloomberg News. He studied Artificial Intelligence at Edinburgh University before going on to work at the *Daily Mirror* and the *Financial Times*. He is the author of *Romps, Tots and Boffins: The Strange Language of News* and *Would They Lie to You?: How to Spin Friends and Manipulate People*, both of which were shortlisted for the Paddy Power Political Book Awards.

🐦 @RobDotHutton
www.roberthutton.co.uk

Praise for *Agent Jack*

'Eye-opening from start to finish. Pacy, original and frequently chilling, Hutton offers a fascinating new take on the story of the Home Front'
Henry Hemming, author of *M: Maxwell Knight, MI5's Greatest Spymaster*

'A gripping book by a talented new spy-writer which illuminates a shocking episode in our wartime history. Fans of Ben Macintyre's books will love this'
Tim Shipman, author of *All Out War: The Full Story of Brexit*

'Robert Hutton's deeply researched, often astounding book describes how a loose network of homegrown fascists plotted to undermine wartime Britain, and explains the ingenious way MI5 attempted to neutralise them . . . Hutton includes transcripts of eavesdropped conversations with these fanatics that would make your hair stand on end' Anthony Quinn, *Guardian*

'Robert Hutton has written a well-researched, highly readable account of Roberts's strange undercover life'
Ben Macintyre, *The Times*

A supporter of the Imperial Fascist League in London in the 1930s

AGENT JACK

The True Story of MI5's
Secret Nazi Hunter

ROBERT HUTTON

WEIDENFELD & NICOLSON

First published in Great Britain in 2018
This paperback edition published in 2019 by Weidenfeld & Nicolson
an imprint of The Orion Publishing Group Ltd
Carmelite House, 50 Victoria Embankment
London EC4Y 0DZ

An Hachette UK Company

1 3 5 7 9 10 8 6 4 2

A CIP catalogue record for this book is
available from the British Library.

ISBN (paperback) 978 1 4746 0513 7
ISBN (audio) 978 1 4091 6918 5
ISBN (ebook) 978 1 4746 0514 4

Typeset by Input Data Services Ltd, Somerset

Printed and bound in Great Britain by Clays Ltd, Elcograf S.p.A.

www.orionbooks.co.uk

Contents

CONTENTS

List of Illustrations

Note to the Reader

This is a true story. It has never before been told in full. The handful of people who knew it were sworn to secrecy. Such oaths are occasionally broken, but unlike some of British intelligence's other Second World War operations, this was one no one wanted to boast about.

Since 1945, Britain has told itself a story about the war. In this narrative, not only did the country stand alone against the military forces of fascism, but it was also uniquely resistant to the ideology itself. While other nations succumbed to such ideas or collaborated with invaders, Britain stood firm. That strength of character saved not just the UK, but all of Europe.

But MI5 knew a different story. By the end of the war, it had identified hundreds of apparently loyal British men and women who longed for a Nazi conquest. A few had gone further, risking their lives to help Hitler.

Even more worryingly, most of these traitors lived in a single ordinary London suburb, and had been identified by a single agent. Underneath the spirit of the Blitz, he had uncovered another set of loyalties.

Much of what that agent found has been destroyed in the decades since. But among the records that have survived are more than 600 pages of transcripts of conversations, made between 1942 and 1944, in which British citizens discuss how best to betray their country to Germany. The tale of what they said, and how they came to be saying it, is one that caused deep unease among the few who knew it. But it is time for those voices to be heard.

Dramatis Personae

MI5*

Jasper Harker – Director 1940–41, Deputy Director-General 1941–46

David Petrie – Director-General from 1941

Guy Liddell – Director, B Division (Espionage)

Dick White – Deputy Director, B Division

Maxwell Knight – Head of M Section (Agents)

Victor Rothschild – Head of B1C (Sabotage)

Theresa Clay – Assistant officer B1C

Tess Mayor – Assistant officer B1C

Cynthia Shaw – Assistant B1C

Tar Robertson – Head of Double Cross

Jack Curry – Head of F Division (Subversive Activities) then Research

Roger Hollis – succeeded Curry as head of F Division

Edward Blanshard Stamp – Officer

Jimmy Dickson – Officer

John Bingham – Officer

Dick Brooman-White – Officer

The Government

Edward Tindal Atkinson – Director of Public Prosecutions

Alexander Maxwell – Permanent Under-Secretary of State, Home Office

---

* Over the course of the war, officers at MI5 arrived, were promoted and left. The organisation itself was restructured twice. Some job titles and departmental names here are simplified, and deal with the roles people were in when they encountered the Fifth Column case.

John Anderson – Home Secretary 1939–40
Herbert Morrison – Home Secretary 1940–45
Norman Birkett – Head of the Advisory Committee on internment
  cases
Duff Cooper – Member of Parliament, Head of the Security Ex-
  ecutive, overseeing MI5
William Strang – diplomat

The Roberts Family

Eric – codenames '102', 'M/F', 'SR'. Alias 'Jack King'.
Audrey (née Sprague)
Max
Peter
Crista

The Leeds Fascists

Reg Windsor
Michael Gannon
Walter Longfellow
Angela Crewe
Private Robert Jeffery
Sydney Charnley
A. D. Lewis, alias 'Mr Wells' – the informer

The Kent Sympathisers

Walter Wegener – Siemens employee
Dorothy Wegener – his sister
Bobby Engert – Dorothy's friend
Edward Engert – Bobby's brother
Friedel Engert – Edward's wife
Martin Engert – father of Bobby and Edward

Other Fascist Sympathisers

Irma Stapleton
Gunner Philip Jackson

The Fifth Column

Marita Perigoe
Bernard Perigoe
Charles Perigoe
Emma Perigoe
Eileen Gleave
Hilda Leech
Edgar Bray
Sophia Bray
Nancy Brown
Hans Kohout
Adolf Herzig
Luise Herzig
Ronald Creasy
Rita Creasy
Serafina Donko
Maria Lanzl
Alwina Thies

1

'A great deal about sabotage and arson'

Mr Jones, assistant controller at the Westminster Bank, put down the phone in a puzzled mood. There was much to trouble any Englishman that day, even one sitting, as Jones did, in the head-quarters of one of the City of London's most important banks. The previous day, 10 June 1940, Italy had entered the war on Germany's side. And while Adolf Hitler was gaining allies, Britain was running out of them: across the Channel, the French were on the point of surrender in the face of an unstoppable German advance. Britain was Europe's final bastion of freedom and Hitler's next target. The country was drawing up plans to face the most serious invasion threat to its shores in almost a thousand years.

But at the front of Jones's mind was the conversation he'd just finished, with a mysterious man from the military who wanted the Westminster Bank's help.

What was most puzzling was the nature of the request. It had come the previous day in a letter – marked 'Secret, Personal' – from the man he'd just spoken to, Lt Col Allen Harker. Harker's question was in itself simple enough: could the bank release one of its staff immediately for special war work? Harker had been vague in his letter about both the work and what he called simply 'my organisation', but when Jones consulted his superiors, the answer was clear: there was no question of refusing. In the country's hour of need, the Westminster Bank would not be found wanting.

In Jones's view, the man the government wanted was no great loss to the Westminster Bank. Eric Roberts had been a clerk there for fifteen years, during which time he had failed to distinguish himself. Indeed, he was best known for playing tiresome pranks on his superiors and even on customers. It was typical of Roberts that at the very moment the future of the nation hung in the balance, and when apparently he alone of the Westminster Bank's staff could make a difference, he had gone on holiday.

Eric Roberts at the start of the war

It wasn't just Roberts's career that was unremarkable. He had married a fellow bank clerk and they now lived with their two young sons in an unexceptional semi-detached house in the unexceptional London suburb of Epsom. Roberts was ordinary in every way.

But Harker had been clear that it was Roberts they wanted. Jones began to dictate a letter, confirming what he'd said in the phone call, that Roberts would be made available immediately. Even Harker's address was mysterious: Box 500, Parliament Street.

To a better-informed man, this would have been the clue. Box 500 was the postal address of the secret state. The day before Jones spoke to him, Harker – Jasper to his friends – had himself received a summons. He had been called to see the prime minister, Winston Churchill, who had appointed him director of the Security Service, MI5.

Jones knew none of this. And although he did know that in wartime one was not supposed to ask questions, he could not help adding a line to his letter: 'What we would like to know here is, what are the particular and especial qualifications of Mr Roberts – which we have not been able to perceive – for some particular work of national importance?'

*

Two months after that phone call, as the sun faded at the end of a fine summer's day, a pair of young men in Leeds set out to burn down a shop.

That night, as every night since the start of the war, the blackout was strictly in force. In an effort to stop lights from the ground helping enemy bombers to find their targets, the country plunged itself into darkness. On top of rationing and the other hardships of wartime, people had the nightly chore of covering every window and doorway with thick black cloth to prevent any possible leak of light. Air-raid wardens patrolled towns whose street lamps were unlit, looking for signs of light and warning transgressors. As pedestrians groped their way through the darkness, forbidden even from lighting a cigarette, cars navigated by the faint glow of masked headlights. Accident rates – and crime rates – soared.

There was no moon as Reginald Windsor and Michael Gannon walked through the pitch-dark streets. Neither man looked like an aspiring arsonist. Windsor, at twenty-seven, was the older of the pair by a year. An unexceptional-looking young man with a tendency to talk too much, he worked long hours in the newsagent and tobacconist he owned, while Gannon worked as a driver. They could have passed for any two young men on a night out. But theirs wasn't a friendship forged over sport or a drink in the pub. Their bond was fascism.

Windsor wasn't very good at making friends. Indeed, Gannon was one of the very few he had. He wasn't a big drinker, he didn't like billiards or card games, and though he'd played a bit of football, he hadn't really got on with the other players. The first person he'd found that he felt he could open up to was his wife, Margaret. They'd married in 1937 and she was now two months pregnant.

It was a hard world to be bringing a child into. Over the previous decade, Windsor had seen the effects of the Great Depression on his city. 'I remember seeing the same persons on the street corners with no prospects at all in life,' he said of the 1930s. He would go home and tell his mother about the indignity of 'men having to wash the clothes while their wives went to work'. The politicians, he said, had 'not nursed the people – from my point of view I honestly believe they have neglected many things in this country'.

Local politicians, as well as those in London, were the target of Windsor's anger. He was pretty sure that Leeds' city councillors were lining their own pockets at the expense of honest taxpayers like himself. And it was these thoughts that had led Windsor, like 40,000 others, to join the fascists of Sir Oswald Mosley's British Union. Mosley argued that the political system was failing the people and destroying Britain and her empire. The age of democracy was over. What was needed was a strong leader with the power to bring about change, unfettered by Parliament. These ideas had enjoyed some wider popularity in the early 1930s, but as people had seen how they worked in practice in Germany, support had ebbed – one reason that in 1937 Mosley had dropped the final two words from the name of the British Union of Fascists. Mosley became increasingly associated with the violence of his Blackshirts, the uniformed young men who were supposed to keep order at his events. He also began to talk more and more about 'the Jewish Question'.

Windsor had joined the British Union around the time of the Munich crisis of 1938, when it enjoyed a small resurgence. The prime minister, Neville Chamberlain, was wrestling with Hitler's demand that he be allowed to annex parts of Czechoslovakia. To Windsor and many others, it had seemed the country might be dragged into war by the same politicians who couldn't even help ordinary people put food on their tables. Two of Windsor's older brothers had fought in the Great War, and one of them had been seriously wounded. So, like a lot of Britons, he had been relieved that Chamberlain had been able to broker 'peace for our time' with Hitler that September. As Mosley said, war with Germany would mean sending Britons to die in a 'Jews' quarrel'.

Like Mosley, Windsor didn't see himself as anti-Semitic. He didn't, he said, hate Jews. But he did blame them for many of the problems he faced. One of the reasons Mosley argued that democracy was a sham was that governments were powerless in the face of 'money power', the bankers of Wall Street and the City of London who manipulated prices so as to profit at the expense of ordinary people. And who were these bankers? 'Throughout the ages Jews have taken a leading part in international usury and all forms of finance and money lending,' Mosley explained in his 1938 book, *Tomorrow We Live*.

To Windsor, it seemed that the Jews had all the advantages. When Mosley railed against 'international finance' and the harm it did the ordinary man, Windsor knew exactly what he was talking about. When he read that Mosley promised to close down 'the great chain and multiple stores, largely created by alien finance', Windsor nodded in agreement.

In the BU, Windsor had found his cause. He'd also found some friends. He became the treasurer of the BU's North Leeds branch. As war loomed in 1939, he, along with other members of the party, campaigned for peace. As Mosley argued, war with Germany would be a 'world disaster'. And the people pushing for it were the usual suspects: the Jews, angry that Hitler had 'broken the control of international finance'.

Once war broke out, a lot of BU members disappeared. Some had been called up to the military, and some simply stopped coming to meetings. But Windsor kept the faith. In March 1940, he signed up to help campaign for the BU candidate in the local parliamentary by-election. In a sign of the shift in public mood, the party won just 722 votes. The only other candidate, a Conservative, swept to victory with 97 per cent of the vote.*

At the start of May, Chamberlain was forced to resign as prime minister after the Allies were routed by the advancing German forces in Norway, and was replaced by Winston Churchill. At the end of the month, France collapsed in the face of a swift German advance. This military disaster seemed, to Mosley's supporters, to vindicate his stance. Why were British soldiers being sent to die to defend France when French soldiers had so little interest in fighting themselves? Hitler had shown himself to be the greatest military commander of the age, but he wanted to come to terms with Britain, so why not do just that?

This view wasn't confined to fascists. The Foreign Secretary, Lord Halifax, put out diplomatic feelers to Benito Mussolini's government in Italy to see if it could help broker peace talks with

---

* Almost a British record, but beaten two months later by the 98.7 per cent of the vote that the Conservative candidate won over the BU in the Middleton and Prestwich by-election.

Germany. Churchill, weeks into his job as prime minister, had to outmanoeuvre his own colleague to win support for continuing the war.

Churchill's pledge to fight on was made more credible by what was to happen that week on the other side of the Channel. With hundreds of thousands of British troops stranded at Dunkirk, the Royal Navy ordered every ship on the south coast of England to sail for France. Over the space of nine days, between 26 May and 4 June, more than 330,000 men were rescued, despite attacks from the German navy and air force. Britain now had the troops to fight Hitler, even if they'd been forced to leave much of their equipment behind.

But this victory in turn raised an immediate question on both sides of the Channel: if Britain could move hundreds of thousands of men from France to England under enemy fire, why couldn't Germany? German planners began to work out how they might pull off such a feat, while in Britain the generals debated how best to fight off the invader. Everywhere there were reminders that the government expected the Germans to arrive soon: obstacles in fields to stop planes from landing; road signs removed for fear they might assist the enemy.

If ordinary Britons questioned whether invasion really was a possibility, the government did its best to remove such doubts when, in the middle of June, it sent a leaflet to every household in the country entitled 'If the Invader Comes'. Its message was that everyone must play their part in the coming struggle. 'Hitler's invasions of Poland, Holland and Belgium were greatly helped by the fact that the civilian population was taken by surprise,' the leaflet explained. 'They did not know what to do when the moment came. *You must not be taken by surprise.*' The public response was mixed. Some people were terrified, while others felt the leaflet's patronising tone was ridiculous.

Everywhere, able-bodied men were being pressed into service. In his late twenties, Windsor was a prime candidate for the military. Failing that, he could have been among the 1.5 million men who by August had signed up for the Local Defence Volunteers. But when he was called up, he secured an extension, saying he needed time to sell his business or find a manager. He was, he claimed later, prepared to sign up as an engineer, but what he wanted 'to avoid if possible was getting into any part of the Army where I might have to walk miles', because it disagreed with his feet.

One of Churchill's first acts as prime minister was to respond to growing fears about the loyalty of the British Union by outlawing the party and locking up Mosley and the group's other leaders. The popular press welcomed the move. 'Britain's pocket Fuehrer is hauled in,' the Daily Express trumpeted. The Daily Mirror felt this was long overdue. 'Precautions that should have been taken years ago are now being applied to the Judas Association (British Branch),' it told its readers.

Windsor had responded to the crackdown by destroying all of his BU branch's paperwork – he said he didn't want the police to find anything that might lead them to other members. But in secret, he fought on. He kept his branch going, organising meetings in the back room of his shop where his little group discussed how Britain had been dragged into war against its natural ally by the Jews, and what they might do to restore common sense to the nation. Which would clearly come only with a swift military defeat for the Churchill government.

How could they help to bring that about? They discussed carrying out sabotage operations against airfields and factories. They considered whether they could gather military intelligence and pass it to Germany. And they talked about whether they could blow things up during the blackout. It was the final idea that Windsor and Gannon planned to put into action that August evening. By starting a fire in Leeds city centre, they hoped to guide the Luftwaffe's bombers in. They would strike a blow against the war effort, against the blackout, and for Germany. And they would do it in a way that chimed with one of Windsor's personal grievances.

Sidney Dawson and his wife Dolly together ran a small chain of shops across Leeds. Known locally as 'the Murder Man', thanks to his slogan 'We Don't Cut Prices – We Murder Them', Sidney was the kind of competitor – undercutting his own business – that Windsor loathed. This was also, he knew, exactly the sort of business Mosley had in mind when he attacked 'alien finance' and 'price-cutting': the Dawsons were Jewish. 'A cheap place where actually it was all rubbish,' was Windsor's verdict on Dawson's.

Even though the stock was cut-price, 'it was not worth the price the fellow used to ask'.

So, Windsor had selected as the evening's target a branch of Dawson's on Wellington Road, which ran south-west out of the city centre. The shop had the strategic advantage of being close to several railway yards and right next to the main London, Midland and Scottish Railway line. Some nearby gas towers would also burn well if bombed.

The buildings along Wellington Road were black with soot and grime. Tramlines ran down the middle of the wide, cobbled street, but there was no sign of activity that night. The two men approached Dawson's cautiously and stood in the doorway. The building was silent. They took turns to peer through the letter box. No one there. But then, just as they were preparing to act, they heard a noise from the flat above the shop. The pair panicked and fled.

Once they'd got to what they judged a safe distance, they collected themselves and considered what to do. They wanted to go through with their plan, but they didn't dare go back to Wellington Road. There was, however, another branch of Dawson's about twenty minutes' walk away. It wasn't quite as central as the Wellington Road branch, but it was right next to a railway viaduct, and another gasworks. Surely those would be useful targets for the Luftwaffe?

This time, the two were determined to go through with their mission. As they peered through the second shop's letter flap, they could see some kind of curtain on the other side, probably a blackout measure. They didn't have much to start a fire with, except a cigarette lighter, so they pulled out the petrol-soaked wool from it, and started to push it through the slit.

Just then, the slow rising and falling wail of the air-raid sirens began. The bombers were coming! Windsor would later claim he'd told Gannon to wait for the raid to pass, but it seems unlikely that the two nervous young men would have been prepared to stay crouched in a shop doorway as the sirens howled above them, especially when their purpose was to help the bombers.

With Windsor standing with his back to the door to conceal his friend, Gannon lit the wool from the lighter and quickly pushed it through the door. They saw a flash as some paper on the floor caught fire, and ran.

The two were therefore not around to see their arson attempt thwarted. After they'd disappeared, someone spotted the flames in the shop and called the fire brigade, who put it out before much damage had been done. In any case, there was no Luftwaffe raid. The enemy planes that had been spotted over England's north-east coast sixty miles away turned back without attacking.

Windsor and Gannon may have been disappointed not to have caused a larger fire, or to have summoned the bombers, but they still succeeded in scaring Sidney and Dolly Dawson. Two weeks after the arson attempt, the couple put their only child, twelve-year-old Olive, on board the *Duchess of Atholl* liner to Canada, where she would spend the next four years living with her aunt. In their view, England wasn't safe for Jewish children any more.

What neither Windsor nor Gannon suspected that Sunday evening, as they hurried away through the darkness with the sirens sounding the single high note of the All Clear, was that MI5 was already on their trail.

Three weeks earlier the Secret Intelligence Service, MI6, responsible for espionage operations outside British territory, had passed a letter to its sister agency MI5, the Security Service. From someone calling himself A. D. Lewis, it warned that some members of the banned British Union of Fascists were continuing to meet in Leeds. A second letter repeating the allegation arrived at MI6 a fortnight later, which, since domestic counter-subversion was MI5's job, they again passed on.

That summer, MI5 was a service in chaos. The declaration of war had led to a huge expansion of its responsibilities, and a recruitment drive to match. In search of more space, the organisation shifted its offices from the seventh floor of Thames House, a few minutes upriver from the Houses of Parliament, to Wormwood Scrubs prison. Sitting in the recently vacated cells – and, on occasion, accidentally getting locked into them – the staff were overwhelmed by reports of German spying and sabotage sent in by suddenly suspicious members of the public.

But the letters from Lewis were noticed, and taken seriously. Three weeks after the first one arrived at MI5, and a couple

of days after Windsor and Gannon's arson expedition, Lewis
visited London, where he was interviewed by MI5 officers responsible for investigating right-wing groups. He had a story
to tell.

Two months earlier, shortly after the BU leaders had been arrested, Lewis had walked into Windsor's shop and, after checking
they were alone, turned back the lapel on his coat to reveal a
badge with the distinctive lightning-bolt-in-a-circle of the BU. 'I
am not a copper,' he'd begun. Instead, he said, he was a bus driver
called Wells, and a fellow fascist. He also claimed that he'd been
sent to make contact with Windsor by a mutual acquaintance in
the West Leeds BU. According to the account he gave MI5, Lewis
was a loyal citizen who had learned that Windsor's group was
still meeting in secret, and had decided to find out what it was
up to.

Business had been hard for Windsor in recent months – a
number of customers had taken to avoiding a shop run by a
fascist – but he'd begun to pick up business from soldiers training
at the Royal Army Medical Corps hospital up the road. On their
afternoons off, they would often come to loaf around his shop's
back room, play cards or darts, or borrow books from the tiny
library he kept there. But on Sunday evenings the room had another purpose, as Lewis discovered when Windsor invited him to
come to a meeting.

As well as Windsor and Gannon, there were around half a
dozen fellow BU members present. Lewis told MI5 that the group
had come up with three plans to further the fascist cause: throw
bombs; sabotage factories and airfields; and pass information on
to Germany.

The first idea had been rejected because they didn't have the
funds (or, in all likelihood, the ability) to make bombs. They
also feared that such a brazen act would lead the government to
decide to arrest those BU members who were still at liberty, such
as themselves. The other two plans, they felt, had merit but so
far had remained simply talk. The only woman in the group, a
nineteen-year-old shop assistant called Angela Crewe, was particularly taken with the idea of passing information to Germany.
Lewis told MI5 that she'd 'said that she could contact serving
officers and could obtain information regarding the location of

aerodromes and vital factories'. How exactly she planned to do this wasn't explained, but she may have seen herself as Yorkshire's answer to Mata Hari.

Windsor would later claim that he had been suspicious of 'Wells' all along, not least because of his initial insistence that he wasn't with the police. But he invited him to the meetings, and agreed that Wells should travel to London to try to make contact with other BU members. Which was what Windsor thought Wells was doing as he sat with the men from MI5.

Lewis's account excited the Security Service. 'Although these people are of no great importance in themselves the case is worthy of mention in that it throws considerable light on the general question of Fascist and "Fifth Column" activities in this country,' a report noted. This was the question greatly troubling MI5 at the time: how many disloyal people were there in the country, and how might they be uncovered?

Around the world it was accepted that part of the reason for Hitler's swift advance through Europe had been networks of agents behind the lines, so-called 'Fifth Columnists' who passed information to the advancing troops, sheltered parachutists and carried out sabotage operations. The *Chicago Daily News* told its readers that the capture of Norway's cities was not the work of soldiers. 'They were seized with unparalleled speed by means of a gigantic conspiracy,' it explained. 'By bribery and extraordinary infiltration on the part of Nazi agents, and by treason on the part of a few highly placed Norwegian civilians, and defence officials, the German dictatorship built its Trojan Horse inside Norway.' The article, which was reprinted in several British papers, claimed that the commander of a Norwegian naval base had been ordered not to oppose the German forces, and that a minefield elsewhere had been disconnected from its control point. If anyone was inclined to doubt these tales, it was undeniable that in the hours after Germany invaded Norway, the country's former defence minister and leader of its fascist party, Vidkun Quisling, had attempted to seize power and order troops to stand down. In Britain, his name rapidly passed into the language as a synonym for 'traitor'.

MI5's job was to find the Fifth Columnists in Britain before the Germans invaded. One avenue was to monitor German citizens still living in Britain, but British fascists were the next obvious people to investigate.

Lewis's testimony seemed to offer both proof that Fifth Column groups existed and a way into the organisation. Guy Liddell, MI5's head of counter-espionage, noting the group's existence in his diary, mused that perhaps the Security Service itself could put the Leeds fascists in touch with German spies in Portugal – the neutral country with links to both Britain and Germany that was the jumping-off point for much of the war's espionage – possibly with the goal of using them to gain access to the enemy's intelligence networks.

MI5 sent Lewis back to Leeds and considered their options. The idea of allowing Lewis to work the case on his own was rejected. Although he was obviously a man of some initiative, and MI5 were inclined to think him both honest and loyal to his country, a case such as this required considerable subtlety. It was vital not to cross the line from undercover operative to agent provocateur – from observing illegal acts to instigating them. As they questioned Lewis, it had become clear to the MI5 officers that he had not observed this rule. Leaving the ethics of such behaviour aside, it would scupper any prosecution if the government's witness was revealed to have encouraged the wrongdoing.

So they decided to send in their own man alongside Lewis. On Friday 23 August, Eric Roberts, late of the Euston Road branch of the Westminster Bank, arrived in Leeds. His orders were to assess Windsor's group for himself, and report on their intentions, what danger they represented – and to what extent their behaviour was the result of Lewis's encouragement.

It was a delicate mission to give to a man who had joined MI5 less than two months earlier, at the start of July. Before he left for Leeds, Roberts was warned about how far he could go as an undercover agent. 'It was impressed on him very strongly that once he was satisfied that these persons either separately or jointly were prepared to act in an illegal manner, it was quite justifiable for him to represent himself as a sympathiser or collaborator,' Sydney Noakes, the lawyer running the case, wrote. 'But that under no circumstances must he make suggestions to them which might in any way be considered provocation.'

The man who walked with 'Wells' into Windsor's shop that

afternoon was six foot tall with tanned skin and dark, close-cropped hair that was thinning on top, making him look older than his 33 years. He was well built, with the controlled move-ments of an athlete. Under the shade of his trilby hat could be seen a distinctive scar on his cheek. It hinted that this man was familiar with danger, and might be dangerous himself. Windsor's immediate instinct was caution.

But then the man began talking.

Eric Roberts's charm was hard to resist. His smile carried warmth and humour but also something more: a sense that he was genuinely pleased to meet you. It was a smile that made other people smile back. Windsor's momentary doubt disappeared. Whoever this man was, he liked him.

Lewis introduced him. This was Mr Roberts, a British Union contact he had made in London. Windsor was enthusiastic. The men chatted briefly, but agreed that it would be best to talk in private. They would rendezvous that evening at Windsor's home.

The shopkeeper lived with his wife a couple of minutes away, on an estate of recently built bay-fronted houses. When they met there, Roberts set about winning Windsor's trust. Smoking cig-arette after cigarette, he took the role of a senior BU man, now operating underground since the arrests of his colleagues, building a network around the country. He played the part with humour and gentleness, coaxing his target to trust him. The introverted Windsor was delighted to have this important man on his secret mission sitting in his house and listening with such interest to his opinions and plans, and his enthusiasm for their mutual cause came pouring out.

Under the affable exterior, Roberts was assessing his target. Windsor was 'violently anti-Semitic', he noted, and 'talked a great deal about sabotage and arson'. But was he a serious threat? He certainly claimed to be: the shopkeeper wanted Roberts to put him in touch with someone senior in the BU who could set him to work.

The next day was Saturday, and Windsor took Roberts round Leeds, keen to introduce some of the members of his network. It proved an underwhelming tour, consisting as it did of an elderly Italian waiter whom Windsor insisted was a keen fascist and an optician who could apparently tell them how to make bombs – but refused to do so.

Windsor was keen on bombs. He asked Roberts for his views on the relative merits of throwing them or planting them: personally, he favoured the idea of hurling them from the top of a tram as it made its way through the city. The height would be a great advantage in increasing the range of your throw, and you would be carried away from the site of the blast before anyone had worked out what was happening.

Just as Roberts was wondering if this man was merely a fantasist, Windsor said something that made him sit up. His talk of arson wasn't all theoretical: he and his friend had set fire to a Jewish shop three weeks earlier.

As he described the attack on Dawson's shop to Roberts, Windsor gave it the air of a spur-of-the-moment act. He didn't mention the first, abortive attempt, but instead suggested their failure to start a bigger fire was the result of not having brought out the proper tools with them.

The conversation moved Windsor into a new category. Arson isn't a difficult trick to master, and one attempt meant another was likely. It was only a matter of time before Windsor succeeded in starting a fire. Even if he didn't summon the Luftwaffe, he could still kill people.

At 6 p.m. on the Sunday, Roberts arrived to meet the rest of the group in the back room of Windsor's shop. Angela Crewe wasn't there, but Gannon and three other men were. Their host introduced their guest, and announced that he would now address them on current BU policy. As the party's leaders were all in prison and the organisation was effectively illegal, this was something of a challenge for Roberts, but he did so as best he could. In brief, he said, Mosley's policy since the start of the war had been to leaven his pacifism towards Germany with patriotism for Britain: the BU believed the war was a mistake, but its members would defend their country if it was attacked.

At least one of those present was dissatisfied with these platitudes. One of four brothers who had joined the Blackshirts in the early 1930s, Sydney Charnley was a baker, a small, tough, angry man with receding hair and a thin moustache. His younger brother John had been the BU District Leader in Hull, and was now in prison. The whole family were veterans of the running battles between fascists and communists of the previous decade. One of those fights, in Manchester, had ended with John being thrown through a plate glass window.

Charnley had come along hoping to hear about how the BU was organising active resistance to the government. He wanted Roberts to explain what part they could play and give them orders on illegal activities to undertake – not simply tell them things they already knew about the difficulties they faced.

But there was another reason for Charnley's presence. Windsor had asked him to come and take a look at Roberts. Despite his enthusiasm over the previous two days, Windsor wasn't completely sure of the man from London. Just as other citizens were on a constant lookout for fascist spies, Windsor and his fellow fascists were on permanent watch for the police. There was something funny about Wells, he reckoned, and that was reason enough to suspect the man he'd brought along. If Roberts was a police spy, Charnley would sniff him out soon enough. Charnley had marched with Mosley, had fought in his black shirt in cities the length of the land. He'd know what to ask Roberts.

After three days of being treated as an honoured guest, Roberts now found the tables were turned, as Charnley began asking him question after question about his past in the BU. Which branch had he been a member of, and for how long? Who did he know there? Who else had he met inside the movement? Any of the questions could have been a trap, and only the senior BU member that Roberts claimed to be would have known which.

Roberts had been with MI5 for less than two months and already he was in danger of exposure. Should he run? How far would he get? Even if he made it out of the room, he would be in a lonely street on the outskirts of a city he barely knew. It wouldn't take long for the gang to hunt him down.

Should he fight? Roberts was a judo black belt, and knew karate as well. He could certainly handle Windsor, and probably Gannon at the same time, but Charnley looked like he could be dangerous. And in the small room the likelihood was that the group would be able to overpower him by sheer weight of numbers.

In any case, to flee or to fight would have blown the operation.

He knew he had only one choice. As the interrogation began, Roberts turned his friendly face to Charnley, and prepared to tell the truth.

Well, some of it.

2

'Thoroughly familiar'

Eric Roberts grew up on the edge of Britain, and moved to its centre at the first chance he got.

Cornwall is the westernmost, southernmost county in England, sufficiently separated from the rest of the country by geography, history and culture that some natives deny they're English at all. It's shaped like a long, thin triangle, stretching away from the rest of the country into the Atlantic. Just at the point where this wedge has narrowed almost to nothing there is the town of Penzance, the last significant outpost of humanity for two thousand miles west. In the early 1920s, the town's population was barely more than a couple of thousand. For those seeking isolation and escape from the world's pressures, it was the perfect refuge. For the teenage Eric, it was a place to escape from. And at the age of seventeen, he set out for London. The city was still then the central point of an empire that stretched around the globe, taking in Canada, India, Australia, parts of Africa and more besides. America's economy had just outgrown Britain's, and the former colony had confirmed its emergence as a global power with its intervention in the Great War, but Britain was not yet eclipsed, and its capital was a good place to go in search of adventure.

What Roberts found, in early 1925, was a job as a clerk at the Westminster Bank, working in the Threadneedle Street branch, in the City. The work was hardly exciting, but it paid ninety-five pounds a year, and there were diversions: Roberts's supervisor at the bank, Audrey Sprague, soon took a shine to her charming new trainee.

They made an odd couple. The teenage Roberts had barely finished growing to his six feet, his dark eyes matching his dark hair that resisted attempts to slick it into a parting. Audrey on the other hand was tiny, barely over five feet tall, with hair that had turned completely white with shock during childhood when she had been attacked by a dog.

Eric Roberts and Audrey Sprague in the early 1930s

She was also seven years Eric's senior. In her mid-twenties, she should really have been married by now. But too many of the men of her generation had died in the mud of Flanders. Besides, Audrey Sprague was a young woman who knew her own mind. She was clever, and not embarrassed by it, proud to show off her ability to swiftly add multiple columns of figures in her head.

Eric was delighted to explore London. In Leadenhall Market, near the bank, he found a pub where he could get a 'substantial' beef sandwich, and half a pint of ale, for sixpence. When he was feeling flush, there was a basement restaurant offering a roast mutton dinner for three times that. Or if he was running short, he would live off bananas. 'I was perpetually hungry, tall and thin,' he recalled.

The main reason for Eric's occasional periods of poverty was the difficulty of making the rent. When Audrey learned he was struggling to find somewhere he could afford to live, she told her widowed mother that they should take the young man into their home in Wembley, north-west London. It was an unconventional arrangement at the time, but if anyone passed comment, Audrey didn't let it trouble her. Roberts seemed to have landed on his feet. But he wanted more than just a steady job and a steady girl.

Eric came from a line of frustrated free spirits. His great-great-great-grandfather had been one of the first convicts transported to Australia, in 1787, for stealing some yarn. His grandfather William had trained as a lawyer but had swiftly tired of the work, and followed his forebears into farming. William's son Arthur had moved to Canada as a young man, working with survey parties in northern Ontario. He returned to England in 1906, but still hadn't settled, and caused a family scandal by getting his sweetheart pregnant. In 1907, months after his wedding and slightly fewer months after Eric's birth, Arthur took his new family back to Canada, where he worked as a telegraphist for four years before deciding it was time to return home to Cornwall. There he got a job on the other end of the Western Union telegraph line where it emerged from the Atlantic.

Two daughters followed, but it wasn't an easy marriage: Arthur was still a little wild, especially about money, and Maud, Eric's mother, was forced to run a tight ship to keep the family finances together. But they could afford to send Eric to local private schools, where he was 'an excellent worker, a good student and most intelligent'.

Though he did well enough to win a scholarship at sixteen to the local school of mining, Eric was already dreaming of life beyond Cornwall. He had grown up in the first great era of the spy novel. Rudyard Kipling published *Kim* in 1901. Erskine Childers's *The Riddle of the Sands* appeared in 1903. Joseph Conrad's *The Secret Agent* came out in the year of Eric's birth, 1907. Sherlock Holmes, brought back from the dead in 1903, also got in on the act, hunting spies in *The Second Stain* and *The Bruce-Partington Plans*. The young Eric devoured these tales of stolen secrets, of police agents hunting revolutionaries, often on the streets of Britain, where it seemed that your apparently ordinary next-door neighbour could be hiding a terrible truth. He began to fantasise about whether he, too, could become such a spy.

A year in mining college was enough to assure Eric, who was never comfortable with machinery, that he had neither aptitude for the work, nor a desire to spend his life mining tin in Cornwall. He quit the course and set off for London, 'full of hope and enthusiasm, and ambition'.

But working in a bank wasn't for Roberts either. His mind found other diversions, largely pranks, played largely on his superiors. He noticed that one manager was regular in his habits, visiting the toilet at the same time each day. So he made the room appear occupied, propping a jacket up on a broomstick against the opaque window in the door, and enjoyed the spectacle of his boss's increasing discomfort. Or there was the visiting bank dignitary who discovered his car had been filled with toilet rolls. Or the Japanese client whose umbrella was loaded with hole-punch confetti. Or the time Roberts hid a dead fish in a drawer, and enjoyed the bafflement of his colleagues as they sought out the source of the smell.

These were all good entertainments, which endeared him to Audrey at least. But they were less popular with his bosses, who saw no reason to promote him. He, in return, couldn't bring himself to dream of the day he would be deputy manager of a suburban branch of the Westminster Bank.

So what did he want to be, this teenager who had moved so far from home? A man of action, perhaps, or a patriot. But in 1925, it wasn't clear what patriotism meant any more. Was it loyalty to King and Empire, the sort of ideas that had just seen millions sent to their deaths in the Great War? Or was it more patriotic to dream of a world in which all men were equal, in which a teenager wasn't doomed to be a bank clerk because his father was a telegraphist? For the first time, such a world seemed possible.

The devastation of the Great War had given fresh urgency to questions that had long existed about the traditional order of things. The men who had fought together in the trenches asked why some were born to rule and others to serve. In Parliament, it was recognised that it was unacceptable to deny the vote to millions of men who had fought in the war simply because they couldn't afford to own property, and in 1918 all men over twenty-one were awarded the vote. Women, too, gained victories in their fight for democratic rights, and were finally given parity with men in 1928.

These new voters had changed the make-up of Parliament. The working classes now had a chance to vote for the party that represented them, Labour. Outside Parliament, trades unions were flexing their muscles on behalf of those same working men.

Meanwhile, although the acquisition of German territories at the end of the war had left Britain's empire larger than ever, there was weakness within, as Ireland's war of independence had just demonstrated.

If things had stopped there, it might have been unwelcome enough to the ruling classes, but for those who looked abroad there were more worrying precedents. Russia's still-fresh revolution had resulted in millions of deaths, and the stated intention of the Soviet Union's new leaders was to export communism around the world. Who was to say they wouldn't succeed? In 1913, the Tsar had been on his throne, and the Austro-Hungarian Empire had stretched across Eastern and Central Europe. Now, just a decade later, both were gone. This was not a time to trust to old certainties.

One woman who wasn't prepared to sit on the sidelines was Rotha Lintorn-Orman. Born in 1895 to a wealthy military family, she had been one of the first Girl Guides, and then volunteered as an ambulance driver during the war, winning decorations for gallantry before being invalided home in 1917. There she ran the British Red Cross motor school, training drivers for the battlefield. But with the war over, she struggled to go back to the place allotted to a young gentlewoman. She drank heavily, cut her dark hair short and wore a shirt and tie, leading others to describe her pejoratively as a 'mannish woman'. As she dug her garden and contemplated the socialist menace that threatened her country, she realised that her calling was to fight it. Financed by her mother, Lintorn-Orman found her model in Benito Mussolini, the new prime minister of Italy, and in 1923 she named her new organisation the British Fascisti in tribute to him.

In her regard for the Italian leader, Lintorn-Orman was hardly unusual. On the British right at the time, Mussolini was more admired than understood. The common perception was that he had imposed order on a chaotic nation and seen off the communist threat. Churchill called him 'the saviour of his country'.

For Lintorn-Orman, the important thing about fascism was less what it stood for than what it stood against: disorder and socialism. Her BF – people joked it stood for 'Bloody Fools' – was, at least at first, deeply conservative, with an enthusiasm for marches and uniforms. Its focus was on recruiting people who would fight back in the event of a communist uprising, not attempting to seize power itself.

Rotha Lintorn-Orman, 1916

One of those recruits was Eric Roberts, who signed up soon after he arrived in London. In later life, he concealed this from his family, so his motives at the time are unclear. A desire to resist communism must have been part of the appeal. Audrey's brother-in-law had been one of a small number of British troops stationed in Russia at the end of the war, fighting the Bolsheviks, and he'd told Eric stories of his time there.

But for a stranger in London, the BF also offered fellowship and community. For a young man who had missed out on the war it offered the chance to wear a smart uniform and to learn military drill. And for a bored bank clerk it offered the possibility of excitement. Across Europe, politics in the 1920s often meant violence. Young men who were struggling to return to normal life after the brutality of the trenches often found a familiarity in the military structure of groups like the BF, and moved easily on to physical attacks on opponents. At the other end of the political spectrum, it was clear that the revolution the communists wanted was likely to involve a lot of killing.

Public meetings, the basic political event of the time, were frequently rowdy as rival groups tried to infiltrate them and break them up. The communists in particular were notorious for trying to storm platforms at right-wing events. In response, some BF members joined together in a secret squad to go and deal violence back to the reds.

Eric did find excitement, but not of this kind. It was through the BF that Eric was to meet the man who would change his life.

Maxwell Knight was seven years older than Eric. This was only the same age gap as that between Eric and Audrey, but with Knight it was enough to make him seem almost of a different generation. Knight had served in the Royal Naval Reserve during the final year of the Great War. As a midshipman in armed merchantmen, he had seen little of the enemy, but he had visited New York on shore leave, giving him the chance to experience the new world. He had fallen in love with jazz, and had realised that the naval career his family planned for him would never do.

Knight was tall, good-looking, socially confident and upper class, apparently just another member of the Bright Young Things who were scandalising and delighting society with their risqué behaviour. But this was a mask. Although he came from a good family, he had no money. His father, a solicitor, had frittered his earnings away on mistresses. The family fortune was held by an uncle who had no desire to fund his nephew's high living. In the years after the war, Knight had worked as a civil servant, a paint salesman, a preparatory school master and a freelance journalist – none of these jobs paying enough to properly fund his social aspirations.

Then, in 1923, Knight was approached by an acquaintance at a political meeting and asked a strange question: would he be interested in some part-time, paid work of a patriotic nature? Short of money and eager for excitement, he replied that he would. Which was how he came to find himself recruited as a spy in an intelligence organisation run by a right-wing industrialist.

Like Lintorn-Orman, Sir George Makgill was both worried about socialism and determined to do something about it. A wealthy man, he decided that what capitalism needed was information about its opponents. To supply it, he set up a freelance organisation which he christened the Industrial Intelligence

Bureau. Its customers were factory owners and companies that wanted to know about potential strikes. Its method was to recruit like-minded people and send them undercover into suspect groups.

Maxwell Knight, 1934

After an interview, Knight was invited to join. But his target wasn't a socialist group at all. It was Lintorn-Orman's British Fascisti.

Why Makgill wanted to keep an eye on the BF isn't clear. It's unlikely he viewed them as a threat: his own views were very much in sympathy with theirs, and in some areas even more extreme. It may simply have been that Makgill thought the BF would be a good place for Knight to recruit more agents.

Knight set off for BF headquarters, offering himself as a volunteer. In the heated atmosphere of 1920s fringe politics, this immediately made him the subject of suspicion: the group believed, correctly, that it was a target for infiltration, though the assumption was that it would be communists, rather than other anti-communists, who would attempt it.

All his life, Knight had been fascinated by nature. He had an extraordinary affinity for creatures of every size and shape – in his London flat he had assembled a menagerie, ranging from mice to a bear. His family had always thought that he would end up making a living working with animals. Now he discovered that the same skills that made for the successful study of timid creatures also made for successful spying: watchfulness, calm, and above all patience.

Rather than push himself on to the BF leadership, Knight hung back, and let them notice him. He was bright and able, and completed the small jobs he was given with ease. Lintorn-Orman identified Knight as someone she thought she could use and, just as Makgill had done, decided that he could have an aptitude for espionage. Within a year of his joining the BF, Knight was appointed its director of intelligence.

This new role allowed him to start running his own agents. The BF's prime target was the same as Makgill's: the Communist Party. Knight hadn't been trained as an agent himself, but he was now in the position of recruiting others. He set about the task with enthusiasm.

From the BF's headquarters in a house in Elm Park Gardens, Chelsea, where the décor was heavy with large union flags and portraits of the King, Knight approached at least fifty potential recruits in his first year. To make so many attempts suggests a scattergun approach, but one of Knight's gifts was to make each of his recruits feel special.

He certainly succeeded with Roberts. A year earlier, he had been an unhappy mining student in Penzance. Now he was being asked to become a spy. It was his childhood fantasy come true.

'I read Kipling's infernal *Kim* at a very early age and read it again several times,' he recalled later. 'Which was the original stimulation that set my mind working in the direction of intelligence.' In the book, Kimball O'Hara is the orphan son of an Irish soldier. He lives on the streets of Lahore where few suspect he isn't just another Indian beggar. His mentor is Mahbub Ali, a Pashtun horse-trader who is also a talent-spotter for British intelligence.

If Roberts was happy to find himself cast as a real-life Kim, Knight excelled in the role of Ali. At the end of the Second World War, he set down what he'd learned about agent-running. Beginning with a defence of the business of espionage, he attacked those who were 'prone to regard an "agent" as an unscrupulous and dishonest person actuated by unworthy motives'. In fact, Knight argued, the opposite was the case. 'An honest and loyal agent, whether he is working for his country in foreign lands, or at home, has often to exhibit some of the highest human qualities.' Knight stated that he preferred to use 'persons whose personal honesty and motives were above reproach', if for no other reason than that such people's reports were more likely to be trustworthy.

This was a little rich coming from Knight. Doubtless he thought of himself as a trustworthy man, but in 1925, he was lying about his family circumstances, and lying about his reason for working for the BF. He was also about to embark on a new, more personal, lie. At the end of the year, Knight married one of the most senior women in the BF, Gwladys Poole. Superficially, they had much in common: she, too, was a Bright Young Thing, and an enthusiastic fascist. But whereas Gwladys was the real thing, on both these matters Knight was something of a fake. As a foundation for a marriage, lying about his personal circumstances and political beliefs was quite bad enough, but a third far more serious lie was quickly added: to Gwladys's growing sadness and frustration, the marriage remained unconsummated. The cause of Knight's difficulty in this area is unclear, but is likely to have been either psychological or medical – the suggestion by one spurned female colleague that he was gay is unsupported by evidence, and he was an enthusiastic flirt with women.

If he was failing as a husband, Knight was at least succeeding as an agent. On behalf of the BF he sent out a series of agents into the Communist Party. One of these was Roberts.

Any political enthusiasm Roberts may have felt for the BF was quickly cast aside once he had met Knight. What were rallies and flag-waving next to espionage? Knight took a long-term attitude to the penetration of suspect organisations. 'It is of little value to employ highly trained agents for the primary purpose of gathering day-to-day information,' he wrote. 'The object of such an agent should always be to penetrate as far into the organisation as possible, with a view to getting himself eventually into a position of responsibility which will enable him to obtain reliable information about the more sinister plans of the organisation.'

This put Knight in the position of defending his operatives from the demands of the bureaucracy that employed them. He rejected the idea that his team should concern itself with 'producing lists of names and addresses, casual movements of individuals, etc'. An intelligence agency, he argued, had other means of collecting that kind of low-level information.

The best way of training an agent, in Knight's view, was 'actual and immediate work in the field'. There was a place for briefing them on the best moments and methods for taking notes, in the memory games that formed such an important part of the instruction of Kipling's Kim, 'but in the main, the real training ground lies in the day-to-day work of the agent'.

This confident assertion of theory hid a more basic reason for Knight's approach: he had very little training to offer his recruits. He knew barely more about espionage than they did, and there was no spy school for these unofficial infiltrators to attend. He and his agents would have to work out their tradecraft for themselves.

For Roberts, this meant being sent along to communist meetings. This was partly to educate him in the movement he was supposed to be studying, and partly in order to set up the next phase of penetration. 'Having spent some time in attending meetings as an ordinary interested individual, it is possible that [an agent] will obtain some casual personal contact with some adherent or official of the organisation in question,' Knight wrote. What he wanted was for the communists to recruit Roberts, not for Roberts to ask to sign up.

'"Approaches" in connection with joining any particular body should if humanly possible always be made by the body to the agent, not the agent to the body,' wrote Knight. 'The importance of this lies in the future, in that if at any time some query is raised regarding the bona fides of the agent, it will nearly always be remembered by the officials of the Movement that the agent did not in any way thrust himself forward.'

More than that, Knight urged his agents to refuse their first invitation: 'A becoming reluctance to join a movement, which is subsequently overcome by the persuasion of the Movement's propagandists, will stand the agent in very good stead.'

Knight set out to flatter the teenage Eric with attention. 'The officer must always adapt himself to the agent, and not the agent to the officer,' Knight wrote. 'Every good agent likes to think that his officer is almost exclusively concerned with him, and with him alone, even though the agent may know perfectly well that the officer has others with whom he deals.'

Knight wasn't an advocate of professional distance. 'The officer running an agent should set himself the task of getting to know his agent most thoroughly. He must at all costs make a friend of his agent: the agent must trust the officer as much as – if not more than – the officer trusts the agent.'

Roberts showed promise with his first report. The Soviet deputy foreign minister was addressing a meeting at a school in north London. It was strictly for Communist Party members only, but Eric managed to gatecrash it. His fountain pen had leaked as he had scrawled his report, but Knight expressed his delight with it.

Spying must have appealed to Roberts's mischievous side: the challenge of talking his way into a place where he didn't belong, the thrill of being the person in the room with a secret. It's unlikely he gave much thought to the potential danger of his work, but it was real. If political activism could turn rough in the 1920s, infiltrators were likely to be on the roughest end of it.

And Knight's agents had no protection except their own wits: no friends waiting within earshot, not even the veil of a false identity. Working under their own names meant they were less likely to be uncovered as an infiltrator, but they also had few places to hide if they were exposed.

Some of those sent into the Communist Party by Knight in those years would go deep: one even followed Knight's path of marrying into the cause while continuing to report on his colleagues and, apparently, his own wife.

Roberts had less success at penetration. Though he did manage to become a Communist Party member, by 1926 Knight just had him doing surveillance work. He was worried about Ivor Montagu, an aristocratic youth who had abandoned his family position for communism.* This was the year of the General Strike, when

---

* Knight was right to be worried about Montagu. By 1940 he was a Soviet agent, under the codename Intelligentsia. However, even though his brother Ewen helped to coordinate Operation Mincemeat, one of the great Second World War deception operations, Ivor's main interests were film-making and table tennis, and he seems to have provided little useful intelligence.

more than a million and a half men refused to work, something that many feared – and others hoped – was the start of a more widespread revolution. Roberts would finish his day at the bank and then go and tail Montagu and 'Silvio', one of his communist contacts.

Knight was now in the position of running the spies of the group on which he was supposed to be spying. But that was only the start of the complications. His covert employer, Sir George Makgill, was passing his reports to Vernon Kell. Before the Great War, Kell had been asked to help establish what would become MI5, of which he would become the first director. In those days, there had been plenty of interest in counter-espionage, but in peacetime, the government could see little point in Kell's work, and he was running a skeleton service. He saw Makgill's organisation as a way to bring in intelligence off the books. And Knight, with Makgill's permission, was also reporting to MI6. Finally, he was also selling information to Special Branch, the police's intelligence arm.

How much did Roberts and his fellow agents know about who Knight was really working for? Knight's general bias was for honesty with his agents, to prevent them feeling betrayed later. And people who had joined the BF in order to protect the nation against communism were unlikely to be greatly troubled at the thought of working for Makgill, or MI5.*

As the 1926 General Strike seemed to be building to a frenzy, Roberts prepared for the possibility that more direct action against the coming revolution might be needed. On 12 May he enrolled as a volunteer policeman, adding three years to his age so as to meet the entry requirements. He was far from alone: the strike saw the number of special constables in London increase from 10,000 to over 60,000. There were troops on the streets of the capital, and on both sides, the idea that an attempted overthrow of the government was imminent seemed likely.

---

* One trace of Eric's reports on Montagu found its way into the official MI5 file on the young communist. 'On May 6th was observed to be in the company of several communists,' a note read, without giving details of who had supplied this information. As an unofficial source of an unofficial source, that was all that Eric Roberts merited.

And then, on the day that Roberts signed up with the police, the strike ended. The revolution hadn't come. In the ensuing relief in government circles, the demand for Knight's intelligence on communists dried up: they'd had their chance at revolution, and they'd blown it. Other anti-communists seemed to agree, and the British Fascisti began to disintegrate. In a further blow to Knight's espionage career, Makgill died a few months later. Knight was without a spymaster, and without customers.

This may explain why, although Roberts remained a Communist Party member for some years, he was, by 1928, at a sufficiently loose end that he re-enrolled as a Special Constable. He was old enough now, but he stuck to his previous lie, telling them he was 24.

The drudgery of the Westminster Bank was by now outweighing the excitement of life in London. 'I grew to hate the life of a clerk,' he recalled. He began to look for ways to improve his lot. 'I studied five nights a week and applied time after time for jobs in South America. I took some nineteen examinations in banking, commerce, commercial law, economics, French, Spanish, German, etc, and hoped vaguely for advancement. I produced the certificates and diplomas but was informed that only a degree would help, which I could not afford.'

Roberts suspected the problem was simpler. 'I lacked that entrée to everything, a public school education.' In an effort to avoid his superiors' snobbery, he took elocution lessons to lose the Cornish accent that he feared made him sound like a country bumpkin.

One thing kept Roberts sane: his blossoming relationship with Audrey. But even here, the bank found a way to obstruct his happiness. As was the norm at the time, the staff of the Westminster Bank were forbidden to marry without their employer's permission. Until Eric's salary reached a set threshold – usually after around a dozen years of service – the bank deemed him unable to support a family.

Not all of Roberts's evening courses were aimed at becoming a better banker. He also learned martial arts. And when he got home, he devoured spy thrillers. He longed to be back in the game.

*

On 8 June 1934, Eric Roberts married Audrey Sprague at Willesden Register Office, without religious ceremony. After a decade of service, he had been allowed to ask the directors of the Westminster Bank for permission, and after a month's consideration, they had graciously consented.

The couple set off on a honeymoon to Germany. It was unusual to honeymoon abroad, and the choice of Hitler's Germany was more unusual still, but Roberts had a German friend he wanted to visit. He may also have hoped that the trip would give him a way back into espionage.

Eric and Audrey Roberts on their honeymoon

In the run-up to the ceremony, he had written at least twice to Knight, the man who had brought him into the secret world. It's possible that, like many men before they marry, he was trying to reconnect with an acquaintance, to keep hold of a treasured part of his earlier life. But it seems just as likely he was looking to renew their working relationship as well. He told Knight about his impending nuptials, and asked whether he would be interested in hearing his impressions of Germany under its new Nazi government. Knight replied with a brief, unsigned note, addressed simply to '102' – Roberts's codename. He would, he said, be delighted to call upon them on their return and hear about their trip.

There had been developments in Knight's own career. After his spying hiatus, a renewed official interest in communism saw him taken on first by MI6 and then, following a turf war between the services over who should spy where, by MI5. Tasked once again with penetrating the Communist Party, he'd reactivated the agents he already had in place. But there had been no work, until now, for Eric. That was to change thanks to the emergence of a new target, one that was a little awkward for Knight.

On the day that Eric and Audrey celebrated becoming man and wife, the British government was facing up to a problem it had long ignored. The previous evening, Sir Oswald Mosley, a Great War veteran who had in the previous decade been first a dashing young Conservative MP and then, after switching sides, a dashing young Labour MP, had held a rally at Olympia in west London for the party he now led, the British Union of Fascists.

The nature of fascism had developed and become clearer since the days of Rotha Lintorn-Orman, and Mosley had become convinced that it was the future. He saw the key elements to its appeal, and copied them. The British Union of Fascists had a distinctive black uniform that had earned them a nickname, a nationalistic message, clearly defined enemies, and an enthusiasm for violence.

Mosley also had some influential supporters. Lord Rothermere, proprietor of the *Daily Mail*, agreed with Mosley's sentiment that 'the new age requires new methods and new men'. Under the headline 'Hurrah for the Blackshirts!', Rothermere set out the case for fascism in January 1934. 'Parliamentary government is conducted on the same lines as it was in the eighteenth century,' he complained, 'though the conditions with which it deals have altered beyond recognition.'

He pointed to the 'gigantic revival of national strength and spirit which a similar process of modernisation has brought about in Italy and Germany. These are beyond all doubt the best-governed nations in Europe today.' What Britain needed if it was to survive, Rothermere said, was a leader 'with the same directness of purpose and energy of method as Mussolini and Hitler have displayed.

MI5 had been reluctant to examine fascism too closely, perhaps in part because the man whose job it would be to do so, Knight, was in sympathy with many of the BUF's views. He was hardly the only member of the establishment who felt that way – Donald

Makgill, the son of the man who had brought Knight into espionage, was also an enthusiastic member of the BUF. The fascists were the sworn enemy of communism, and communism was the threat that most worried Britain's ruling class.

That view began to shift in 1934, in large part because of what happened at Olympia on 7 June. The Blackshirts had held other rallies in London over the previous two years, but this was the largest. Outside, police tried to keep protesters and ticket-holders apart. Inside, order was kept by the Blackshirts. But this wasn't simply a case of trying to see off the sort of disruption in which their communist opponents specialised. Mosley understood that the violence wasn't a distraction from his message: it was part of the appeal. Whenever someone stood to heckle the leader, the spotlights would pick them out, and then Mosley would wait while his uniformed enforcers grabbed the perpetrator and administered swift and public punishment.

But this meeting was different from previous BUF rallies in another way. This time, the audience included members of parliament and churchmen, there to see the character of British fascism for themselves. They were horrified.

'I am not very sympathetic to Communists who try to break up meetings,' Geoffrey Lloyd, a Conservative MP, wrote afterwards. 'But I am bound to say that I was appalled by the brutal conduct of the fascists. I saw with my own eyes case after case of single interrupters being attacked by ten or twenty fascists. Again and again, as five or six fascists carried out an interrupter by arms and legs, several other Blackshirts engaged in hitting and kicking his helpless body. I can only say it was a deeply shocking scene for an Englishman to see in London.'

Others gave similar accounts. 'A woman who intervened in another scuffle in the body of the hall was manhandled first of all by male Blackshirts and then flung to the "tender mercies" of the fermale Blackshirts,' recalled a witness. 'There was tearing and clawing, with the woman screaming. She was stripped naked to the waist . . . A woman behind me rose indignantly and shouted "Disgraceful." A Blackshirt steward leaned over towards her and said menacingly: "It will be better for you if you sit down."' But Lloyd's words were the ones that mattered. He was not simply an MP, he was also the Parliamentary Private Secretary to the former prime minister, Stanley Baldwin. In 1934 Baldwin was Lord President of the Council in Ramsay MacDonald's National Coalition, and on his way to returning as prime minister the next year. As Baldwin's parliamentary bag-carrier, Lloyd had his ear.

If the public and political outcry at the behaviour of Mosley's followers wasn't enough, events in Germany at the end of June added an extra spur to action against fascism. As the Robertses were returning from their honeymoon hiking along the Rhine, Hitler ordered the arrest and execution of dozens of his enemies and former allies.

Hitler was unlikely to have known or cared, but the timing was especially poor from Mosley's point of view. 'The almost simultaneous occurrence of "the night of the long knives" and the ruthless beating up of their opponents by Mosley's fascists at Olympia had the double effect of discrediting Mosley's movement in the eyes of many people who had tended to sympathise with it, and of drawing attention to its close affinities with the Nazis,' wrote one of Knight's colleagues.

The time for leaving British fascism alone was over. Knight was ordered to target the movement just as he had done the communists. And that instruction came just as Eric Roberts had got back in touch, wanting to discuss German fascism and possibly angling for a job. It was a happy coincidence. Although Roberts had failed to make much headway infiltrating the communists, Knight clearly had faith in his abilities. He decided he'd found his man.

Two months after Eric and Audrey married, Knight wrote to him again, this time in more specific terms. 'I am anxious to see you as soon as possible,' he said. 'I have what might be a very interesting and mildly profitable proposition to put to you. It is one that I cannot discuss on paper.'

Knight's proposal was identical to the one that Sir George Makgill had made to him a decade earlier: penetrate the fascists. 'Get in touch with our friends at their head office,' he told Roberts. 'Put in some evening work there as and when it is most convenient to you.'

Knight liked to pay his agents 'a small regular sum'. He argued that payment by results created the wrong incentives for people whose work he needed to trust. For Roberts, whom he suggested would be working two evenings a week, he proposed a 'retaining fee' of a pound a week, plus half as much again to cover expenses. A little over a quarter of the average annual wage at the time, it was hardly a fortune, but it would help.

As with Knight's other agents, Roberts would be working under his own name. That carried a series of risks. Roberts's manager at the bank disapproved of the BUF, so it might harm his already limited prospects if it became known that he was a fascist. Much more seriously, both Knight and Roberts were very well aware of the Blackshirts' propensity for violence. The Olympia rally had shown what they could do to hecklers. What would they do to spies?

To the teenage Roberts of 1925, such dangers must have seemed exciting, and in any case remote. To the 27-year-old of 1934, they were more serious. He had a wife now. Was he putting Audrey in danger?

While Eric's life was becoming more exciting, Audrey's horizons were shrinking. The bank required women to resign when they married. Her job now was to keep house and wait for mother-hood. She occupied herself playing the violin in a symphony orchestra.

Roberts didn't keep her in ignorance of his activities. One Sunday evening in February 1935, Knight even visited the couple at home. To some, this would seem an extraordinary step for an intelligence officer to take – a breach of security protocol. For Knight, it was essential to his approach of winning his agents' complete trust by getting as close to them as possible. 'The officer should take an interest in the agent's home surroundings, family, hobbies, personal likes and dislikes; and must bear all this in mind when setting an agent to work on any particular task.'

But Knight's idea of intimacy involved control: both with his menagerie of animals and with the spies he ran, it was clear who was in charge. In his private life, he continued to struggle. In 1936, Gwladys died of an overdose of barbiturates. Although her family suspected that Knight had driven her to suicide or even murdered her, her death was likely accidental, as she was suffering from acute back pain and had been prescribed the medicine to ease it. The following year, he married again, to Lois Coplestone, a country-loving woman a decade his junior, with whom he had fallen in love while they were fishing together. But again, he was unable to consummate the marriage.

In 1934, the BUF headquarters were on the King's Road in Chelsea, in a former teacher training college named Whitelands House. The locals had renamed it 'Black House' in honour of its new occupants, and the threatening name suited the building. Even the exterior brickwork was dark. It felt more like a fortress than a political headquarters. Indeed, there were sentries posted regularly around its quarter of a mile of corridors, on the lookout for intruders and infiltrators. The rumour was that in an emergency, 5,000 fascists would be able to live in and defend the building.

As Roberts approached, he was determined that this time he would make a success of espionage. Knight's instructions were clear: 'Nothing is too small to report'; 'Do whatever task is allotted to you as well as you can, and allow yourself to drift along with the tide'; 'You have to be very patient in this game'.

It was easy to say, but hard to do. Roberts's early attempt to join the BUF's Foreign Relations Department, where he had hoped his language skills might be appreciated, was rebuffed. Knight reassured him. 'They will obviously regard with suspicion any new recruits,' he explained. 'I should not make any more obvious attempts to get in touch with them or find out about them for a week or two.' Instead, he advised Roberts to read a couple of foreign newspapers each day and clip out items of interest, which he could pass on to the department. 'In this way you will gradually establish confidence. The great thing is not to be in too much of a hurry.'

It was a difficult time for Roberts to be joining the BUF. Following the uproar over Olympia, they were suffering from a 'spy mania'. Indeed, Roberts himself suspected that one of his fellow activists was an undercover journalist. Knight repeatedly urged his agent not to be anxious about results, or to push for information in any way that might arouse suspicion. Roberts's reports were already excellent, he assured him.

But three months into his mission, Roberts sought Knight's advice. He had encountered a group of apparently disgruntled BUF members. Should he now drift along with them instead, in the hope that they would be loose-lipped? Knight suspected a trap.

'Don't utter a single word or phrase that could be used against you on some future occasion,' he urged, going on to explain that one of the senior BUF members, William Joyce, had his own internal intelligence service, keeping him informed of the views of the party's various factions. For all his talk of honesty with agents, Knight omitted to mention that he knew this because he was still in regular contact with Joyce, a friend from their early days together in the British Fascisti.

The caution was well advised. Roberts learned a week later that an entire conversation he'd had with a disaffected BUF member had been reported back. 'One has to tread very warily in these organisations,' Knight sighed.

For the next five years, Roberts worked his way steadily up through the BUF, rising to the senior rank of inspector. He would leave the bank after work, and find somewhere to change into his uniform before reporting for duty. 'I rather liked myself in my blackshirt, knee boots and breeches,' he later recalled. 'But found it awfully embarrassing after leaving the bank to change in some public toilet.' Once, he was pursued from the facilities at Sloane Square by an outraged janitor who had taken offence at his jackboots.

Roberts was Knight's first successful infiltrator of the BUF. His reports, under his new codename M/F – M for Knight's 'M Section' within the Security Service, F probably for 'fascist' – formed the basis of much of MI5's knowledge of the organisation.

It wasn't just fascists that Roberts supplied information on. In the middle of 1935, he handled a transaction at the bank. A woman wanted to cable £25 to a Hungarian who was staying in Zurich. Roberts was struck that the woman seemed 'excited and urgent'. As she was married to a member of one of Britain's more prominent communist-sympathising families, the moment seemed worth noting. Looking through her account, Roberts saw that she gave money to the King Alfred School in Golders Green – a location burned on his memory as the place he'd carried out his first work for Knight, spying on the Soviet deputy foreign minister a decade earlier. The woman's name was Edith Tudor-Hart. He reported back to Knight. 'She is of interest to us, and anything further about her will come in useful,' Knight's assistant replied.

Some of Knight's agents came close to cracking under the strain of a double life, but Roberts thrived on it. Knight's confidence in him was rewarded as he proved a natural agent, able to inhabit his life as a fascist without losing touch with reality. His likeable nature meant that, even as war approached and fascism became unpopular, he wasn't cut off by family or neighbours, something that probably helped him to keep his grip. At home, his first son was born in 1936, and named Maxwell, after Knight. Another boy, Peter, arrived the following year.

The Roberts family at play

With the arrival of children, some wives would have urged their husbands to give up a hobby as dangerous and all-consuming as spying. But whether because she believed in the national importance of the work or because she simply knew how much it mattered to Eric, Audrey supported her husband's frenzy of covert activity. She even took part herself, helping to entertain their local BUF parliamentary candidate and his wife for dinner.

In Roberts's secret life, he was meeting leading BUF figures and joining every fringe group he could find. Though Knight advised him not to mention his past membership of the British Fascisti, it helped him understand the thinking of those he was now infiltrating. Kind-hearted, fond of a joke and a drink, on the surface he couldn't have been further from the image of the guarded, furtive spy. But the friendliness was a front. The keenly observed, occasionally waspish reports that he passed on to Knight revealed his true opinions. 'Capt. Hick struck me as a most unpleasant piece of work,' he wrote of one senior fascist. 'Extremely guarded in what he said and beyond grunts committed himself to nothing.'

The people he was spying on were completely taken in by his impression of 'the most loyal pro-German'. Shortly after war broke out in 1939, a fellow BUF member sought Eric out to warn him to distance himself from the group – 'my best and safest plan during the next six months would be to steer clear of politics in any shape or form'. It was good advice, meant kindly, but Roberts had no intention of following it. War was going to give him the chance to play on a bigger field than ever before.

Roberts hadn't just found purpose in his work for MI5, he'd found friends, too. In particular, he got to know Jimmy Dickson – codename M/3. A couple of years older than Roberts, Dickson was another free spirit whose mind was wasted in his day job – in his case, as a civil servant. In the evenings he wrote thrillers, chased women and spied.

Like Roberts, Dickson had begun his espionage career in the early days of the British Fascisti, where as a young recruit he'd been ordered to spy on Knight – while working for him – by the BF's previous head of intelligence. 'To be an accomplished double-crosser in one's early twenties is nothing to be proud of, but by God it was fun,' he recalled. By the start of the 1930s, he'd regularised his position somewhat as one of Knight's agents inside the Communist Party. Then, in 1937, Knight asked him to turn his attention to fascism.

He and Roberts enjoyed letting off steam together, in particular employing the skills as a burglar that Dickson had learned in Knight's service. They'd break into pubs after closing time to help themselves to a final drink. Their plan if interrupted by a policeman was to tip a glass of Scotch over Roberts's head and then for Dickson to apologise and explain that he was trying to rescue his inebriated friend and get him safely home.

Roberts also began seeking out other contacts within MI5. This wasn't straightforward: Knight avoided the Security Service headquarters, and operated instead out of his own flat. Those who deal in secret information are often reluctant to share their sources. Some of the reasons for this are good: security, a desire to ensure a clear chain of command. Some are less good: a fear that the customer will go direct to the source and cut out the middle man, or embarrassment about the source's identity.

In the case of Roberts, though, Knight felt no need for shame, and apparently didn't object to his meeting more senior men. So in 1935, Roberts received an invitation to dine at the East India Club. The grand Georgian building in St James's Square, decorated with hunting trophies sent in from around the world by members, including the head of a hippopotamus, was not a place bank clerks often visited. For Roberts, walking in could well have been a more intimidating experience than walking through the entrance of Mosley's Black House. That it wasn't was down to his 'excellent host', Jack Curry. After a twenty-five-year career in the Indian Police, Curry had returned to London and joined the Security Service, in the section responsible for finding German spies. He had taken an interest in Knight's new agent in the BUF, and wanted to meet him.

Despite their different backgrounds and a twenty-year age gap, Curry and Roberts enjoyed each other's company. Both were men who had experience of practical action but who were capable of stepping back and looking at the larger picture. As they discussed the BUF, Roberts suggested that many of the problems of fascism might be dealt with by outlawing the wearing of political uniforms, which gave its members their militaristic swagger. The older man agreed.

Until then, Knight had been Roberts's only experience of MI5. Now he began to see that there might be a world beyond his spymaster, and he started to consider whether he might better flourish out of Knight's shadow. There was no immediate prospect of escaping it, but Curry and Roberts kept in touch.

The opportunity came with war. MI5 needed recruits, and when in the middle of 1940 the BUF was wound up, there was little point of Roberts continuing to infiltrate it. It was time for him to go official. At the end of May, a note was sent upwards. 'Roberts is thoroughly familiar with everything connected with the various pro-Nazi organisations in this country and Maxwell Knight has the highest opinion of his character and abilities,' it read. A few days later, Mr Jones at the Westminster Bank received the letter marked 'Secret And Personal'. Its subject was a clerk at the Euston Road branch.

'Would it be possible for you to arrange for him to be spared to my organisation for the duration of the war?' Jasper Harker asked.

Fifteen years after filing his first report for MI5, Eric Roberts was formally joining the Security Service.

3

'A splendid beacon for the Germans'

The interrogation Roberts was given in the back room of Windsor's shop in Leeds might well have exposed a simple police spy. That was exactly what Charnley accused him of being, as he fired names at him, asking who he knew and what he knew about them, all with the goal of tripping him up.

He was a good choice for the job of inquisitor. Unlike Windsor, a relatively recent recruit to the British Union, Charnley had been in from close to the start. He'd joined in 1933, a year before Roberts, and had been a serious member, lucky to escape being locked up along with his brother. But he had been living in Hull, meeting senior members of the group only when they visited northern England. Roberts, who had been in London, was equipped to match Charnley name for name. As Charnley asked about northerners that Roberts had never heard of, the MI5 man shot back with questions about London, putting his questioner on the back foot.

Roberts began to sense he was winning the room. The Leeds fascists desperately wanted to believe him: if he was genuine, he was their link to a wider world of resistance to Churchill and the war, and proof that they were part of a movement, not just lone partisans. 'They spent the whole evening cross-examining each other,' Windsor said afterwards. He wasn't convinced by the effort to make him doubt Charnley, but he was certainly reassured about Roberts.

Eventually, Charnley too was convinced. Indeed he felt he had to justify himself after his initial suspicions. He was, he assured the group, loyal to the British Union. If its leaders had a plan for revolution, he would play his part. He said he was sure Germany would invade in the coming weeks, and if fascist leaders called for an uprising, he was certain that every Blackshirt in the north of England would answer. Personally, Charnley drew the line only 'where it would lead to British soldiers losing their lives'. On this issue, Roberts noted, 'the other members present did not appear to agree with Charnley's reservation'.

The following day Roberts woke to the news that every Londoner had dreaded: the Luftwaffe had bombed the city over the weekend. The Battle of Britain had been raging for a month and a half, but until now, the German bombers had targeted RAF airfields and warning stations. The Roberts family, south-west of London in Epsom, ought to have been away from the main point of danger. The morning papers suggested that few people had been killed, but they did say that the suburbs had been hit. Security restrictions on printing the exact locations meant that, for Roberts far away in Leeds, the reports were frustratingly vague. Like most homes, his didn't have a phone line, so there was no easy way to establish if the family was safe. The wider question was whether the dramatic pictures of the capital city's skyline lit by flames signified a shift in enemy tactics.

In fact, it was unintentional: the bombs had been meant for an oil depot and an aircraft factory down the Thames. But Churchill retaliated with a raid of more than ninety bombers on Berlin. The prime minister's assistant private secretary, John Colville, feared Germany would respond in turn with a 'big raid' on London.

Despite the threat of bombing, the Roberts family had decided not to leave Epsom for the country. Eric still had family in Cornwall that Audrey and the boys could have gone to stay with, but his wife wanted to stay relatively close to her mother and sisters in north London. Audrey and the children would have to trust themselves to the Anderson shelter that Eric, never a handyman, had paid some builders to put up in the back garden.

Turning to the matter in hand, Roberts took stock. He had won the Leeds group's trust. He had established that they were committed to fascism and willing to talk about overthrowing the government by force. But how dangerous were they really? Was Windsor and Gannon's arson attack on Dawson's a one-off or the start of something bigger? Had it even actually happened, or was it simply the boast of a fantasist?

More importantly, how much of this talk had been inspired by Lewis? After two and a half days in Windsor's company, Roberts had concluded that, although he was undoubtedly keen to be involved in sabotage, 'he was a person of such vague mentality that it was extremely difficult to decide how many of his plans were of his own devising and how many had been put into his head'. If ideas had been put there, Roberts had a good idea who was responsible. Lewis hadn't impressed him as an undercover operator – 'too inept to be much use', MI5's file observed. At best, he was probably too committed to proving himself right about the Leeds group to be a reliable judge of how much danger they actually posed.

But Roberts was sure that Lewis had been encouraging Windsor in his plots. If this were true, it was a serious problem. MI5 couldn't simply round up people it was worried about. Indeed MI5 had no formal powers of action at all. The British state had reconciled itself to the need for something as un-British as a secret police by having one, but not acknowledging it. So the Security Service could investigate, but once it had identified a suspect, it was supposed to work with the police – usually Special Branch detectives who dealt with sensitive cases – and the Director of Public Prosecutions, to put them on trial like any other criminal. And just as in ordinary criminal trials, the prosecution would fail if it became clear that MI5 officers or their informants had persuaded the defendants to break the law.

Lewis might have been the person to expose the Leeds group, but if he had overstepped the mark, as Roberts feared, he might also have made their prosecution impossible.

In an effort to undo this damage, Roberts set about testing Windsor's resolve. When the pair met that day, Windsor, now convinced that the man from London was genuine, 'talked somewhat wildly of various things which he intended to do to help the enemy'.

In response, Roberts gave the shopkeeper a chance to back out. He warned him of the dangers in what he proposed, and especially of espionage. Three months earlier, Parliament had rushed through the Treachery Act in two days. This forbade, among other things, 'any act which is designed or likely to give assistance to the naval, military or air operations of the enemy', if it was done 'with intent to help the enemy'. It was a line that Windsor had already crossed. The new law also made it easier to convict someone of treachery, requiring only a single witness.

And it specified just one penalty: death. If Windsor were caught, it would mean the noose.

But Windsor wouldn't be dissuaded. The work needed to be done, he told Roberts. 'He did not like leaving the dirty work for other people to do if he was not prepared to do it himself.'

With Windsor's commitment confirmed, Roberts headed to his next appointment of the day. Three months short of her twentieth birthday, Angela Crewe was a shop assistant living with her parents a mile up the road from Windsor's shop. She had got to know him some weeks earlier, having declared herself 'pro-German and anti-Jew'. She now told Roberts that she wanted to be a spy. Posters were already appearing around the country warning that 'Careless Talk Costs Lives'. But where the government saw threat, young Angela saw opportunity. She would collect that careless talk and send it to Germany, if only she could find a messenger. She showed Roberts two cameras that she was contemplating using to photograph aerodromes.

Roberts was troubled. He thought her probably 'more stupid than dangerous', and even more emphatically than with Windsor, he warned her of the dangers of what she proposed. He asked her why she wished to do this to her country. 'Because I am a National Socialist and a follower of Oswald Mosley,' she replied, before adding that she would also like to be paid.

When he saw that he couldn't dissuade her, Roberts changed course. If Crewe was determined to pass information to Germany, he should make sure she didn't succeed. Acting on what seems to have been a flash of inspiration, he suggested that he might know a way to get secrets to Berlin. He was, he revealed, much more than a fellow fascist: he was a German agent. This was information she must keep in the utmost confidence.

Crewe was thrilled. She promised to use her charms to obtain information from some of the soldiers posted locally and send it to him in London. Roberts gave her an address, and she promised she would prove herself.

His final meeting was with a soldier. Robert Jeffery was a private in the Royal Army Medical Corps. Stationed near Windsor's shop, he was among those who came to pass their time in the back room. It had been in the course of one of these visits that he had mentioned that his father had owned a sweetshop, and revealed he shared Windsor's loathing of cut-prices stores. Windsor had sensed a sympathetic mind, and begun setting out the case for fascism to the soldier.

By the time he met Roberts, Jeffery was a convert to the cause, although his motives were at least partly financial. He'd already offered to steal chemicals that could be used to make bombs from the hospital where he worked, but, upon meeting the man from London, he asked how much he'd be prepared to pay for weapons. Roberts suggested a price of 30 shillings for a service revolver and ammunition. Jeffery agreed, and added that he could definitely get a service gas mask for 21 shillings. He promised to write to Roberts in code, with any number he gave being the number of revolvers he'd stolen. 'After thanking him for his offer of help, I left him,' Roberts wrote.

Back in London, Roberts's masters at MI5 were impressed with their new recruit's work. Guy Liddell, the head of counter-espionage, recorded 'melodramatic developments' in his diary. 'There is now a definite conspiracy to obtain military information through a young girl who is friendly with an officer and to pass this information to the Germans. There is also a scheme to obtain arms and explosives.' The machinery of the secret state swung into action. Orders were imposed to intercept and copy Windsor's, Crewe's and Charnley's letters.

MI5 drew several conclusions from Roberts's report. First, the decision earlier in the year to ban the BU and round up its members seemed to have succeeded in its aim of putting the organisation out of action. 'The Leeds group are quite isolated and in spite of all their efforts have failed to contact fascists elsewhere,' a case summary read. 'They are also considerably hampered by lack of funds.'

Second, 'although they are so anxious to help the Germans, they have no contact with Germany'. While it was quite possible that the Germans were approaching individual BU members, 'the BU as an organisation is not in touch with the German Secret Service'. This made sense to the men in London. They assumed that the Abwehr – Germany's intelligence service – had been setting up networks in Britain before the war, but that their recruits would have been told to drop political activities.

Third, and more worryingly, 'the case of Miss Crewe in particular shows how an otherwise perfectly normal and decent person can be completely subverted by Nazi doctrines. It is unlikely that the majority of BU members are fanatics of this type, but the movement undoubtedly contained a fair number.'

As it seemed unlikely that the Leeds group were going to lead MI5 to bigger fish, the most sensible thing was to lock them up before they hurt anyone. Knight set off to see Sir Edward Tindal Atkinson, the Director of Public Prosecutions.*

Atkinson had little time for traitors. However, he advised Knight that what Roberts had brought back from Leeds wasn't enough. The only evidence against the group was the word of an undercover MI5 man, corroborated by Lewis, who seemed an unreliable witness. He'd need more before he could prosecute under the wartime emergency powers. As he'd helped draft the relevant legislation, there was no point in Knight arguing.

Roberts had already written to Windsor since his return to London, and now he awaited a response. Nearly three weeks after he'd left Leeds, two letters arrived: one from Windsor, and the other from Angela Crewe in which she sent the locations of factories near Leeds. 'This information is amateurish and would probably be of little use to the Germans,' a report noted. Obviously convinced by Roberts's claim to be acting for the Germans, she begged him to give her specific work to do.

Windsor's letter was in code. 'The organ is working quite well,' he wrote. 'In fact a friend of mine, a Mr Wells, intends calling upon you re the service it's giving him. Its activity is slow but sure and is most reliable. If nothing develops in the next week, shall try my utmost to come down and see you.'

A week later, Windsor wrote again, announcing that he would visit London on 25 September. But MI5 wasn't the only organisation in chaos in 1940: delays in the post meant the letter didn't arrive until the 26th, and Roberts missed the proposed meeting.

---

* Atkinson hadn't expected to become DPP: when in 1930 he was summoned to the Home Office to discuss 'a certain matter', he assumed that he'd made a mistake in his work as a recorder – the most junior sort of judge – and prepared for a reprimand. When he was told the real reason he was there, he refused to believe it and walked out of the room.

The check on Windsor's mail, meanwhile, had turned up a disappointing lack of incriminating communication. An explanation for this came out of the blue, when another military recruit contacted MI5 to report Windsor as suspicious. The most troubling thing about this account was that it revealed Windsor had been told by a friend in the Post Office that his letters were being opened. The checks had begun after Roberts's visit. Surely Windsor would make the connection?

The following month more communication failures led to missed meetings in London with Gannon and Charnley, so it was with relief that Roberts received a letter from Windsor at the end of October inviting him to visit Leeds again. In his letter Windsor said that 'Mr Jay' had left the city some time ago, but 'gave me an Xmas sample for your approval'. With high hopes that it would be a stolen Army revolver – proof of a crime – Roberts set off for Yorkshire.

On Tuesday, 5 November, Roberts arrived in Leeds. It was Bonfire Night, but the blackout meant no bonfires, and no fireworks either. For many children, this was the privation that particularly hit home. One Leeds shopkeeper reported children asking if he had any rockets in stock 'just to look at'. The indoor fireworks he was offering instead – small pyrotechnics that floated to the ceiling before burning out, or fizzed and wriggled into snakes on a plate – were poor substitutes.

The *Daily Mirror* depicted Hitler as a guy on top of a bonfire, with the caption 'Fireworks supplied by the RAF'. The reality was less cheerful. In the House of Commons, the prime minister reported on the progress of the war: 14,000 civilians had been killed and 20,000 wounded by the bombing so far, mainly in London. Churchill also warned that the fighting could last another three years.

The day after he arrived in Leeds, Roberts went to see Windsor and Gannon. They lost no time in bringing their visitor up to speed on their activities since August. 'We've done a job!' Gannon told him. Asked for more details, they explained how they'd set fire to a factory. Feigning enthusiasm, Roberts requested to be taken to see the evidence. The Leeds men were suddenly reticent, but Roberts insisted, and so the three boarded a tram.

In many ways, the war was being good to Leeds. Despite Windsor and Gannon's efforts, there had been little bombing there – the local joke was that the Luftwaffe couldn't see through the clouds of industrial smoke hanging over the city. And the demands of war had brought back manufacturing work after the decline of the 1930s. The Avro aircraft plant north-west of the city was reckoned to be the largest factory in Europe. It was carefully camouflaged to look like farmland from the air, with hedgerows, scattered buildings, even a duck pond.

The place to which Windsor and Gannon were taking Roberts was part of a much longer tradition. The wool trade had been important in Yorkshire for centuries, and clothmaking had been crucial to the development of Leeds. With the industrial revolution had come giant mills on the western side of the city, taking in wool from all over the world and turning it into cloth. Having struggled in the aftermath of the Great Depression, the mills now had a purpose once again: hundreds of thousands of men needed uniforms.

Windsor and Gannon were taking Roberts to Stanningley, one of these mill districts, but they had a small problem: they were lying to him. Gannon had simply got carried away with his claim to have 'done a job', and when Roberts had asked for more details, Windsor had suggested Stanningley because he knew there had been a fire there. Unfortunately, he didn't know where. As their tram got closer to its destination, Roberts sensed 'some hesitation on the part of both men', and he wondered again if Windsor and Gannon were more fantasists than dangerous fanatics.

They hopped off the tram and Windsor went into a shop, hoping to find out where the fire had been. To his horror, the shopkeeper didn't know, so he and Gannon led Roberts aimlessly between the mills, in the hope they might spot something. In the end, Roberts put them out of their misery. He pointed to some new buildings, and asked if that was the site of their arson. Windsor and Gannon gratefully agreed that it was, and described how they'd started the fire during a recent blackout.

As they made their way back into the city, the conversation became 'somewhat strained'. But what Roberts initially took for embarrassment was actually suspicion. Finally, Windsor and Gannon challenged him: when they hadn't heard back from him

about their proposed September visit to London, they'd decided
to go and find him. They'd had two clues: the address he had
given them, and the place he said he'd worked. Although Roberts
was working under his own name, he wasn't so foolish as to have
given his own address. Instead he'd used that of his MI5 colleague
and drinking partner Jimmy Dickson.

Windsor and Gannon had found no sign of Roberts at Dickson's Fulham flat. They'd had more success at the Euston Road
branch of the Westminster Bank. People there knew Eric Roberts
all right. But they hadn't seen him since he joined the Army.
Windsor protested: he'd seen Roberts not two months earlier, and
he hadn't been in the Army then. But the bank staff insisted that
Roberts had left long before that, about six months ago. 'It was
very mystifying,' Windsor observed later.

For Roberts, this was a moment far more dangerous than the
interrogation by Charnley. On that occasion he had escaped detection because he had, in a way, the truth on his side. Here, he
was caught in a lie. His former colleagues at the Westminster
Bank had inadvertently given him away. Combined with Windsor's discovery that his post was being opened, surely the game
was up?

But there was one possible glimmer of hope. If Windsor and
Gannon had drawn the obvious conclusion from their trip to
London – that Roberts was, in some capacity, working for the
government – they would hardly have taken him to see evidence
of an arson attack, even a fictional one. That meant that whatever
their doubts about him, they wanted him to dispel them.

Roberts didn't record what he said to Windsor and Gannon that
day. He simply reported that, in the course of the tram journey
back into the city centre, he 'succeeded in allaying their suspicions
on these points'. Their desire to believe in the man from London
was a huge asset, as was Roberts's skill at inhabiting the role he
played. But for all his coyness about the conversation, this moment
was a sign to his MI5 employers of the extraordinary extent of
his abilities as an undercover operator. Eric Roberts could make
people trust him, even when they had no business doing so.

Having decided to put their faith in Roberts, Windsor and
Gannon again wanted to impress him. The conversation turned
to their favourite subject – arson. Gannon had identified Morley's

plumbing supplies warehouse, just off City Square in the centre of Leeds, as a target. He'd already made two attempts to burn it down, but each time he felt he'd been let down by his assistant. The first time he'd taken Walter Longfellow, a sheet-metal worker who was in the group, and a can of petrol. But his companion had become scared at the last minute and ran away. The second time he'd enlisted Private Jeffery, who was also supposed to be stealing guns for Roberts. But although they'd successfully pushed a home-made incendiary bomb through the building's letter box, it hadn't ignited properly. 'The attempt had been further wrecked by a sudden spasm of weakness of the knees on Jeffery's part, followed by a swift run for safety,' Roberts reported drily. Two days later the soldier had been transferred to Lincoln, sixty miles away. Windsor complained that although he'd given Jeffery money to fund fascist activities, they hadn't heard from him since. They suspected he'd lost his nerve.

But Gannon wasn't downhearted. He was sure the warehouse would burn furiously if they could get a blaze started, and he had two more home-made firebombs. Windsor had another idea to help Germany: they should make a map of Leeds, marking munitions factories, railway junctions and other targets for Roberts to pass to Berlin. Gannon, excited, had his own suggestion: in his search for places to set fire to, he'd noticed that bomb shelters were constructed from timber, which would burn beautifully. Windsor agreed they'd be good targets, and 'proposed that shelters should be chosen with an eye to old buildings which would blaze well, either above or at the side'.

The two men were now throwing out all sorts of ideas, although Roberts 'strongly discouraged' Gannon's proposal that they try to contact local agents of the Irish Republican Army – the previous year had seen a bombing campaign by republicans against English cities. The conversation moved on, with Gannon proposing to burn a military parking depot.

It was clear to Roberts that the Leeds group had become more determined since his last visit. While much of their talk was fanciful, they were determined to set fire to something, and even a fire set by a fool could kill.

The following evening he met Windsor and Gannon again. The shopkeeper, Roberts reported, 'felt they ought to do something ambitious'. He liked the idea of trying again at the warehouse Gannon had mentioned. 'His great wish was to cause a big blaze in the centre of Leeds to attract the attention of Jerry planes.' The pair insisted Roberts come with them to take a look at their proposed target.

In September, City Square had been at the heart of 'War Weapons Week', an effort to persuade people to help finance the war effort. A barometer board had been set up in front of a local landmark, the statue of the Black Prince, to show how many bombers had been bought. On the first day alone, £1.4 million was raised – seventy bombers. Now Windsor and Gannon were planning to strike back. As they approached Morley's warehouse, 'they kept reiterating the fact that once alight it would make a splendid beacon for the Germans'.

Gannon slipped down an alley at the side of the building and came back in a state of high excitement. The door didn't seem to be padlocked. They could break in and start a fire there and then. Windsor agreed, pointing out once again that the place was full of straw packaging, which would make excellent kindling.

That was the last thing Roberts wanted them to do. He urged caution, suggesting they take time to prepare and plan. To his immense relief, while the two men were considering his plea, a policeman appeared in the distance. Windsor and Gannon agreed it might be wiser to wait.

Over the following days, the group was busy. Gannon announced he had got hold of a Michelin map and he committed 'with some glee' to work with Windsor to mark ammunition factories on to the maps. He had also bought a small saw, of which he was very proud, for hacking through the lock on the door at Morley's.

The men were keen to reassure Roberts of their loyalty to fascism. Windsor had decided that a defeat for National Socialism in Germany would mean its defeat in Britain. Gannon said that he'd studied British Union policy deeply, and that he had denied himself 'every little pleasure in order to save for the movement'. He told Roberts that 'his most treasured possessions' were his collection of BU pamphlets and his copy of Mosley's 1938 manifesto, 'Tomorrow We Live'.

On Sunday 10 November, they met in the back room of Windsor's shop, joined by Longfellow, the timorous sheet-metal worker, who explained that while he was keen to help, his wife was dying, and so he couldn't come with them on the actual attack. But Windsor and Gannon were ready: they would set fire to Morley's the following day. They planned carefully, drawing up a map of the warehouse approaches and testing Gannon's hacksaw on a nail, to see how long it would take to cut through a padlock. Then came the high point. Gannon produced one of his home-made firebombs. He'd managed to get hold of some gunpowder – possibly from some now-forbidden fireworks – and placed it in a piece of paper, then wrapped a cloth around it and secured it with a rubber band, to make a ball about three inches in diameter. A fuse stuck out of the top. It looked like the kind of bomb a villain would throw in a cartoon.

The men decided to test it. They placed the bomb in the grate of the fireplace, lit the fuse, retreated to the corners of the room, and watched eagerly. The fuse burned down, and then there was a flash and a foul smell, but no fire. Despite this, 'it was decided that in straw a fire would certainly start'.

Roberts told the gang that he would be returning to London on the Tuesday morning, the day after their proposed attack. If they wanted to give him maps to send to Germany, they needed to have them ready by then.

They set about their task with relish. Windsor and Longfellow numbered important sites on the map, while Gannon wrote out descriptions of the targets in a notebook. They agreed that Gannon would take the map, notebook and other material, including fascist literature and a list of likely supporters, with him when they set fire to the warehouse the following day. Once their mission was completed, they would split up, and he would meet Roberts at the Red Lion Hotel to hand the material over. When they'd finished, Windsor took everyone through the plan for the following evening from start to finish. Watching him coordinate it all, Roberts was, despite himself, at least a little impressed with his organisational skills.

They carefully cleared the room of evidence, and agreed to meet the next day at 8 p.m.

In the meantime, Roberts had his own preparations to put in place. Working with MI5's local man, one Major Hordern, he arranged for the police and firefighters to be lying in wait that night. He would signal them by flashing a torch, and they would pounce and arrest the whole gang. Everything was ready.

Before his rendezvous with the would-be arsonists, Roberts had a meeting with Sydney Charnley. Two months earlier, Charnley had been accusing Roberts of being a police spy. Now he was sure Roberts was a genuine fascist.

He wasn't coming on that night's raid, as he was doubtful about both the means and the end. 'He did not really favour the sort of activities which were being carried out by the others,' Roberts reported. Like many of Mosley's followers, Charnley was a patriot at heart, and his loyalty to King and Country was clashing with his loyalty to fascism. 'He did not want to see a German victory unless such a victory could tally with a National Socialist victory in England.' But he did need money, and he had a proposal: he would work for Roberts, and for the fascist cause, for two pounds five shillings a week. Charnley, Roberts wrote, 'salvaged his conscience by the thought that if he did work in this fashion, although he was working indirectly for the Germans he would not be working against his own country'. Roberts committed himself to nothing.

When he met Gannon and Windsor that evening, they were in a state of high excitement. They'd brought with them a 47-year-old clerk called Albert Miller who was keen to meet Roberts – a feeling that wasn't entirely reciprocated. Miller took them to his office, where he had a postcard of Mosley pinned up behind the door, and, in Roberts's words, 'wasted a lot of time explaining what he had done for fascism'. Roberts was beginning to tire of Windsor's endless stream of enthusiastic fascists.

Miller, like Charnley, had his doubts about the evening's enterprise. He offered to provide the others with an alibi, but he warned about the danger of 'Watchers', and when that didn't work, proposed they target a Jewish business instead of Morley's. Finally, he suggested they telephone the plumbing warehouse to at least ensure that there wasn't a nightwatchman present. Windsor thought this would be a sensible precaution, and so they set out to find a phone box.

After cultivating them for weeks, Roberts didn't want to give his conspirators an excuse to pull out at this point. As they approached the phone box, he pushed ahead, and made the call himself. Someone did pick up at the other end, but Roberts said nothing, simply hanging up and telling his companions that there had been no answer. The operation was on.

As they approached the warehouse, Roberts tried to see where the police were lying in wait, hoping they hadn't left signs of their presence. To his relief, there was nothing to spook Windsor and Gannon. They approached the warehouse door, and found it locked. Gannon produced his saw and set to work.

This was the moment for the police to pounce. Roberts pulled out his torch and shone it on the door, on the pretext of helping Gannon to see. No one came. Feigning incompetence, Roberts flashed the torch around. Still no one came. Windsor cursed Roberts for a fool who would give them all away, and confiscated the torch.

By now Roberts was worried: the police were supposed to be catching Windsor and Gannon in the act. As important, they were supposed to be stopping them from starting a fire. Roberts might be a fake, but Gannon's firebomb was real, and so was the straw inside the warehouse.

Fortunately, Gannon was discovering that padlocks are harder to saw through than nails. Despairing of his saw, he pulled his firebomb from his pocket, lit the fuse, and shoved it through the letter box. He and Windsor walked away as calmly as they could manage and, having agreed a later rendezvous at the Red Lion, Roberts made off in the other direction, still expecting the police to pounce.

But there were no running footsteps, no shouts. Instead, Windsor and Gannon disappeared into the blackout and a confused and frustrated Roberts walked round the warehouse only to find the police lying in wait on the other side, patiently watching a different door.

The trap had failed. Some of the policemen had, they admitted, seen Windsor and Gannon walk away, but hadn't stopped them, because they hadn't realised the attempt on Morley's had already been made.

Roberts was exasperated. But he saw another chance. Gannon was still carrying the suitcase full of fascist literature, with maps marking bomb targets. That was incriminating evidence enough. He was due at the Red Lion later for the handover. Officers were sent there to arrest him. Meanwhile Roberts took Hordern to look at the real scene of the crime.

The good news when they got there was that Leeds's fascists were apparently as bad at starting fires as the city's police were at setting traps. There was no obvious sign of an arson attempt. Roberts showed his colleagues the padlock that Gannon had tried to saw. But though the Security Service colleagues could see marks on it, Inspector Buchanan of the Leeds police was of the view that he had been sent on a fool's errand. He denied he could see any sign of tampering with the lock, and announced he was not going to waste any more time searching the premises.

His officers had meanwhile failed to arrest Gannon. Realising that Leeds had no Red Lion hotel, they had guessed that he must have meant either the Black Lion or the Golden Lion. With a fifty-fifty chance of being correct, they went to the former while Gannon waited at the latter, before losing his nerve, leaving and getting rid of the contents of his suitcase.

His trap failed, his evidence destroyed, Roberts returned to London. But if he was downhearted, his superiors weren't. He had established that Windsor's group were determined, even if they lacked competence. That determination was enough to make them dangerous. It was surely only a matter of time before they managed to set fire to something, and Leeds was home to many of Britain's most important factories. The risk of leaving them at large was too great.

Even if they couldn't be prosecuted, there was another option open to MI5. Under emergency wartime laws, the government had the power to lock people up, indefinitely and without trial, if they were suspected of being Nazi sympathisers. At the start of December 1940, Windsor, Gannon, Longfellow and Jeffery were arrested. They swiftly confessed their support for fascism and their attempts to sabotage the British war effort, blaming the mysterious man from London, Mr Roberts, for leading them astray.

MI5 had considered arresting Charnley and Angela Crewe as well, but rejected the idea. There was a mix of reasons for this. Partly, it was that neither had moved from talk into action. Crewe 'was not likely to do any serious harm by her communication'. Charnley 'did not appear to have taken any part in the attempts at sabotage'. But there was raw calculation behind the decision, as well. MI5 was trying to find active fascists, and so was Charnley. Why not let him carry on, and see who he turned up? 'It was decided that he might be of more use to the authorities if left at large, at least for the time being.'

One risk was that the arrest of his four fellow fascists might sow suspicion in Charnley's mind about Roberts, and that was why it made sense to leave Crewe at large. Given the things she'd said to Roberts, leaving her alone would suggest that he couldn't be the person who'd betrayed them. It seemed to work: Roberts and Charnley stayed in occasional contact for at least another year, though without much apparent result.

It seemed that Roberts's first official case for MI5 had been a success. But unknown to him, there were moves at the highest level of the government that threatened to end his MI5 career just as it was beginning to take off.

4

'Every person within the fortress'

Sir Alexander Maxwell, the permanent under-secretary of state at the Home Office – its chief civil servant – had been at the department for thirty-six years, his entire career. The son of a Congregational minister, he was passionate about juvenile delinquency and reform, and had deeply held views about the need to balance public security with the liberty of the subject. He had a powerful intellect, but was gentle, humorous and modest. Those around him relied on him for advice and guidance, and held him in deep affection. He was the rock upon which the Home Office stood. MI5 found him a nightmare.

Shortly before Christmas 1940, just as the Leeds case seemed settled, the Home Office began to take an interest in it. Over at MI5, the director of counter-espionage, Guy Liddell, sensed danger, and prepared for battle. Liddell was a veteran of the Great War, during which he'd won the Military Cross. After leaving the Army, he'd joined Special Branch, where he'd displayed a gift for counter-intelligence. In 1931, he'd moved over to MI5, as part of a reorganisation of intelligence across government. He was shy and gently humorous, but like Maxwell concerned for his subordinates, who sought him out for advice. After meeting him in 1940, the novelist Somerset Maugham included in a memoir a description of an unnamed Security Service officer: 'a plump man with grey hair and a grey moon face, in rather shabby grey clothes. He had an ingratiating way with him, a pleasant laugh and a soft voice. I do not know what you would have taken him for if you had found him standing in a doorway where you had sought refuge from a sudden shower – a motor salesman perhaps, or a retired tea planter.' At least one of Liddell's friends recognised him, though another colleague would have disputed the suggestion of shabbiness: 'always beautifully dressed, with handmade shoes'.

Sir Alexander Maxwell, left, and Guy Liddell

Liddell had been at loggerheads with Maxwell since the very start of the war. In July 1939, the Security Service had just thirty-six officers with which to thwart German intelligence and keep the country safe from home-grown threats. As it prepared for the coming war, its most pressing problem was what to do about the 70,000 Germans and Austrians living in the country. Many of them resented Hitler as much as any Briton, but might some not feel the pulls of patriotism? Might some, indeed, be agents sent over in advance? Even if one assumed that most of the Germans in Britain presented no threat, how was MI5 supposed to identify the dangerous ones?

To Liddell, the problem was so difficult that it wasn't even worth attempting. He calculated it would take at least eight months to interview every German and assess their case. 'In the meantime the Germans will have an opportunity of working on enemy aliens in this country and organising them into some kind of intelligence agency,' he wrote. Instead, he and his colleagues assumed that the government would repeat the policy adopted in the First World War: lock up every German man until they could prove they should be released. This would free MI5 to deal with more urgent matters.

But Maxwell had other ideas. The view of the Home Office was that the Great War policy of internment, as it had been known, had been a cruel mistake. Applied far too widely as a result of public panic, it had resulted in thousands of innocent men being held in overcrowded conditions for years.

On top of that, if it was difficult for MI5 to screen tens of thousands of people in a few months, locking them all up was hardly straightforward, either. Where? For how long? Even if the government restricted itself to men of military age, there were 28,500 of them. The Home Office had managed to identify space to intern only 18,000.

There were also compassionate considerations. Many of the Germans in Britain were refugees, mainly Jewish. Had they fled barbed wire at home only to find it in their place of sanctuary?

Two days before war broke out, Maxwell wrote to the Security Service, telling them that there would be no mass internment. Tribunals would review the case of every male enemy alien over the age of sixteen. If MI5 thought someone should be locked up, they would have to make the case for it. Liddell's judgement on this decision was blunt: 'Farce.'

Three months later, he felt his assessment had been proved right. 'Large numbers of enemy aliens are at large and they have freedom of movement,' he complained. He estimated that simply processing their cases was taking up four-fifths of MI5's time. The general view within MI5 was that the Home Office neither understood nor cared about the problems the Security Service faced.

Those problems weren't limited to foreigners. MI5 was also concerned about Britons with questionable loyalties. Oswald Mosley was an admirer of Hitler. Could he and his followers be trusted? The Home Office responded that it couldn't lock people up on the basis of what they might do, only for what they had done.

The Security Service position was summed up by its director, Jasper Harker: Britain was a castle under siege. 'It is essential,' he said, 'that every person within the fortress must either be harnessed to the national effort or put under proper control.'

In the summer of 1940, Adolf Hitler's advance across Europe began to shift the argument in MI5's favour. In April, Germany overran Denmark and invaded Norway, starting a two-month campaign that would end in defeat for the Norwegians and humiliation for the British forces sent to push the invaders back.

But two months was longer than other European countries held out. On 10 May, Hitler invaded France and Holland and rolled forward with astonishing speed. The British Expeditionary Force, which had been deployed the previous year to hold the line in Belgium, found that the French line to the east had collapsed. The British were ordered to abandon their weapons and flee from Dunkirk. Six weeks after the offensive began, Germany's territory stretched from the border of the Soviet Union to the Atlantic.

With German forces suddenly just across the Channel, British high command tried to understand how they had moved so far and so fast. The concept of Fifth Columnists had originated in 1936, in the Spanish Civil War, when General Franco's fascist forces claimed to have four columns of soldiers ready to march on Madrid, and a fifth column of sympathisers inside the city ready to rise up in their support. As it took another two years to take the city, this claim seems doubtful, but at the time the reports led to the arrest and assassination of suspected fifth columnists within the besieged city.

The idea gripped imaginations across Europe, already impressionable thanks to the boom in spy novels and films. John Buchan's *The Thirty-Nine Steps* had entertained Tommies in the trenches of the First World War. Brought to the silver screen by Alfred Hitchcock in 1935, it thrilled another generation, with a plot which now emphasised that even the most respectable citizen could be a secret traitor.

Behind Hitler's victories lay good fortune, new military tactics and strategy, superior military forces, and opponents who were poorly equipped and led. But none of these explanations was as beguiling as the idea that the Germans had won in an underhand way. News reports suggested Norway had been betrayed from the inside. After Holland's collapse, an apparently even more authoritative report came from no less a person than Sir Nevile Bland, the British ambassador.

He had fled the country the day before it surrendered, and returned home to describe how it had been overrun in less than a week. His thousand-word report, entitled 'Fifth Column Menace', claimed that is was parachutists, assisted by foreign domestic servants, who had delivered victory to Germany. 'The paltriest kitchen maid . . . not only can be but generally is a menace to the safety of the country,' he wrote.

MI5 had its own word for such an organisation: 'Kriegsnetz' – war network.

And that was just the threat posed by Germans and Austrians. Evidence of the apparent duplicity of those from countries where Britain hoped for support came days after the fall of Holland, with the arrest of an American diplomat, Tyler Kent. Kent was a cipher clerk at the US embassy in London. His job meant he had seen private cables between Churchill, then First Lord of the Admiralty, and President Franklin D. Roosevelt. These messages showed Roosevelt was secretly moving away from America's iso-lationist policy – something Kent strongly opposed. In the hope of exposing this, he began collecting documents at his flat.

Kent had formed links with the pro-German Right Club, set up by Captain Archibald Ramsay, a Conservative Member of Parliament determined to root out the 'Jewish influence' he saw in his party. There he befriended Anna Wolkoff, one of its keenest members. He passed her some of the papers, which she in turn passed to the Italian embassy. British codebreakers reading Italian cables to Berlin reported that Rome was sending on most of the contents of Ambassador Joe Kennedy's messages from London to Roosevelt.

But MI5 was watching Kent. Maxwell Knight had at least five agents inside the Right Club: three women and two men. One of those men was Eric Roberts, who had added it to the portfolio of right-wing groups he'd joined in the service of MI5, although he hadn't filed a report of any significance on Ramsay in a year. The day after Churchill became prime minister, Wolkoff boasted to one of Knight's women that she had seen some of Churchill's pri-vate papers. Nine days later, Knight, along with three policemen, arrived at Kent's flat. They were accompanied by a US embassy official, who informed Kent that he had that day been dismissed from the diplomatic service, and so lost his immunity from pros-ecution. The searched yielded 1,500 secret papers.

Following Kent's arrest, MI5 renewed its case against the BUF. Knight briefed the Home Secretary, Sir John Anderson, arguing that Mosley and Ramsay were in close touch with each other, and that there was overlap between the memberships of their groups.

'Anderson began by saying that he found it difficult to believe that members of the BUF would assist the enemy,' Liddell, who was also present, recorded. 'He seemed to have a great aversion to locking up a British subject unless he had a very cast-iron case against him.'

The Home Secretary explained he was worried about the long-term impact on British democracy of locking Mosley and his supporters up. Liddell seethed inwardly. 'I longed to say that if somebody did not get a move on there would be no democracy, no England and no Empire, and that this was almost a matter of days.'

The following day, Churchill persuaded the Cabinet to extend regulation 18B of the Emergency Powers (Defence) Act, which currently allowed the internment of those with 'hostile origin or associations', to cover anyone who had been a member of a proscribed group. Mosley and his fellow BUF leaders were swiftly rounded up.

Sir Alexander Maxwell and the Home Office were losing the argument on internment. The final blow came on 10 June, as German troops prepared to take Paris. Benito Mussolini, hoping to share some of the spoils of victory, announced that Italy was entering the war on the side of its fascist allies.

Officials had worked out a plan for the limited internment of Italians in Britain once war was declared, but Churchill had no time for such niceties, and gave a brief instruction: 'Collar the lot.' By July, 753 BUF members, 22,000 Germans and Austrians and 4,000 Italians had been interned.

This led to grave injustices. Refugees from Germany found themselves being dragged out of their new homes by the very government to which they had come for protection. Even advocates of internment knew that most of those arrested were harmless. 'We do not necessarily believe that there is a high percentage of fifth columnists among these people,' Liddell mused. 'There may be a few. Our main point is that as a category these aliens will be an embarrassment if hostilities commenced in this country.' Already his department was deluged with tip-offs about suspicious foreigners. It only needed one of them to be revealed as a spy to trigger a public outcry.

But those internees kept in camps were at least relatively safe.

The low point of the internment policy came at the start of July. Churchill didn't just want 'enemy aliens' locked up, he wanted them out of the country altogether. Canada was persuaded to take thousands of them, and the internees were loaded onto ships. On 2 July, the SS *Arandora Star*, carrying over 1,200 internees, was torpedoed by a German U-boat. More than 800 of those on board were killed.

The sinking caused outrage in Britain. Many of those killed were Italians who had made their lives in Britain, and, as Liddell noted, 'everybody is reluctant to believe that there could be any harm in their pet waiters and restaurateurs'. Even Liddell, the longstanding advocate of the wholesale arrest and deportation of 'enemy aliens', now seemed to disown the policy.

Having spent close to a year arguing for such action, and detailing how it would work, he expressed puzzlement that the Italians had been on a ship to Canada in the first place: the plan had been to send them back to Italy 'to create focal points for discontent' against Mussolini. 'Why this policy was never carried out I cannot think.'

This was disingenuous at best. Liddell had been aware of the plan, and had supported it only weeks earlier. He was beginning to realise something that Maxwell, his opponent at the Home Office, had long known: national policy decisions could have a tragic impact on individuals.

Germany was happy to stoke the atmosphere of terror in Britain that summer. In the middle of August, Churchill's War Cabinet was informed that forty-five Nazi parachutists had landed in Britain. Near one of the parachutes, some maps had been found. The next day ministers were told this had been a hoax by the Germans, who had dropped parachutes – but not parachutists – across the country, hoping to sow confusion. Nazi propaganda radio meanwhile broadcast English-language instructions to Fifth Columnists in Britain.

MI5 was overwhelmed by reports of suspicious activity pouring in from across the country. The vast bulk of them were groundless, but each report required at least momentary consideration, and many took more than that. People spotted suspicious markings on walls and telegraph poles: these turned out to be the work of 'children, boy scouts, lovers, tramps and lewd fellows'. Some Royal Air Force pilots reported seeing markings on the ground just north of the port of Newquay in Cornwall that might be a signal to enemy aircraft: they were in fact heaps of lime that a farmer was preparing to spread on his fields. A similar investigation close to nearby Truro found that some fencing had indeed been placed in a cross shape on a field: it had been installed by a different branch of the RAF, to deny German planes a landing ground.

Another RAF photo showed an arrow on the ground, pointing towards a nearby ordnance factory. Examination of a map showed it coming from a church belonging to the sinister and slightly Germanic-sounding 'Unden Order'. An investigation on the ground revealed that the church was 'Undenominational', and that the head of the arrow was a car park, built at the insistence of the local council, which then had a drive leading to the church itself.

Sometimes the military didn't wait to consult MI5. A retired soldier and his wife were arrested for a week because his surname sounded German. Liddell was told that some local units 'appear to have prepared a kind of Black List of their own. When the balloon goes up they intend to round up or shoot all these individuals. The position is so serious that something of a very drastic kind will have to be done.'

A new MI5 recruit named Anthony Blunt reported on his first day's work, and Liddell was sufficiently amused by the summary to record it in full in his diary:

1. Dealt with letter from lady pointing out danger of sentries being poisoned by icecreams sold by aliens.
2. Report from a man who heard a colonel (name not given) making indiscreet statements (no details) at places and time not stated.
3. Report about a mark (lover's sign) on a telegraph post.
4. Report about a Christadelphian* conscientious objector giving training in engineering to prospective members of HM Forces.

---

* A religious group whose teachings forbade fighting.

5. Report on a hotel keeper in Scotland thought to have German
   blood in him . . .

The inquiries didn't just come from the public. A Home Office
minister, Osbert Peake, passed on information from a constituent
about a German woman in Yorkshire who owned several caravans. 'Ostensibly these are said to be let out to holidaymakers
but they obviously provide possibilities of espionage, wireless etc.'
Someone in MI5 took this one seriously. 'One of the centres of
fifth column activities may be a caravan circus,' an officer noted.
'This was proved to be the case in Holland, where it was found
that large holes had been dug beneath caravans to conceal radio
transmitters and arms.'

The police investigated, but found nothing suspicious. Another
MI5 officer closed the file, expressing doubts about the idea of
Dutch clowns and strongmen having been secret Nazis: 'The very
fact that a circus is always on the move makes the digging of holes
under caravans seem absurd.'

A thriller writer, Dennis Wheatley, produced a paper on possible German invasion tactics which was largely dismissed by
General Hastings Ismay, Churchill's chief military adviser, as 'too
far-fetched even for Hitler', but a few points caught his eye. One
idea was, he thought, 'just the sort of fiendish trick that the Nazi
mentality would conceive'. And he asked an aide, Duncan Sandys
– Churchill's son-in-law – to look into it. A month later, Sandys
sent back a dry reply. 'You asked me to enquire about measures
to prevent the unleashing of prisoners, lunatics and wild beasts,'
he noted, before explaining that the first two issues had been
considered and that the third, given the current ratio of soldiers
to zoos, wasn't a concern.

All this activity was watched keenly from abroad. In an encrypted
message sent back to Moscow at the start of September, Semyon
Kremer, an intelligence officer at the Russian embassy in London,
reported that 'the police have found pieces of metal polished to
a mirror finish round important objectives. An expert thinks they
were scattered by the Fifth Column to help the Sausage-Dealers'*
aircraft to get their bearings when they dropped light signals.'

---

* The Soviet code for Germans. France was 'Gastronomica'.

MI5 had investigated these aluminium discs, which were found in a circle on the ground near an aircraft factory, and concluded they had been dropped by accident.

But among the many false trails there were enough real cases – like Reginald Windsor's group – to feed the Security Service's strong belief that there were dangerous people in Britain who needed to be monitored.

When it came to the Leeds group, MI5 considered the case settled: they had their men behind bars, and that was an end to the matter. Unfortunately, it quickly became apparent that Roberts had done too good a job: the Leeds group were over-qualified for regulation 18B. When the new Home Secretary, Herbert Morrison, was asked to sign the detention orders, he had a question. Internment was intended for those who were judged dangerous, but against whom criminal charges couldn't be brought. Given what these men had done, he observed, surely they should be put on trial? Could he see a full report of the case?

The request, which arrived just before Christmas 1940, set off alarm bells at MI5. A prosecution would mean Roberts having to give evidence. Even if he did so in private, his identity would be obvious to the men on trial, and it would be impossible to stop them communicating that back to Charnley. 'We shall inevitably lose Roberts as an agent,' director Jasper Harker was warned.

Harker consulted Liddell. 'We must make up our minds at once as to whether we are prepared to sacrifice Mr Roberts's future usefulness,' he wrote.

Liddell was firm. 'I do not think that there is a case without Roberts,' he replied, and it would be impossible to retain his anonymity in a trial. 'His identity would be bound to leak out,' he said, citing the case of 'Miss X', another Knight agent, who had helped catch three communist spies in 1938. After their trial, Miss X – real name Olga Gray – had been paid off. But while Gray had found the undercover life a strain – at Knight's request she had worked as a secretary inside the Communist Party for much of the 1930s – Roberts showed no signs of wanting to be pensioned off.

MI5 began preparing its lines of defence against the Home Office. The first was delay. It was the end of January before

Harker sent the report on the Leeds case to Morrison – a month after the Home Secretary requested details 'at the earliest possible moment'.

As 1941 began, the war seemed to move to a new phase. There was no longer the prospect of imminent invasion, though that threat might return again in the spring. Britain was taking the battle to the enemy in Africa, advancing through Libya from Egypt, but it was beginning to sink in that the fight was going to be a long one.

At home, MI5 had found itself drawn into an internal row within Charles de Gaulle's Free French government in London. The British were shown letters which apparently revealed that Émile Muselier, the commander of the Free French naval forces, had been passing information to the Nazis' puppet Vichy government. Although MI5 had doubts about the veracity of the documents, Churchill ordered Muselier's arrest. To Liddell's evident amusement, this was delayed as the French admiral had been 'down at Windsor spending the night with a lady friend'.

De Gaulle was furious, convinced that the letters had been forged by British intelligence in an effort to discredit Muselier. He was half-right: they had in fact been forged by a French intelligence officer, who confessed after he was arrested a week later.

As Liddell shuttled between Scotland Yard and the Foreign Office, trying to disentangle the threads of this plot – for which de Gaulle remained determined to blame the British – he discussed the Leeds case with the Director of Public Prosecutions. Atkinson confirmed his view that there was 'no hope whatsoever' of a prosecution without Roberts giving evidence.

When it was eventually sent, Harker's note to Sir Alexander Maxwell, enclosing a report on the case, was brief. 'I appreciate it may be thought desirable that publicity should be given to this case,' he wrote. 'A public trial would, however, inevitably destroy our agent's usefulness. He is a much valued agent, and I should be most reluctant that this should happen.'

Maxwell's reply ran to three pages of typically elegant prose. The aim of such a trial, he said, would not be to expose the activities of 'the more disreputable riff-raff which has been attracted to the British Union' but to punish the guilty and to deter other 'little pockets of scoundrels'. And he had a final point: just because under emergency war regulations the government had the power to lock people up without trial, it was 'very important' that MI5 shouldn't 'drift into the view' that this was an alternative to 'criminal prosecution against persons who engage in criminal activities'.

Harker's reply went through several drafts, each stronger than the last, before it got to Maxwell. He insisted he needed Roberts in order to monitor the remnants of the British Union. 'It is owing to the fact that he has been working for us for over seven years in the party that he is able to do this,' he wrote. 'There is no other agent who is in such a unique position, and if we are deprived of his services we shall be working under serious disadvantages.' And he raised a further point: 'The disclosure of the agent's identity might have undesirable consequences, so far as he personally is concerned, and an undesirable effect upon other agents.'

This wasn't an idle warning. Lewis had introduced Roberts to the group. Roberts had given Jimmy Dickson's home address to them. But the greatest threat was to Roberts himself. He had spent years working inside the BU under his own name. He'd been involved with his local fascist group. If he was revealed to be a spy, his whole family would be at risk from attacks by anyone inclined to take revenge.

But Maxwell had someone else weighing in on his side. Norman Birkett was one of the most celebrated barristers of the day. In his youth, Birkett had been set for a life as a Methodist preacher, but at Cambridge he discovered the law, and the pleasure of public debate. After joining the chambers of the great advocate Sir Edward Marshall Hall, he had defended the notorious Maundy Gregory on charges of selling government honours, as well as taking high-profile murder and libel cases. When war broke out, he'd been put in charge of the Advisory Committees, which heard the appeals of people who had been interned. As far as MI5 was concerned, Birkett was a good-hearted pest. This was his job. The way the Home Office had squared the internment policy with its conscience was by putting men in charge who would ask awkward questions.

The Leeds group had come before his committee, and Birkett too wanted to know why they weren't being put on trial. 'I am bound to say that I think your view was right,' he told Maxwell.

'The most satisfactory course is to put the papers into the hands of the Director of Public Prosecutions and to ask him to proceed according to the law.'

Harker had had enough. 'The only person who is in a position to give evidence which would result in a conviction is our agent,' he wrote to Maxwell at the end of March. 'And after very careful consideration I have come to the conclusion that I cannot allow him to appear in court.' The Home Office weren't going to get Roberts, and that was that.

The characteristic of the fights between MI5 and the Home Office was that both sides were in the right. Roberts was, in Harker's words, 'an agent upon whom we place the very greatest reliance'. The Leeds case had shown the value of having someone who had been inside the BU since its early days. It had also revealed to MI5 officers beyond Knight the extent of Roberts's skills as an undercover operator. If his cover was blown, there would be no way to replace him.

But Maxwell was equally correct to have deep anxieties about the abuse of emergency powers. The usual rules preventing arbitrary detention and allowing suspects to see the evidence against them had been suspended. Britain, in fighting totalitarianism, was adopting the characteristics of a totalitarian state. The Leeds fascists might well have been dangerous, but they were being locked up in large part on the word of an anonymous agent working for the secret police. Maxwell and Birkett were fighting to keep a Britain whose values were worth fighting for.

For Windsor, Gannon, Longfellow and Jeffery, Harker's decision had mixed implications: they wouldn't face a trial for the serious crimes of which they were guilty. There would be no prison terms and no criminal records. But they would, instead, face summary justice. The following month, Windsor spent two days being questioned by one of Birkett's Advisory Committees. He and the others were told that they would be locked up indefinitely with other designated undesirables on the Isle of Man.

In the middle of the Irish Sea, halfway between the Lake District and Ireland, the Isle of Man was an ideal spot for the government to dump its problems. Even if internees could escape the barbed wire, there was twenty miles of sea to cross to get to the mainland. The prison 'camps' were, in reality, groups of buildings, houses and hotels, surrounded by wire and guards. There were eleven camps in all, covering Germans and Austrians, Italians, and Britons, and both men and women. The randomness of internment meant that refugees from fascism found themselves being held alongside British fascists – though in separate camps.

An internment camp on the Isle of Man

The main enemy in the camps was boredom, as internees waited for the war to end, or for the government to relent and release them. And the internees were at least safe from bombing, which was more than could be said for the families many of them had left behind.

Roberts, too, was worrying about his family. Every day the face of London was being changed, as bombs ripped fresh holes in familiar streets, wiping out landmarks in an instant. At such times, and surrounded by so much death, little seemed safe or solid. While Epsom wasn't a prime bombing target, it was still hit by planes that were lost or simply dropping their payloads before heading home. The house four doors up from the Roberts family was blown to bits by a high-explosive bomb, killing a friend of Max's.

Audrey, meanwhile, was fearful for the safety of the man she loved. He may not have to wear a uniform, but he had swapped the dangers of the battlefront for a less quantifiable peril. Hunting traitors and spies carried its own risks. As Audrey struggled with the stress of war, Roberts advised her to start smoking, to calm her nerves.

Though his wife knew the truth about his work, their neighbours knew nothing. Many of the husbands had joined up, and Roberts had faced questions about why he wasn't doing the same. A vague reference to a job in the War Office would have been problematic for someone so well known locally as an enthusiastic Blackshirt. Instead, he said he was a conscientious objector, and had registered for non-combat service. To cover his long absences, Roberts said he was working on a farm 'up north'. His son Max hated this. Other boys, whose fathers were in uniform, told him that his old man was a coward. In fact his father had a far better understanding of why fascism needed to be fought than the average conscripted soldier. And dealing daily with traitors, he felt in more imminent peril than many of those wearing khaki.

Not all the neighbours were convinced. At least one reported Roberts's suspicious pattern of movements to the authorities. Still, the likeable nature that had made Windsor and Gannon trust Roberts seems to have generally protected him. His returns home on leave, often without notice, would begin with him catching up with his sons and then, in the early evening, he and Audrey would walk to the pub for a drink. The stroll together, in which the couple could exchange their news and discuss their worries, was as important for settling Roberts's mind as the beer at the end of the journey.

Now that Roberts was an MI5 officer, he had his own desk. Initially, this had been in Wormwood Scrubs, but when the prison was hit by a bomb in September 1940, most of the staff – Roberts among them – were moved to Blenheim Palace, the Duke of Marlborough's country seat in Oxfordshire. Senior officers were left behind in London, in a headquarters on St James's Street that was camouflaged behind a 'To Let' sign. The autumn was proving to be as pleasant as the summer had been, and the vast Blenheim estate provided an agreeable respite for many of the staff after spending most of the year working in a prison. Desks were set up under tapestries. From the balcony near his, Roberts could see the young women of the Registry, as MI5's archive of files was known, relaxing in their lunch breaks on the lawns. There was a lake for swimming in or, when it froze in the winter, for skating on. When it snowed, staff discovered that their in-trays could serve as toboggans.

Pleasant though his surroundings were, Roberts found sitting behind a desk little more enjoyable at MI5 than he had at the Westminster Bank. He wanted to be in the field, not shuffling papers. But at the start of 1941, he was doing the bread and butter work of MI5, sending memos to other branches of government requesting information about people of interest.

Roberts would be rescued by a young man who, like him, had a mischievous, enquiring mind, and nerves of steel. Like Roberts, he'd worked in a bank but hadn't enjoyed it. This was slightly more awkward in his case, as the bank in question was the most famous in the world, and it carried his name.

5

'He is quite ruthless where Germans are concerned'

On a Saturday afternoon in March 1941, two women arrived in the courtyard of Swan Court, a modern nine-storey red-brick block of flats just off the King's Road in Chelsea. They walked into the entrance hall, where they had arranged to meet a man who lived there. One of the women, Molly Hiscox, had been introduced to him a few days earlier, by an acquaintance of hers from the now-closed Right Club. She had been told he was a German agent, who could help her with a mission she'd given herself.

She had a friend, Norah Briscoe, with her. The man took them up to flat number 74. In the sitting room, the two women looked at the view from the window, admiring the damage done by a bomb that had fallen on Shawfield Street, over the road. Molly asked the man if he'd seen the big crater near the Bank of England. 'Wasn't it marvellous?' she said. The high-explosive bomb that had fallen there two months earlier, leaving a huge crater that was still disrupting traffic, had killed 111 people.

The two women sat on the sofa, while the man sat in the armchair opposite. If the guests hoped for a cup of tea, their host made no move towards the kitchen. The man said to Norah that he'd heard she had a son living in Germany. This was true. The boy, now ten, had been born in Britain, but after Norah's husband died, she'd travelled to Germany and become infatuated with Nazism. When she'd returned to England before the war, she'd left him behind, to be raised by her German lover. As war approached, she'd made no effort to get him back.

The three discussed places in Germany they all knew, and how much they preferred Germany's food and climate to Britain's. Molly quoted another friend as saying that it was a pity they had been born in the wrong country.

Norah moved things on. 'We might as well get down to

business,' she said, opening her handbag. She showed the man her pass from the Ministry of Supply, where she worked as a typist. Though her job was unimportant, she said she saw a lot of official files. She paused, nervous. 'Can anybody hear us here?' she asked. The man reassured her that the flats had been very quiet since the bombing, with residents staying away.

Norah pulled a bundle of papers from her bag and put them on the small table between them, then began to explain what they were. The first, dated two months previously, gave the location of factories in Northern Ireland. Another showed supplies to be sent to Turkey. She could, she said, sometimes get the dates of shipping, although she apologised that she couldn't always find out which ports the ships would be sailing from. Other papers covered different firms, their labour conditions and shortages.

Then the door opened, and two more men walked in from the kitchen. One of them identified himself as Inspector Evan Jones of the Special Branch. He informed all three occupants of the room that they were under arrest. The other man was Maxwell Knight. The supposed German agent, to whom Norah had been trying to pass documents, was one of his men, Harold Kurtz, codename M/H. Having left Nazi Germany for London, he had been recruited by Knight three years earlier with a promise of help towards British citizenship if he spied on his fellow émigrés. He was now being used on short-term operations like this one.

Two days later, on the Monday, Knight had lunch with Liddell. 'He told me all about the Briscoe case and showed me the documents,' Liddell recorded afterwards. 'They are voluminous and cover a wide field. If the information had leaked it would certainly be a serious matter.'

In the total war in which Britain and Germany were now engaged, factories and supplies were as important as troops. These delivered the aircraft, tanks and bullets without which victory would be impossible. This was just one of the technological aspects of modern warfare for which MI5's staff were ill-equipped. It was for that reason that Liddell had brought in a most unusual recruit the previous year.

Nathaniel Mayer Victor Rothschild, always known as Victor, used to say that his family could be divided into those who made money and those who spent it. Born to be the former, he soon determined to be the latter.

When Victor was born in 1910, his gender came as a great relief to his family. A century earlier, the dynasty's founding father, Mayer Amschel, had decreed that only Rothschild sons could inherit a stake in the family bank. While this ensured that the House of Rothschild remained in the hands of Rothschilds, it created a practical pressure to produce boys: in 1901 the Frankfurt branch of the bank had closed for want of a male heir to run it. And at the start of the twentieth century, it was an area in which the English branch of the family was also struggling.

The patriarch, Nathaniel, had two adult sons, Walter and Charles. The elder, Walter, wasn't suited to banking. At the office, he threw his correspondence unopened into huge wicker crates where it lay undiscovered until some years later. His private life was equally chaotic. He hadn't married, but had several mistresses, one of whom was blackmailing him. Another bore him a daughter. Only one subject truly engaged him: the study of animals and insects. On this, he spent his fortune, amassing one of the world's largest private collections of specimens, living and dead. It ranged from butterflies and moths – he had two million of those – to giraffes and giant tortoises. He even had a team of zebras to pull his pony trap. At the family home of Tring Park, north-west of London, he built a museum to house his collection. Every item was carefully catalogued and cross-referenced.

His younger brother shared his passion. But as he was more capable of dealing with the real world than Walter, Charles at least attempted to become a serious banker. This effort was stifled by his overbearing father, and a reluctance within the bank to adopt his novel ideas. In particular, his suggestion that Rothschilds should invest in a new invention called a 'gramophone' was rebuffed.

Charles was more successful in his marriage, however, falling in love with a woman he met while on an expedition to catch butterflies and fleas in the Carpathian mountains in central Europe. Rózsika von Wertheimstein was a great beauty, known as 'the Rose of Hungary'. She was also considered quite daring, as among other things she had been the first woman in Europe to serve a tennis ball overarm, a motion that revealed an unlady-like amount of information about the shape of her breast. But she was in her late thirties when they married, seven years older than Charles, and their first two children, Miriam and Liberty, born in 1908 and 1909, were girls. So the arrival of a healthy boy in 1910 allowed the entire family to breathe a little easier, knowing the bank's future was secure for another generation at least.

Victor was doted upon, especially when Charles and Rózsika's final child, born in 1913, proved to be another girl, Nica. As an infant, the young heir was delighted by the sight of flames, and so a servant was told to walk backwards in front of his pram, lighting matches. He looked back on his childhood as 'simul-taneously spoilt and regimented'. Both his father and his uncle instilled in the children their shared love of natural history, and in so doing taught them the value of precise observation. Victor's earliest memory was of being sent into the garden aged four by his father to catch a rare butterfly. But his youth was overshadowed by a tragedy from which no amount of wealth could protect him.

As Charles had grown older, he had suffered increasingly from depression. His daughter Miriam would later attribute this to the Rothschild tradition of inbreeding, noting that Charles's parents had been cousins – but the growing responsibilities of work can't have helped. Nathaniel Rothschild had died in 1915, leaving Charles partly responsible, with his uncles, for running the British branch of the bank just as Europe was being ripped apart by war. The bouts of illness increased, and Charles was sent away to Switzerland to recuperate. Then in 1916 he contracted encephalitis, an inflammation of the brain. Although he recovered, the disease seems to have been the final blow to his mind.

Charles returned home from treatment in December 1919, a shell of a man. On his arrival, he didn't even acknowledge his eager children. In the following years, his moods would swing wildly, and staff and children found themselves dreading the next manic episode. Finally, in 1923, he walked into the bathroom and cut his own throat.

The children weren't told how he'd died. Servants were forbid-den from speaking about it, and any newspapers that might carry

a report were banned from the house. Two years later* Victor, by
then fifteen years old and away boarding at Harrow School, called
Miriam in distress, asking his big sister to come at once. When she
arrived, he told her the other boys had been teasing him, saying
that his father had killed himself. Miriam assured him this wasn't
true, and drove back to Tring to confront her mother. Instead,
Rózsika confirmed the bare fact, refusing to say another word on
the matter.

School had already exposed Victor to some of the harshness
of the world outside Tring Park. He described his preparatory
school, Stanmore Park, as 'a hell hole'. But at Harrow things were
a little easier. His skill as a cricketer, augmented by private coach-
ing, meant he wasn't a target for bullies. Naturally intelligent and
particularly gifted at biology, he was tempted to slack off in other
subjects. This his mother wouldn't tolerate, and the teenager was
forced to spend his holidays writing daily essays on the Punic
Wars until he mended his ways.

By the time Victor arrived at Cambridge University, he had all
the makings of a playboy: limitless wealth, good looks, enviable
sporting skills and the prospect of an inherited title. He played
cricket for Northamptonshire, facing the bodyline bowling of
Harold Larwood – fast deliveries aimed directly at the batsman
with the goal of terrifying him into a mistake – without protection.
He played jazz piano, signing up for lessons from American swing
legend Teddy Wilson. He drove fast cars, setting a Cambridge-
to-London record in his Bugatti – 60 miles in 49 minutes. He
motored down to Monte Carlo for his vacation to try his hand
in the casinos, and completed another area of his education by
visiting a brothel in Rheims on the way.

But there was more to Victor than the search for pleasure. His
mother's attempt to instil in him a sense of the responsibility
that came with his name had left him terrified that he might not
live up to it. He knew that people sneered, as only the British
could, at his wealth. Having been blessed with every advantage,
a Rothschild who wasn't a success was without excuse. 'I don't

---

* The exact timing is unclear. Kenneth Rose, *Elusive Rothschild* (2001), says 'a
year or so'. Hannah Rothschild, *The Baroness* (2012), relying on Miriam's vivid
recollection, says Victor was fifteen.

like failing at jobs I do,' he said. 'In fact I'm very determined not to fail. The idea of my walking out of a job or being sacked is repugnant to me.'

Victor Rothschild, c. 1930

Victor in particular had not just money, but intellect. Now, at Cambridge, he found he could put that intellect to work. He determined to follow his father and his uncle – and his sister, for Miriam, who as a girl had been denied a formal education, was proving to be a brilliant self-taught scientist – into the study of natural history.

This was not, of course, what the family intended for him or needed from him. Rózsika pleaded with Victor to at least try banking. He gave it six months and, bored, returned to his laboratory in Cambridge. He was happy enough to spend the family money, but Victor simply wasn't very keen on being a Rothschild.

The family duties weren't to be escaped quite as easily as that, though. The death of his uncle Walter in 1937 meant that Victor became the third Baron Rothschild, and a significant personage in the country. He was uneasy with that. Although he now had a seat in the House of Lords, he didn't speak there, even when he privately opposed the Munich Agreement.

Instead, he began to prepare for war. At the start of 1939, now aged 28, he visited the US, telling friends he was going for more piano lessons from Teddy Wilson. The more significant part of the trip was an invitation to the White House from the president, Franklin D. Roosevelt. While in Washington, he met a series of other leading government officials. J. Edgar Hoover invited him to tour the FBI, and he met the head of the US Chemical Warfare Service.

Rothschild owed this particular encounter to his scientific patron, Sir Harold Hartley. The two had first met a decade earlier, when Hartley had examined Rothschild for a scholarship to Cambridge. Hartley was an Oxford don, a chemist who, having joined the Army at the outbreak of the First World War, was assigned the task of protecting his fellow soldiers from German gas attacks. He would spend the next three decades advising successive governments on chemical warfare.

Hartley recognised that Rothschild's mind would be of use in the coming fight, and when war broke out, he invited the young man to become his assistant. The work was important, but Rothschild was the wrong kind of scientist: he was a biologist, and the field was physical chemistry. He began looking around for something else to do. He occupied part of his mind by recruiting a tutor to improve his grasp of pure mathematics, doing exercises in his spare time. By now Rothschild was thinking about the military possibilities of sabotage, and through the intelligence connections he had already made, secured a meeting with Guy Liddell of MI5 in February 1940.

Liddell took an immediate liking to Rothschild, and set him a problem. 'I told him that broadly speaking we wanted to give an answer to the factory manager who said, "You tell me that in the event of trouble sabotage may take place on a wide scale. What do you expect me to do about it?"'

Rothschild didn't know, but he said that he would get to work on the question.

He started sketching out a solution when the two men met

again the following month, and by April 1940, Liddell, who was on the lookout for interesting minds that he could put to work, had invited Rothschild to join the Security Service full-time. Rothschild replied that he 'will have as much as five days a week free'. He was hired on a 'part time' basis, working initially for three days a week. The aristocrat scientist was now an aristocrat spy-hunter.

Liddell was pushing fifty, with two decades in the secret world and a series of successful cases under his belt. His professional success relied partly on his ability to hold his tongue and gently guide his superiors towards conclusions. On the face of it, he had little in common with Rothschild, not yet thirty and a proud man accustomed both to high living, and to telling people exactly what he thought – with an abruptness that some of those closest to him thought was actually a mask for shyness. But the two quickly became friends, dining together regularly. In an effort to free himself of his family burdens, Rothschild had sold most of his family's estates, but he opened one house he'd kept, in the grounds of Tring Park, to fellow MI5 staff members who needed relief from the Blitz. Liddell was a frequent guest.

They shared a love of music. While Rothschild had his piano, Liddell was a fine cellist. He told friends that in the previous war he'd owned three cellos, stored in different places so that he could get to them in the event of advance or retreat.

But the two men also had private sadnesses in common. In 1926, Liddell had married the aristocratic Calypso Baring, heiress to another banking family. Theirs must briefly have seemed a charmed life. Over the next five years, they had four children. Her father commissioned Sir Edwin Lutyens to design them a house on Cheyne Walk in Chelsea, overlooking the Thames. The project was the height of style, to which Calypso added an eccentric touch by papering some of the walls with front pages of *The Times*. The marriage wasn't to last. In 1935, Calypso left Liddell for her stepbrother in California. The couple would spend the subsequent years in a custody battle, and the marriage was dissolved in 1943.

Rothschild too was unhappily married. He'd met Barbara Hutchinson in 1931, and they'd married in 1933. They had different expectations of what marriage was. For all his discomfort with his heritage, Rothschild had grown up around women who stayed at home and focused on the family. Barbara's had been a more bohemian upbringing. Her mother was a cousin of the writer Lytton Strachey, and the young Barbara had been exposed to more modern ideas than previous Rothschild wives. There was passion in the marriage, and three children, but also frequent fighting. Barbara increasingly complained she found Victor cold, and began a series of affairs in search of warmth. 'I never thought he cared,' she told a friend later. 'But he remembers every man – some I'd forgotten myself.'

Perhaps what most united Rothschild and Liddell, though, was their approach to their work: patient, methodical, dedicated. All his life, Rothschild had been viewed through the prism of his family, its bank and its wealth. In Liddell, he met someone who was interested in his mind.

To be a Rothschild was to be rich and powerful, but it meant something else as well. In 1934, shortly after his marriage, Victor and some friends had stopped on a whim at a well-known London restaurant. 'Soon after I had entered, a man whom I took to be the manager came up and said: "Excuse me, sir, are you a Jew?"' Rothschild saw no point in denying it – 'my appearance is hardly Aryan' – so he replied that he was. 'He then said that he was sorry but in that case he would not serve me and I would have to leave. No explanation was offered.'

No explanation was needed. His great-grandfather, Lionel de Rothschild, had been elected to the House of Commons five times as a Liberal between 1847 and 1857, but had been forbidden to take his seat each time because he was Jewish. His obstinacy – and that of the electors in the City of London who kept voting for him – was rewarded in 1858, when the government changed the law. But that was only the lower chamber of Parliament. A decade later, Queen Victoria expressly rejected the suggestion that Lionel be given a seat in the House of Lords, saying she could not consent to making 'a Jew a peer'. It wasn't until 1885 that the Queen changed her mind, making Lionel's son Nathaniel the first Baron Rothschild. But that didn't mean acceptance. Five years later, when Victoria visited Waddesdon Manor, the home of Nathaniel's brother-in-law, the Queen had her lunch with only her daughter present, while her host ate with the other guests in the next room.

Victor's father Charles had had his own formative experiences. 'If I ever have a son he will be instructed in boxing and ju-jitsu before he enters school,' he wrote to a friend, a decade after he left Harrow. 'Jew hunts such as I experienced are a very one-sided amusement.'

The restaurant manager might have been encouraged in his refusal to serve Jews by events in Germany, where Hitler had just taken power – indeed, Victor made the link at the time – but England had no need to import anti-Semitism from the continent. It was a centuries-old force that had seen every Jew expelled from the country in the thirteenth century, not to return for more than 350 years. It could be found in the work of England's greatest writers: Geoffrey Chaucer, William Shakespeare and Charles Dickens. The English hadn't invented anti-Semitism, but they'd invented their own forms of it.

In the 1930s, Oswald Mosley's rhetorical attacks on Jews as a separate group who used their wealth to undermine the national interest weren't that far out of line with many people's private views. Although a sense of British politeness meant that Jewish jokes had disappeared from music hall stages once large numbers of refugees began arriving from Germany and Austria in the mid-1930s, the sentiments behind them were still expressed in conversation. Jews were not entirely to be trusted. They observed different religious days, and ate different foods. They lived in the same areas as each other, and stuck to the same types of work – much of it, such as banking and diamond-dealing, highly lucrative. Like Roman Catholics, they owed allegiance to something other than King and Country: one didn't have to believe in an international conspiracy to note that Jews in one country seemed very interested in the welfare of Jews in other countries. The result was a muted suspicion that permeated all levels of society. While there were no longer any legal barriers for Jews, they would struggle to get into the better regiments in the Army.

Victor wasn't a religious man, but he accepted his status, an attitude summed up in his instructions to a waiter: 'I am Lord Rothschild. I do not eat pork. Bring me a ham sandwich.' He wasn't just a Jew, he was a Rothschild. That meant he was the de facto head of Anglo-Jewry. He observed Jewish holidays because it was expected of him. He had persuaded Barbara to convert to Judaism before their marriage so as to spare his mother's feelings, and so that their children would be accepted as Jewish. And although he was shy of public speaking, in the 1930s he recognised his duty to stand up for those fleeing Hitler, and organised relief funds for the Jews of Europe.

But to millions, the very name Rothschild was shorthand for Jewish scheming. Everyone knew the story of how his great-great-grandfather, Nathan Mayer Rothschild, had made a fortune by rushing from the scene of Britain's victory at the Battle of Waterloo and spreading rumours of defeat, before going to the stock exchange and buying up shares in the depressed market. When the good news arrived, his profit was a million pounds. Everyone of quality had a view of what they saw as the family's vulgar extravagance, the houses piled with oranate eighteenth-century French furniture, the fine pictures that were hung, over-varnished, in over-gilded frames. Rothschilds might have more money than anyone else, they might sit in the House of Lords, but England's gentry could still sneer at them.

The claims of excess were undeniable, but the Waterloo story was a lie – an archetypal anti-Jewish slur. Nathan hadn't been in Belgium watching Wellington fight Napoleon, he'd been in London. He probably did get early wind of the victory, but if so, it seems he took it straight to the government. One story tells that he was unable to convince Lord Liverpool, the prime minister, of the truth: official reports were still that the battle was going France's way. Whatever the truth of that, Nathan had felt that having informed the government, his duty was done, and he went to the stock exchange, convinced that his sources were more reliable than the government's. The market wasn't in fact depressed, but it did rise when official news of the victory came in. Nathan made a profit, but nothing close to the claimed million pounds.

The story was so famous, so aligned with the legend of amoral Jews profiting from the blood of Gentiles, that in 1940 it was the subject of a Nazi propaganda film. *Die Rothschilds* had the Waterloo trades as a central moment in a Jewish scheme to enslave Europe. The film closed with an image of a Star of David burning across the continent.

For Victor, the war was one of personal as well as national survival. He was well aware that if the Nazis reached Britain, he and his children would be at the top of their list for arrest and murder. 'He is quite ruthless where Germans are concerned,' Liddell observed after their first meeting, 'and would exterminate them by any and every means.' He was determined at least to avoid torture: when invasion seemed imminent, he equipped himself with a suicide pill.

MI5 had responded to its wartime staffing crisis by encouraging those officers it did have to recruit anyone they thought suitable. That tended to mean lawyers and academics – agile thinkers used to asking questions and approaching problems in creative ways.

But there was one area where Liddell knew they were deficient: science. The dons and barristers were ill-equipped to understand the complexities involved in this new high-technology warfare of factories and machines. As Liddell noted, they were struggling to communicate with the manufacturers. Rothschild could see why. He viewed his new colleagues as 'scientifically sub-human', people who 'did not know the difference between sulphuric acid and a sonar wave'.

Rothschild's advantage was that he was a polymath. He had studied English at Cambridge alongside his biology, and discovered a taste for collecting eighteenth-century books and manuscripts. The fact that he felt at home in both science and the arts perfectly qualified him to be MI5's bridge to what he called 'technical' people.

Though he was given a uniform, and the rank of colonel, such things counted for little at MI5. The less formal atmosphere suited Rothschild. Life as a junior officer in the regular military would have been a struggle for someone who had been a guest of Roosevelt and royalty. While Rothschild was used to working hard, he was also used to doing it under his own direction. As an intelligence officer, he had the freedom to act as he pleased, and his self-assurance was a positive benefit when it came to having to deal with the top level of government.

Four months after he joined MI5, in August 1940, Rothschild became concerned about a group of Germans working in one of the factories supervised by Lord Beaverbrook, the Minister for Aircraft Production. Beaverbrook's overriding concern was to get every available pair of hands to work on building planes for the ongoing Battle of Britain. To that end he was pleased to have skilled German engineers playing their part. Rothschild's job was to keep the same factories safe from sabotage or attack, and started from a point of suspicion of any German. Beaverbook regarded MI5 as excessively anxious on the subject of security. MI5 regarded the man they called 'the Beaver' as cavalier about it.

Rothschild went to see the Beaver, to demand that eight German engineers be removed from a factory in Poole. He reported the conversation back.

'I am surprised that somebody with your name, your liberal views, your position and reputation, should go in for this witch-hunting,' Beaverbrook told him, in Rothschild's account. 'Those poor Jews have been hunted out of Germany, and now when they come here they are hunted back into concentration camps. You should not be involved in this persecution and you should not be in MI5 witch-hunting.'

Rothschild replied that the people in question weren't Jews. 'They are what is known as Aryan,' he said drily.

'They are Jews,' Beaverbrook said.

'They are not,' Rothschild told him.

'They are Jews,' Beaverbrook insisted, unused to being contradicted.

'They are not,' said Rothschild, certain of his ground.

Beaverbrook gave up on this aspect, but not the whole matter. After agreeing to look at Rothschild's evidence, he appealed to his fellow peer to quit MI5: 'You should not be in that organisation with witch-hunters. It ought to be abolished.' The workers, he argued, were too closely watched to be able to commit sabotage, and even if they were able to communicate the location of their factories to Berlin, it would be difficult for the Germans to bomb them accurately. 'I do not think there is any danger from Nazi spies in this country,' he concluded. 'I do not think it matters if they are at large.'

Rothschild thought it mattered a great deal. Three weeks after Liddell had asked him to think about sabotage, the men dined together, and Rothschild laid out the problem in a way that the MI5 man had simply never thought about before. Every tank, gun and aeroplane was manufactured from thousands of precision-engineered components, made by hundreds of suppliers. A flaw in any single piece could delay production or cause the final weapon to fail. For an organisation used to thinking about counter-espionage in terms of catching individuals and protecting military targets, the prospect of having to secure all the stages in a modern manufacturing process, from the smallest workshop to the final assembly line, was a daunting one. But Rothschild had already worked it out.

'He thought we should first try and classify our vulnerable points and factories in this country and place them in groups,' Liddell recorded afterwards. 'We should then get the opinions of some of the managers as to how it would be possible to put the works out of action or damage the products without undue risk of detection.'

Then there was the question of protecting technology. Rothschild described to Liddell a 'rocket bomb' that was under development. 'I gather that this is a somewhat epoch-making invention,' a clearly baffled Liddell noted. 'It is the first that I have heard of it. It is obviously very desirable that every possible step should be taken to prevent a leakage about this information to the Germans. We shall probably find that it is being made in a small tin shack in a corner of a field and that anybody can get inside with the aid of a tin-opener.'

The day after that meeting, Liddell spoke to an official at the Ministry of Supply, and realised he wasn't the only person who hadn't thought about the problem. The official saw 'no danger in the employment of German firms and Germans' and had given no thought to the possibilities of espionage or sabotage.

By September 1940, Rothschild was running his own section of MI5, tasked with counter-sabotage. He was told he could have a small staff, and asked that they should include an engineer. He also brought in two women, to act as secretaries. Neither was inclined to let that be the limit of her ambitions.

As it happened, they were both Tesses: Teresa Mayor and Theresa Clay. Mayor hadn't been Rothschild's first choice. He'd wanted her flatmate Patricia Rawdon-Smith, but she suggested Mayor instead. For the unhappily married Rothschild, there was an appeal to her suggestion: one of the few women who had studied at Cambridge, Mayor had been known as an 'unearthly beauty'. Her friends called her Tess, or sometimes 'Red Tess' – as a student, she'd flirted with communism.

Tess Mayor, left, in 1933 and Theresa Clay in 1938

Clay was a friend of Rothschild's sister Miriam, and like her a biologist specialising in parasites – in Clay's case, lice. Another biologist wasn't particularly what the team needed, but Clay, like Rothschild, would be able to speak science unto scientists. She also had another advantage as far as Rothschild was concerned: impeccable intelligence connections. She was in an intense relationship with Colonel Richard Meinertzhagen, then Britain's most famous spy.

The 62-year-old Meinertzhagen had made a name for himself two decades earlier, during the Great War, fighting against German-Turkish forces in Palestine. Every schoolboy knew the tale of how, as an intelligence officer in 1917, he'd conceived and executed one of the great deception operations of the war. On his horse, he'd set out towards the Turkish lines carrying a haversack containing papers suggesting the British would make a feint on the enemy's eastern flank before attacking in force in the west.

Meinertzhagen rode within sight of an enemy patrol, and then pretended to flee. When they fired, he pretended to be hit, slumping in the saddle and dropping the haversack and his rifle, before spurring his horse away.

The Turks found the plans, were fooled, and the British attack, sooner than expected and from an unexpected direction, was a total success. Jerusalem was captured within two months, and Meinertzhagen was a hero.

The only problem with this story was that it was a lie. There had been a satchel full of documents and Meinertzhagen had been involved in the production of its contents, but the operation hadn't been his idea, and he hadn't been the man on horseback. The Turks also disputed that they had believed the ruse.

Few knew the truth: the man who had been the brains behind the operation had been killed in action the following year, and the one who'd dropped the bag had stayed in intelligence, and so was not going to make a public fuss. Meinertzhagen exploited this to claim credit, and vigorously propagate the myth of the haversack.

Meinertzhagen's word was questionable in other areas, too. His main preoccupation was ornithology: he was an enthusiastic explorer and collector of birds, a crack shot who brought back specimens from his expeditions across the globe. But he'd been banned from the British Museum for stealing specimens.

Meinertzhagen was an expert at deception, but not in the way people believed. He was a fantasist who told stories about his own acts of daring that lay somewhere between exaggeration and fraud.

The precise nature of his relationship with Clay was also a mystery. In 1940, she was 29, less than half his age, and had known him most of her life. After his wife, and the mother of his children, died in a mysterious shooting, Clay became his travelling companion, nanny, and assistant. She didn't share his house, but hers was linked to his by an interior door. She was undoubtedly devoted to him, and may have assisted him in his ornithological frauds. The only person recorded as having had the nerve to ask whether she was sharing his bed was Victor Rothschild. Meinertzhagen told him to mind his own business.*

*

---

* In a coincidence that reflected the tight circles in which Britain's leading families moved, and from which the intelligence agencies were recruited, the two Tesses were second cousins: Meinertzhagen was Mayor's uncle. There were more family intelligence connections: Rothschild's sister Miriam worked among the Bletchley Park codebreakers, along with Mayor's brother Andreas.

Counter-sabotage turned out to mean bombs. Not the ones dropped from the air, but ones smuggled on to ships bound to Britain from supposedly neutral ports. Rothschild complained of the 'benevolent' attitude taken by Spain towards the German secret service, which allowed the enemy to bribe Spanish dockers to facilitate their work. Germany was trying to starve Britain into submission, and to that end, destroying a ship's cargo could be as effective as sinking the vessel with a torpedo. So their engineers devised ingenious ways to secrete the explosives: flexible explosives disguised as raincoats, with the detonators concealed in their hangers. Or inside thermos flasks, hidden under an inch and a half of hot tea.

If one of these hidden German bombs was discovered, either as a result of good security or because it had failed to go off, it was Rothschild's job to study it. But first, it had to be made safe, and this too was a job Rothschild took upon himself. His years dissecting the eggs of frogs and fish had given him a steady hand, and he found the work more exciting than terrifying. 'When one takes a bomb or a fuse to pieces, one really is so busy that one doesn't have time to be frightened,' he said. 'One's also very, very interested. Some of them are beautifully made.'

The first bomb Rothschild tackled did, he conceded, make him 'rather nervous'. The only other person to have attempted that type of fuse had lost an eye and an arm when it exploded. In the absence of more sophisticated protection, Rothschild defused the bomb while kneeling behind an armchair, hoping that if it went off he would at least be able to save his eyes.

Even bomb disposal he did as only a Rothschild could. One day, shopping at the Cartier store on Bond Street, he was asked about his work by a staff member. Was it difficult? Was it frightening? Rothschild gave his usual self-effacing reply, and then added that there was one problem: his tools weren't really up to the job. 'It was difficult to get hold of the first-class screwdrivers that were necessary to undo the extremely small screws in the delay mechanisms.' It was important, he remarked, 'that the screwdrivers should not slip'. A month later, to his delighted surprise, the company sent him a 'superb' set of seven screwdrivers, 'including some marvellously small ones'.

Rothschild's job wasn't simply to defuse the bombs but to

understand them, so as to guide others in dealing with them. He was, typically, impatient with the draughtsmen who were supposed to be producing diagrams of the devices: the images they produced were too technical for a layman to understand. When he vented his frustration to Inspector Donald Fish, a detective who had been seconded to MI5, the policeman suggested that his son Laurence, a self-taught graphic designer, might be able to do the job. Laurence had joined the RAF in the hope of becoming a pilot, but having failed the eye test, he was peeling potatoes when Rothschild tracked him down. Presented with a bomb fuse, he was enthusiastic: 'If you can explain to me how it works, I think I can draw it.' The result, Rothschild said 'was beyond my most optimistic expectations' – a picture both practical and beautiful.

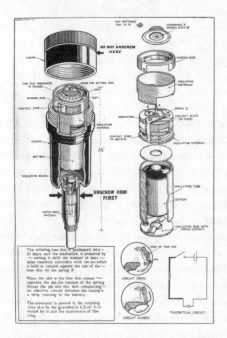

Laurence Fish's diagram of a German 21-day fuse

For the rest of the war, Fish Junior was regularly called in to illustrate MI5 reports on German technology: a fake bar of chocolate designed to blow up seven seconds after it was opened, or a mess tin concealing a bomb under sausages, mash and peas. If Rothschild appreciated him, he was occasionally careless with his safety: one device that Fish took home to study, a bomb disguised as a cigarette box, spent the night under his bed before he discovered that it was still live.

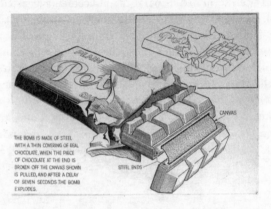

THE BOMB IS MADE OF STEEL WITH A THIN COVERING OF REAL CHOCOLATE. WHEN THE PIECE OF CHOCOLATE AT THE END IS BROKEN OFF THE CANVAS SHOWN IS PULLED, AND AFTER A DELAY OF SEVEN SECONDS THE BOMB EXPLODES.

CANVAS

STEEL ENDS

Fish's sketch of a bomb disguised as a chocolate bar

Then there was the problem of the prime minister. Churchill was regularly sent gifts, mainly cigars, by well-wishers. Rothschild was asked to take a view of the dangers. He concluded that it would be 'too easy' to coat one end of a cigar with 'cyanide or better (in one sense) botulinus toxin' or to hide a small high-explosive charge inside, to be detonated when the cigar was lit. The safest thing would have been to destroy them all, but Churchill was very much inclined to consume them, taking, Rothschild noted, 'obvious pleasure' from personal danger. Rothschild calculated statistically what proportion of the cigars he needed to test to be confident they weren't dangerous. After each box was X-rayed, he would take his sample, grind it up in saline and inject the result into mice. Churchill was 'amused by the experiments but displeased by the delay'.

A more difficult problem was presented by a French general who accosted Churchill as he walked across Parliament Square and presented him with a Virginia ham. Churchill was delighted, and announced he would have it for breakfast the next morning. This caused panic among those tasked with his protection: how could they test the gift in time, and without the prime minister realising? In an 'intricate surgical operation', a very thin slice was removed without disturbing the ham's surface. But there was no time for the usual tests. After a 'high pressure conference', some of London's best scientific minds came up with a solution: they fed the slice to the Medical Research Council's cat, and then watched it closely. When it survived, Churchill was allowed his breakfast.

But there was the occasional compensation for the prime minister's testiness: when Churchill was given a case of 1798 Armagnac, Rothschild insisted on a thirteenth bottle, which he and his colleagues took it upon themselves to test.

Amid such glamour, the original purpose of Rothschild's hiring wasn't forgotten. He and his team set about understanding Britain's defence manufacturers, looking at how they related, and their weaknesses. They assessed vulnerabilities, and identified people who shouldn't be allowed near sensitive installations. The work quickly led them to develop deep suspicions about one company in particular, a household name that MI5 had long believed was a cover for sinister activities.

6

'Agents in every country in the world'

For nearly a century, the Siemens company had been at the cutting edge of technology. In 1848, it began building the first long-distance telegraph line in Europe, from Frankfurt to Berlin. Its founder, Werner Siemens, had a combination of business acumen and an eye for how an invention could be improved. His engineers built a telegraph line from London to Calcutta, and laid another from Ireland to America. Werner developed a dynamo, allowing the generation of electricity with enough power for industrial applications. That in turn allowed the company to build an electric tram service in Berlin, and an underground electric railway in Budapest. And he made innovations as an employer, too. He offered profit-sharing for staff, a nine-hour working day and a generous pension fund. His brother Wilhelm, meanwhile, settled in Britain, and built the firm up there. The business flourished: by the time of Werner's death in 1892, his company was on its way to employing 5,000 staff.

That growth continued after his death. Despite losing most of its overseas assets after the First World War, by the mid-1920s the firm was one of the top five electrical businesses in the world, with Werner's son Carl at the helm. By the start of hostilities in 1939, it made everything from household appliances to railways, a success story in its founder's image.

None of that impressed MI5 very much. At the start of the war Jack Curry, the officer who had taken Roberts under his wing, began looking at Siemens. It was a large German company that was operating in Britain, and operating in some highly sensitive fields, particularly supplying machine tools to other manufacturers. Could its staff be trusted? Curry quickly realised that to check it would be a large job, and he was already too busy. He was in his fifties, and had had a serious eye operation the year before, so he seized his moment when Rothschild complained of having too little to do. The scientist was handed MI5's thick file on Siemens.

It dated back to 1914, when a Member of Parliament had received an anonymous letter from Chile. Signed 'Britannicus', the letter claimed that the local Siemens branch, 'although professedly an English firm, is the rendezvous of all the Germans in the place, and is said on good authority to possess a clandestine wireless installation which has been used to communicate with their cruisers on this coast'.

The reports continued to trickle in throughout the war. In 1916, MI5 was told that the company's technical manager in Madrid was, along with his wife, suspected of spying. By 1917, Siemens was classed as an 'enemy firm', and having worked there was sufficient grounds to refuse a visa to a Norwegian consulate clerk.

As the Great War ended, reports came in of Siemens staff behaving in suspicious ways all over the world. The company was receiving letters from the Dutch East Indies written to a cover address in The Hague. An employee in Stockholm was in touch with German agents there. Two of its employees in Japan were said to have been ordered to Moscow by the German admiralty. They arrived in July, but left the same month, and were suspected of travelling under false names, with the goal of committing 'sabotage outrages in China or Japan'.

By this point, the firm was associated within MI5 with all kinds of wickedness. It was noted that it had managed to regain control of its factories in communist Russia, and in 1921 it was suspected of channelling weapons from the Bolsheviks to Irish republicans.

During the 1920s, when a slimmed-down MI5 was preoccupied with turf wars and the threat of communism, it had little time for Siemens, but as war with Germany approached again in the 1930s, intelligence agencies around the world began looking into the firm.

This wasn't irrational. If a country wanted to spy on industrial targets, an electronics company would be a good place from which to do it. Engineers working for German companies including Siemens had 'obtained direct or indirect access in the normal course of their work to Navy, Army and Air Force establishments and re-armament factories', an MI5 memo on the subject noted in April 1940. 'Even if his visit to a factory is not directly concerned with the production side of the work, any trained engineer would obviously acquire important information about its exact location, the physical structure of the buildings and the general type of the work carried on there.'

Rothschild and his team were particularly impressed by a recently published book, *Inside the Gestapo*, written under the pseudonym Hansjürgen Koehler by a man claiming to be a former Nazi agent. It asserted that 'all German subjects travelling abroad are forced and obliged to carry on industrial espionage on Germany's behalf' and claimed that the Nazis had 'a huge filing system of most of the factories of the world', which told them 'the points which were most vulnerable and could be used for putting the factory out of working order'. The book explained that 'a handful of sand suffices to make a sensitive dynamo or turbine useless for a long time. In other places a small detonator is enough to start a terrible fire.'

But Rothschild didn't need to turn to sensationalist publications such as Koehler's to find proof that German citizens were willing to spy for the Fatherland. He only needed to look across the Atlantic, to a case that showed both the reality of the threat, and the specific focus on factories.

In 1938, MI5 had received a tip-off from Dundee. Mary Curran, a cleaning woman, had found suspicious maps in the hairdressers where she worked. One was hidden behind the till, and another was concealed under the linoleum on the shop's floor. Encouraged by her husband, Curran went to the police, who were sceptical. Curran, however, persisted, and contacted the Security Service. The owner of the shop, 51-year-old Jessie Jordan, had recently moved back to Scotland, the country of her birth, from Germany, where she'd lived for the past three decades. MI5 had known about her, but not her shop. They began intercepting her post, and quickly realised that she was acting as a clearing house for letters from spies in the United States to their masters in Berlin.

Liddell passed this information to his American counterparts, who identified Jordan's correspondent as a 26-year-old US Army deserter, Guenther Rumrich. When he was arrested, he led the FBI to his fellow spies, including Ignatz Griebl, a New York gynaecologist. Griebl in turn identified Nazi agents working on the P-47 Thunderbolt fighter and at the Curtiss-Wright aircraft factory in

Buffalo. 'In every armament factory in America, we have a spy,' Griebl boasted under interrogation. 'In every shipyard we have an agent. Your country cannot plan a warship, design a fighting plane, develop a new instrument or device that we do not know of it at once!'

This was a huge exaggeration, but it served to alert the American authorities to the dangers they faced. The FBI agent leading the case, Leon Turrou, wrote a bestselling book on the back of it, *Nazi Spies in America*, which inspired a 1939 film, *Confessions of a Nazi Spy* – the first American movie in which the words 'Adolf Hitler' were uttered. Neither dwelt on the fact that the FBI had bungled the case, allowing several of the spies, including Griebl, to escape the country – a failure for which Turrou had been dismissed from the Bureau.

For MI5, the case had a clear lesson: 'The accused showed it was quite natural for them to work for the Fatherland against the country in which they had made their homes.'

All Germans were suspect, and Germany was using engineers to do its spying. And the German engineering company Siemens had an international network that any intelligence organisation would have envied. In 1939, it had 26,000 employees abroad, working for around 200 subsidiaries.

Rothschild leafed through report after report of dubious activity associated with the company. Koehler's book claimed, in passing, that the Siemens Madrid office had been used by Germany to process aerial photo-reconnaissance pictures during the Spanish Civil War. France's Deuxième Bureau listed Siemens employees in Cairo as Nazi agents. The same was reported of its staff in Panama, Athens and Singapore. There was suspicious behaviour from the company's agents in Tehran, Argentina and India. In 1939, a decrypted telegram had led Liddell to write to the Commissioner of the South African police warning that the company's workshop in Johannesburg 'may be earmarked for some ulterior purposes'. To protect the secret of Britain's ability to read the German Alpha code, Liddell had attributed this information to 'a source whom we consider very reliable, but who wishes to remain unnamed'.

In May 1940, Rothschild submitted his report on Siemens to Liddell. 'This combine has branches or agents in every country in the world,' he wrote. 'There are also subsidiaries of their own subsidiary companies, so that unless the name Siemens appears in the title the connection is hard to trace.'

Some of Rothschild's information came from those close to or inside the firm. He drew on an interview with Henry Wright, managing director of Siemens Brothers. This had been the British branch of the company, but it had been confiscated by the British government during the First World War, and Rothschild noted that it was 'now regarded as an English company'. Although separate from the rest of Siemens, the ties of history meant Wright was able to offer a picture of the parent firm's link with the German government.

According to Wright, Carl Friedrich von Siemens, who now ran the company his father had founded, was 'far from pro-Nazi'. He was a social democrat, like his father, and had refused to sack Jews from the firm 'until the pressure had been too great', and 'only his importance had saved him from a concentration camp'.

But if the picture from Berlin was one of passive resistance to Hitler, Wright was less warm towards the company's new British branch, Siemens Schukert, which he described as 'a rabid Nazi cell'. An employee had been dismissed there in 1938 because she had Jewish blood.

Some of the British staff at the company's two small factories in west London had deep reservations about their colleagues. Anthony Bramley had joined at the start of 1937 as a manager, and found the company mystifying. For a start, it seemed to be run at a loss. The firm would always cut a price if to do so would win a sale. Bramley thought perhaps the German parent firm was desperate for foreign currency, or perhaps it was trying to promote the Siemens name in Britain. But then he noticed other things.

Some of the firm's German staff spent far more time on the road visiting factories than could be justified by the sales they generated. These men also returned frequently to Germany, and when they were in Britain, they were always asking questions. When they heard that he knew the manager of an aeroplane manufacturer, they were highly excited. Bramley started to wonder if it was possible his employer was actually a cover for German espionage.

After war came, Bramley felt it was his duty to go to the police and tell them his suspicions, but they weren't very interested in hearing that one of the world's biggest electrical firms might also be a nest of spies.

That would change after they realised that one of his colleagues had disappeared.

Willy Muller was 33 years old in September 1939, and had been working for Siemens for seven years. Though he'd been born in Hertfordshire, his German parents had moved home when he was twelve. In 1932, he'd moved with his wife and stepdaughter to Harrow, west London, where he took a job as a 'consulting engineer' for Siemens.

For the next seven years, Muller lived a life of glamour, at least by the standards of Northolt Road, where the family lived a conventional suburban existence in their semi-detached house. He travelled extensively around the country, visiting factories, and took regular flights back to Berlin. His neighbour, a retired policeman, concluded that he had 'funds beyond his salary in view of his mode of holidays and frequent air trips'.

Muller was tall for the time – just a shade under six foot – and, according to his police report, had, with his blond hair combed back, a 'typical German appearance'. He was also deeply committed to the Nazi cause, so much so that in the summer of 1939 his own cousin had reported him to Special Branch.

MI5 had actually opened a file on Muller the previous year, after intercepting a letter to him that suggested he was involved in the Nazi Party's political activities among Germans in Britain. When the Security Service began to draw up its list of Germans who should be interned at the outbreak of war, the Mullers were on it.

But in late August 1939, Muller and his wife drove their new Triumph Coventry to the port of Harwich, in Essex, where they boarded an evening ferry to Antwerp. They'd told their neighbours they were going for a two-week driving tour of Germany, and asked them to water their plants while they were away. Their daughter had gone ahead of them. When the police arrived at their home to serve them with their internment orders on Friday 1 September, they learned that they were away until the following Monday. A watch was put on the ports.

But the Mullers didn't return. Two months later, their neighbour, still watering their plants and no doubt increasingly troubled by the pictures of Hitler on display, reported that the house had been broken into. When the police searched it, they found swastika flags in the garage, and paperwork that showed Muller had been an active Nazi organiser among Germans locally.

All that certainly explained why the Mullers might have decided that Germany was a more comfortable place for them to stay now that war had broken out. A report came in from a relative that Willy had spent the winter of 1939 working somewhere in eastern Germany. At this point MI5 and Special Branch lost interest.

They revived it when Rothschild began looking at Siemens. The story of Muller seemed to demonstrate that the company was suspicious. He was 'outspokenly anti-British', Rothschild noted, and 'described as a "pig": disgusting in his treatment of British employees'. Here was a known Nazi who was a qualified engineer and had been visiting factories the length of the country 'with no apparent results'. He also appeared to have a secret source of income, and had been making frequent trips to Germany. He could have come directly from the pages of Koehler's book about the Gestapo. It was true that Muller had been working with printing and textile machinery, rather than weapons, but Koehler had offered a comment on that. Munitions and aeroplane factories were important of course, he wrote, 'but the rubber factory supplying the pneumatic tyres for lorries or gas masks is just as important. And the otherwise innocent oil distillery whose by-product is glycerine is just as vital: glycerine is needed for nitro-glycerine and dynamite. And what about the tar factory with its by-product, benzol, which is a fundamental element of ecrasite and lyddite, the deathly contents of grenades and shrapnel?'

Siemens had been a cover for spying, Rothschild was sure of it, and it might still be. 'An organisation like Siemens Schukert, which had been so well organised before the war, might perhaps have left some kind of Kriegsnetz behind,' he mused.

One option was simply to shut down the company and intern all its dangerous staff. But Rothschild was more ambitious than that. His colleagues had failed so far to find the network of German spies that they were certain must be operating in Britain. Perhaps he could do it. If there were agents in Siemens, they might reveal others. The question was how to tease them out.

Rothschild's report listed fifteen members of Siemens staff who might be of further interest. Some, like Muller, had already left Britain. Others had been interned. Neither category applied to the man who was thirteenth on the list. A clerk in his early thirties who had been in the company's Brentford office for two years, he had been born in London, of a British mother and a German father. 'Very pro-German,' the report said. 'Reported to have had numerous Nazi visitors from Germany. Denounced by Mr Bramley as being unsafe.'

The clerk's name was Walter Wegener, and in him Rothschild saw an opportunity.

7

'So stupid and so obvious'

Eric Roberts had now been an MI5 officer for a little over six months, and was finding the experience a mixed one. The investigations and the undercover work he was good at, but he'd known that when he'd been one of Maxwell Knight's agents. His disappointing discovery was that the Security Service was home to just as much bureaucracy, officialdom and snobbery as banking. A clue lay in the nickname that staff gave their headquarters: the Office.

Sat behind his desk in Blenheim Palace, Roberts read the files that the Office had built up on fascists and other persons of interest. These were folders to which he had made his own contributions over the years. So it was disturbing to him to find that many of the files were, in his words, 'grossly inaccurate'. He had personal knowledge of these people, and found mistakes about them everywhere. Worse than that, from the point of view of the person who now found himself reading them, the files were 'hopelessly boring'. Intercepted letters, agents' reports on meetings, Special Branch background checks, internal notes between case officers and their superiors, the institutional memory of MI5 was held in paper. To Roberts, this was not what being a spy was about. He enjoyed the face-to-face work, using his gifts for deception to win people's confidence.

He found his immediate superior difficult, as well. Edward Blanshard Stamp was a promising lawyer whom MI5 had recruited at the start of the war. Stamp disliked Roberts only slightly less than Roberts disliked him. He had a low opinion of Roberts's abilities, and repeatedly reported him to Curry, who privately assured Roberts that he paid no attention to such complaints.

Stamp was uncertain about why he had a bank clerk in his section at all. The other men who had been swept into the Security Service at the start of the war were brilliant minds like himself and Rothschild. Roberts hadn't been to university, and only a provincial school. He was clearly not officer material, yet he was held in strangely high regard around the office. What background, Stamp asked Roberts during one row, did he have for intelligence work? Roberts sourly replied that his only qualifications were years of undercover and surveillance work.

Seeing MI5 from the inside, aware of its weaknesses, Roberts started to have doubts, too, about its security. British intelligence was trying to understand the Abwehr. Surely the Abwehr was trying to do the same to them? As he knew better than most people, there were plenty of people in Britain who had felt warmly about the Nazis before the war began. Might not some of them have been recruited? It wasn't as though fascism had been a movement restricted to the lower classes. The man who recruited him to MI5, Maxwell Knight, had been a supporter in the 1920s. Could his support have lasted longer than that? And who else had he brought in, alongside Roberts, from the British Fascisti?

And then there were the geniuses that had swept into MI5 at the start of the war. Stamp's comments about schooling had stung Roberts. But they also revealed something of the way that the English upper orders thought: you judged a chap by the school he'd gone to. That attitude didn't lend itself to the effective screening of recruits, especially when most of the recruits were coming from the top schools and the top universities.

As Roberts considered the organisation he'd fought for so long to be a full member of, a doubt had lodged itself in his mind about whether all of these people were themselves to be trusted.

And then, in early 1941, just as Roberts was pondering all this, he was summoned to MI5's counter-sabotage section, known as B1C, to meet its chief, Victor Rothschild. There was a job that required his special talents. The briefing for the operation covered the Siemens company in general, and the Wegener family in particular.

In 1900, at the start of a new century, Carl Wegener stepped ashore in England. He was nineteen years old, and had left his native Germany three years earlier. After living in Paris and Brussels, he had decided to seek his fortune in London. And if not a fortune, he found a life: work as a hairdresser, and, in 1904, marriage to a local girl. A daughter, Dorothy, swiftly followed, and then in 1907 a son, Walter, was born.

Carl was prospering, and had begun applying for British citizenship, when war came. A month after Britain declared war on Germany in July 1914, the British government ordered the arrest of every German male of military age – between seventeen and fifty-five – in the country. Along with 25,000 other civilians, Carl was interned.

Just as in the Second World War, the Great War internees were held on the Isle of Man, though not in the relative comfort of houses. Instead, they spent the years, muddy and under-nourished, in a vast camp of hastily thrown-up huts that only partially protected them from the wind and the rain, with the Army, the island government and Whitehall engaged in circular arguments about whose problem they were.

The separation had a deep effect on Carl's young family. More than twenty years later, his son could still remember how long his father had been locked up – four years, two months. Neither of them yet ten years old, Dorothy and Walter discovered that the land of their birth viewed their father – and by extension, them – as enemies. By the time Carl was finally released, they were also vanquished enemies. But one day, their father told them, being German would be something to be proud of once again.

When Walter was sixteen, his father decided to take him to discover his roots. It was 1923, and London was shaking off the effects of the Great War. Unemployment was falling as the men back from the front found work. An exciting new technology, the wireless, was revolutionising communications – the British Broadcasting Company had just launched. In Egypt, Lord Carnarvon had opened the tomb of Tutankhamen.

But in Berlin, the Wegeners found little to be optimistic about. Germany was a defeated nation, and the victors were determined it shouldn't forget it. Punitive reparation payments were demanded from the struggling new democracy. 'People were still walking about then without shoes and stockings,' Walter recalled later. 'There was a mother and two children who were physically weak from lack of food. They were holding onto the railings from weakness.' As his son looked on, Carl wept for his country.

Although he continued to live in London, Carl never renewed his application for British citizenship. When Walter had needed a passport for their trip, Carl had applied for a German one for him. To be treated as an enemy by his adopted country and locked up for so long had left deep scars. Carl died in 1929, aged forty-eight.

Their mother had died two years earlier, so Dorothy and Walter were now alone in the world. Walter had a head for figures and by now he was working for a stockbroker in the City of London. He would stop for a beer sometimes at Schmidt's German restaurant on Charlotte Street, whose owner had been interned with his father. The year after Carl's death, Walter and Dorothy visited Germany together, both on German passports. Then in 1932, Walter moved there. Staying initially with a friend he'd met in Schmidt's, he lived in the industrial city of Erfurt, in the centre of the country, learning the language, teaching English and doing translation work.

Nine years after his first visit, Walter found a different country. He liked the newly elected leader, Adolf Hitler. 'He had only been a paper hanger, and had assumed the position of Chancellor of Germany,' Walter said a decade later, trying to explain his feelings. 'I have always admired a self-made man, and a man who has worked himself up by his own efforts. But my main liking for fascism was that it was directly anti-Communistic.'

The Nazis were also restoring some national pride to Germany. 'I admired the strict discipline of the youth,' Walter said. Seeing a picture in a German paper of Sir Oswald Mosley taking a march past from fascist women in Hyde Park, Walter wrote to BUF headquarters in London, applying to join.

After just over two years in Germany, Walter had a row with his landlady and decided to return home. He said later that he was made to feel uncomfortable there as a foreigner, but it didn't seem to dent his enthusiasm for Germany, and in 1938 he took a job with a German firm in England, Siemens Schukert.

Here he found enjoyed a special status as one of the few English staff who spoke German. As a supporter of fascism, he was drawn into an inner group within the firm that was working on the Nazi state's behalf. By his own account, he'd restricted himself to propaganda, rather than getting involved in spying. He was

confident that most of the company's British staff were unaware
of their activities, though the arrest the day after war broke out of
one of his colleagues, an engineer with both British and German
citizenship, caused Walter some doubts on that score. 'Everybody
at the office thought the British authorities have found out something,' he recalled.

But though he didn't know it, he was outspoken enough to be
the subject of a Special Branch investigation the following month.
'There is no doubt that both Walter and Dorothy Wegener are
strongly in sympathy with Nazi Germany,' it concluded.

When news came through in the middle of September 1939 of
an early engagement between the Royal Navy and Germany's
U-boat fleet, which had ended with the torpedoing of a British
aircraft carrier, Walter hadn't bothered to conceal his feelings.
'Has recently gloated over the sinking of HMS *Courageous*, and
the fact that so many of the staff of Siemens have been called up
for service whilst he is free,' reported MI5's file on him.

When Churchill gave the order in May 1940 to widen the internment of Germans, Walter got a knock at the door. The police
searched his house, and took him to Brixton Prison.

The day after his arrest, Walter wrote to the Home Office
asking to be released. 'I have at no time in the whole of my
thirty-three years of my life acted in any way hostile to this
country or to the reigning government of His Majesty's Crown,'
he began. But he had a humanitarian case for release, as well:
Dorothy. 'My sister is at present living alone and her health is in
a very critical state,' he explained. 'She is suffering from severe
depression.'

Dorothy had attempted to kill herself that January, Walter
revealed. 'It was purely due to a miracle that the hospital
doctors were able to save her life.' After a month in a mental
hospital, she had been allowed to come home, on condition that
her brother would care for her. 'Doctors and specialists who
have attended her have given me specific instructions not to let
her live alone,' he wrote. 'The reaction would certainly prove
fatal.'

Walter offered to put up with any restriction in exchange for
his freedom: he suggested he could register daily at a police station, and agree not to travel more than five miles from his home.

He signed off with an emphasis on what was at stake: 'My sister's life may probably depend upon your decision.'

If Walter was melodramatic, his concern for his sister was genuine. But his pleas cut no ice with MI5. They had good reason to be suspicious of Siemens, and good reason to be suspicious of him. Besides, they already knew all about his sister.

They knew in particular that Dorothy was thirty-five years old, unmarried, and unhappy about it. She worked from home, designing blouses. This was not work that brought her into contact with many potential husbands. So she had to resort to other means to meet men.

In October 1939, as they turned their attention to Walter, MI5 had begun intercepting the Wegeners' post. The Home Office Warrant system was the Security Service's main and most powerful investigatory tool. A six-sentence note was sent to the Home Secretary, setting out the reasons to suspect both Walter and Dorothy. Two days later, the warrant came back with his signature. Under an agreement put in place by Churchill when he had been Home Secretary three decades earlier, this piece of paper allowed MI5 to read every letter sent to the Wegeners.

This was a labour-intensive business. Few people had telephones in their homes, so the post was the only way to communicate over any distance. That meant a lot of letters. In a secret office in London, rows of technicians – wearing rubber gloves to avoid leaving fingerprints – sat with rows of constantly boiling kettles, steaming open envelopes, photographing the contents, and then resealing the letters.

At first, the intercept on the Wegeners revealed little of interest. Long before Walter was arrested, MI5 knew about Dorothy's mental condition: they had read the letter the hospital had sent her brother at the start of February. They had also discovered something else rather interesting about her: in May 1940, she began getting letters from strange men. Most only signed their first names: 'Trevor', 'Arnold', 'Bill'.

Dorothy, it turned out, had joined a correspondence club. For five shillings a year, she was sent the names and addresses of six men who had joined the same club. They could write to each other, and take things from there. 'The reasons that persons join correspondence clubs are usually financial (swindling), sexual or owing to loneliness,' MI5 noted.*

Dorothy's motives fell somewhere between the second and third categories. And in her willingness to correspond with strangers, Rothschild thought he'd found a way into the Siemens spy ring.

Rothschild felt that with some staff at the company having fled the country, and others having been arrested, remaining subversives at Siemens 'would be keeping extremely quiet'. He wanted to put an agent in touch with them, in the hope that he could tempt them to reveal themselves. Dorothy's correspondence club offered a way to do that. The medium was one in which people were already acting covertly, so it lent itself to the sharing of confidences.

First, they would need an introduction. They set about talking to Dorothy's correspondents. In what must have been alarming moments for the men, each was approached in turn and asked what he was doing writing to her. The first man they spoke to was, unsurprisingly, married. The second 'was unable to explain his reasons for indulging in this correspondence'. The third was simply 'unsuitable', though he did hint that there had been 'some form of fascist propaganda' in Dorothy's letters.

They found what they wanted with the fourth man.† He claimed, implausibly, to have been 'writing to Dorothy merely out of curiosity'. But whatever his motives, Rothschild decided that he 'appeared reliable', and put a question to him: would he give them an introduction to Dorothy? He agreed. Under MI5's direction, he wrote to her saying that a friend of his, 'Jack King', was anxious to write to her. Dorothy responded enthusiastically.

---

* Not all such clubs were motivated by vice. In 1935, a letter in *Nursery World* magazine began with a plea: 'Can any mother help me?' The author, writing under a pseudonym, explained that she had no neighbours, couldn't afford a wireless, and that once her children were in bed, she was alone and desperately bored. The response inspired the *Cooperative Correspondence Club*, a private magazine sent from member to member, with each writing her thoughts on the pages, and submitting a fortnightly article for the next edition. It would go on to run for more than five decades.

† More than seven decades later, the section of the file dealing with this man is still redacted. He might have been Trevor, Arnold, Bill or someone else entirely. There is a hint in the Wegener file that MI5 was especially interested in a Trevor Williams in the summer of 1940.

It's possible that the name 'Jack King' was a private joke.* Nancy Mitford's novel *Wigs on the Green*, published a few years earlier, had satirised Oswald's Mosley's supporters – and her own sisters – as followers of the fascist 'Captain Jack'. 'King', meanwhile, was one of Maxwell Knight's aliases. But when it came to creating the lure for Dorothy, Rothschild worked with great seriousness to build a man in whom Dorothy could place her trust. His assistants, the two Tesses, offered different insights into a woman's mind.

Theresa Clay was closer to Dorothy in age, but her life had been one of academia, travel and intense, unconventional relationships. Teresa Mayor's life was more conventional, though by that stage, only slightly. She and Patricia Rawdon-Smith had been bombed out of their flat, and Rothschild had offered them rooms in a house he had rented but wasn't using on Bentinck Street, near Selfridges. Their fellow tenants were two of Rothschild's friends from Cambridge, men who were also working for British intelligence: Anthony Blunt and Guy Burgess.

The last was never one to restrain his appetites, but war, the Blitz and the threat of imminent death provoked him to reckless abandon. He brought home 'a series of boys, young men, soldiers, sailors, airmen', according to one account. When the police warned Rothschild that they suspected his house of being a male brothel, he laughed it off. 'How easily in these darkened streets,' he observed, 'the amateur can be confused with the professional.'

All this was a long way from the life of Dorothy Wegener, who had fled the bombing of London to a quiet village near Canterbury, in Kent. But Rothschild and his team began creating her fantasy man. He needed a respectable job, but it also needed to be one that would allow him to express anti-Semitism – this seemed to them the best way to draw out the sympathy they were sure Dorothy felt for fascism. The perfect solution had the advantage of being another joke: Jack would be an employee of Rothschild's bank. In order to give him a reason to discuss engineering, he

---

*It is also possible to read some of the files as suggesting that King was the real name of the MI5 officer writing the letters. But although Eric Roberts had operated under his own name in his days undercover in the BUF, it's hard to see why Rothschild would have adopted such a policy at this point.

would work in die-casting at the Royal Mint Refinery, which the bank owned. Victor had worked there in his six-month attempt to be a conventional Rothschild, and was now offering the Mint scientific advice.

The plan was for Jack's approach to the subject of fascism to be a gradual one. But the Rothschild team's first letter sowed the seeds. With a shyness that was supposed to endear him to Dorothy, he admitted he'd never written to a stranger like this before. But he offered one passing observation: 'In the part of London where I work, the bombs have been pretty bad.'

In the atmosphere of 1940, with people being arrested for spreading 'alarm and despondency', even such an apparently bland remark, put in writing, could be enough to land the person who said it in front of the courts. Rothschild wanted Jack to have an air of naivety that would engender trust. He also wanted to prepare the ground for future, more explicit anti-war statements.

Dorothy responded in kind. 'I had some very narrow escapes and suffered very severe shocks,' she wrote of the Blitz. 'I found living alone during air raids too terrible for words.'

For Rothschild, this was the signal to go further. 'The firm for which I work is owned by Jews,' he had Jack write. 'Sometimes when I have time to think I remember what one hears so often about them.'

Dorothy again responded. 'I assume that you do not like Jews,' she replied. 'Well neither do I. What I do so dislike about them is the way in which they exploit people.'

Rothschild had mixed feelings about the alacrity with which Dorothy had taken the bait. He wanted to ensure that she wasn't simply trying to please her new friend. So Jack's reply attempted to cool things down.

'I felt rather guilty about having written to you about Jews in my last letter,' he said. 'But I know you will keep what I say to yourself and your letter seems so understanding that I feel I can say it to you. I hope it is not wrong of me to dislike them like that, but there seem so many countries and people everywhere who agree. But I sometimes feel a little ashamed of it. What do you think?'

Dorothy knew what she thought.

'You can feel very proud of your dislike,' she said. 'Nearly everybody hates them. Only they will not admit it, they are too cowardly to do so. I utterly loathe and detest them, and I feel more than certain that the Jews and nobody else are purely responsible for this war. If England had not had such an influx of Jewish refugees, she would not have entered this war. Jews have complete monopoly of everything here at the moment and I sometimes think the British Empire is in pawn to the Jews.'

Rothschild didn't record his feelings on reading these words. The head of the family that more than any other epitomised what Dorothy hated, he was at once the possessor of much of the power she attributed to him, and completely powerless. He sat in the House of Lords, he could send money around the world or withhold it, he was even part of the secret state. But none of that was enough to keep his own family safe. His sister Nica, who had married a Frenchman, had been in the chateau they shared near Paris when the city fell to the Germans in June 1940. With her children, she fled for the coast and then to England, barely escaping in time. Her mother-in-law refused to leave, and was arrested by the Nazis. She would die in Auschwitz. Victor's French cousin Philippe would learn after the war that his estranged wife had died in Ravensbrück. Victor's aunt was beaten to death with meat hooks on a railway station outside Buchenwald.

Their fates were unknown to Rothschild as he considered Dorothy's response. But he had been closely involved with the cause of German Jews, and had a better sense than many British people of the Nazis' capacity for acting on their hatred.

His next step was to see whether Dorothy's hatred of Jews did indeed translate into support for Germany.

'I know very little about how these things were dealt with in Germany but one hears that the Chosen race were too badly treated over there,' Jack wrote. 'I rather doubt it. The leaders in Germany were quite right and if only we had as much sense this pointless war might never have taken place.'

'Why Germany and England must always be at loggerheads is beyond me,' replied Dorothy. 'If only common sense had prevailed here, this awful war would never have taken place. But there is not the slightest doubt that this war was made for the last stand for Jewish capitalism.'

*

'Jack' and Dorothy had been corresponding for three months now. It was time for them to meet. Dorothy jumped at the chance. Her letters hinted that there was more she wanted to say, but that she feared her post was being opened. In this, she was actually wrong. MI5 had cancelled the Home Office Warrant on her in September, possibly to prevent exactly this kind of suspicion.

Rothschild was not going to manage the operation on a day-to-day basis. That job would be done by Clay. She had the scientific approach that Rothschild valued, and was better equipped than him to judge how the relationship with Dorothy should be handled. That left the question of who would do the handling.

Jack was going to have to be more than a name on a page. They needed someone with experience of undercover work, who would be able to pass plausibly among fascists. Jack Curry, who had passed the Siemens file to Rothschild, now also passed him his protégé, Eric Roberts. The Leeds case had shown that Roberts had the temperament and ability for exactly this kind of job. More than that, he was tall, athletic, good-looking – if losing his hair – without being intimidatingly handsome, and about the same age as Dorothy. She was expecting to meet a romantic prospect, and he fitted the bill.

Despite the differences in their backgrounds, Roberts and Rothschild got on well. Both men liked a joke, either played on someone else or against themselves. Both felt driven, for different reasons, to prove themselves. Rothschild, frustrated by people's focus on his name, was more interested in whether people could get things done than where they had gone to school.

As the two men discussed the next moves in approaching Dorothy, a couple of problems presented themselves. Rothschild and Clay had written the part of Jack King as an expert engineer, something that came naturally to two eminent scientists. It was a less easy role for Roberts to play. He had largely managed to avoid technology during his career at the Westminster Bank, but had eventually been ordered on a machine accountancy course. The highlight had been the moment that the tabulator he was operating had caught fire, requiring a white-coated mechanic to put out the blaze with a fire extinguisher.

In April 1941, Roberts paid a visit to the Royal Mint Refinery's wartime operation on the Rothschild estate at Tring. In a nineteenth-century silk mill, painted in camouflage colours, with an anti-aircraft gun on the roof, engineers used the expertise they had gained minting coins to make precision parts for artillery and planes. The MI5 man did his best to take it all in, but Rothschild subsequently summarised his agent's level of understanding of die-casting: 'total ignorance'. Roberts's best hope was that none of the Siemens spies would attempt to engage him in technical small talk.

Then there was the question of Roberts's handwriting. It was nothing like that in the letters that Dorothy had been reading. In an attempt to work around the problem, Jack wrote to Dorothy that he'd injured his hand, and would be typing his letters. Roberts, meanwhile, set about learning to copy Jack's signature. The ruse troubled Rothschild. 'At any moment, this may cause serious difficulties,' he pondered.

Despite these problems, Roberts liked Rothschild and Clay, and in him they too saw the professional agent that they needed. Not that he needed to deploy many of his impressive powers of deception on Dorothy Wegener. She wasn't, he swiftly concluded, clever enough to see through him. In any case, she was too smitten with her new soulmate.

She quickly opened her heart to him. She asked him to call her 'Annalisse', her favourite German name. She explained she was eagerly looking forward to Hitler's invasion; she had a swastika flag ready to hang on her house when the moment came, and was particularly pleased that the police had failed to find this when they arrested Walter. They had also missed some very incriminating letters, she confided.

If Dorothy wasn't going to detect Roberts, nor did she seem to be in a position to lead him to the Siemens spy ring, as Rothschild had hoped. But she did bring Roberts into her circle of like-minded friends. Within months, he had twenty more suspects. One was interned, and others had been locked up before being released. Eight were connected with Siemens. The material he was accumulating was all hearsay, but it was promising.

'Dorothy is not an intelligent woman,' Rothschild observed. But this proved to be an advantage in using her as a cipher. Roberts, he reported, 'can put ideas and queries into her mind', leading her to ask the right questions of the 'trickier and more experienced Nazi sympathisers with whom she comes into contact'.

Her very nature meant she could get away with this. 'No one suspects Dorothy of being an agent for the British Secret Service, the fear which is constantly in the minds of all Nazi sympathisers, because she is so stupid and so obvious.'

When one of her friends told her they had strong suspicions that her new man wasn't who he claimed to be, Dorothy simply told the MI5 man, putting him on his guard.

Rothschild dismissed any thought of prosecuting Dorothy, and indeed MI5 began to become rather protective of her. Their difficulty was managing her expectations of Roberts. She had joined the correspondence club to meet a man, and she'd met rather a nice one. It was becoming clear that she expected more from him than cups of tea and discussions about fascism, and more than he felt, as both an MI5 officer and a married man, that he could offer. He told her that he was putting aside thoughts of marriage until the war was over, and began announcing business trips to the Midlands whenever he felt she was becoming too keen.

'Dorothy is a neurotic and lonely woman who has unfortunately become much attached to "King",' Rothschild wrote. 'It is obvious that at some future date their relationship will have to be severed, and we do not want to do this in a way which will cause unnecessary distress.'

But first, Rothschild wanted Roberts to do what he'd come for: penetrate the Siemens ring. Dorothy might not know who they were, but her guileless nature could still help to draw them out. It was time to set a trap.

This would involve a Vickers tank, a blueprint and, thanks to Dorothy, a jar of marmalade.

For weeks, Roberts, in the character of 'Jack', had been telling Dorothy that he wished he could help Germany. But what could ordinary people like them do? She sympathised: she felt exactly the same way. If only, he mused, someone could offer them advice. But he didn't know who to ask. Dorothy agreed: she didn't know either.

Rothschild and Clay believed her. 'It is doubtful if Dorothy knows any German agent in this country,' they concluded. But might a German agent know her? To get them to reveal themselves, what was needed was a tasty piece of bait.

In the middle of 1941, 'Jack' came to Dorothy in a state of high excitement: he had discovered something important. Through his work at the Royal Mint Refinery he was, as she knew, an expert in die-casting. With the country transformed into a huge factory for highly engineered guns, planes, tanks and ships, this process of moulding precisely shaped pieces of metal was vital to the war effort. It was his skills in this area that kept taking him away on business, to Dorothy's frustration.

Roberts explained that his most recent trip had been to the Kryn & Lahy metalworks in Letchworth, north of London. This plant specialised in the production of aircraft parts, advertising the 'Stronger Steel' from its foundry as outperforming that of lesser rivals. But in Roberts's telling, it was having problems casting small components for tanks and he had been asked to advise. While discussing the problem, he had seen a blueprint for a Vickers tank lying unattended. Unwatched for a moment, he had grabbed it and smuggled it out of the factory.

Roberts showed Dorothy his precious contraband. He was now guilty of espionage. If the loss was noticed, and he was suspected, his home might be searched. Could she keep it for him? More than that, could she get it to Berlin?

Dorothy was excited: at last she had a clear opportunity to help Germany, and hit back at Britain for the way it had treated her father and brother. She would try her best.

She began making discreet enquiries among the friends that she knew were sympathetic to the German cause. Did anyone know a way to get the blueprint out of the country? She had no success.

Roberts, in an effort to increase the pressure on her, wrote complaining about her failure. He had taken a great risk and nothing had come of it. Dorothy redoubled her efforts. Now, as Rothschild and Clay had hoped, a fish rose to the bait. Unfortunately it was the wrong fish.

Soon after Dorothy had begun introducing Roberts to her circle, he started to develop suspicions about one of them. The man was 'virulently anti-British and so childishly pro-German'. Roberts, a professional infiltrator, could spot an amateur. He had told Rothschild they were dealing with an informer. If he wasn't one of MI5's, he must be someone passing information to the local police. But when Rothschild confronted the force, he got nothing except 'bland denials'.

The tank plan changed all that. Shortly after Roberts handed it to Dorothy, the Kent Constabulary called MI5: they'd just been told that a suspected fascist near Canterbury had got hold of the blueprint for a tank. They were going to search her house at once. Just as with the Leeds case, Roberts found an operation in jeopardy because of the conflicting aims of the different arms of the British state.

Rothschild couldn't simply tell the police to ignore the tip-off. That would only reveal that MI5 was up to something, and put Roberts under suspicion. Instead, he needed to find a way to sabotage the police's operation without it looking deliberate.

He opted for that most reliable of routes to failure: the government's love of bureaucracy. Doubtless to the frustration of the Kent detectives who hoped to capture a nest of Nazi spies, MI5 asked them to begin by taking statements 'in the ordinary police way' from their informant and his wife. Rothschild may only have been hoping to stall the investigation, but the result was better than he could have hoped for: the police informant's wife was so outraged to discover that her husband was informing on her friends that she immediately went to Dorothy and warned her.

Dorothy was terrified, and in her panic she went to a friend. Doris Engert – everyone called her Bobby – was staying with her half-brother Edward, who ran a garage up the road, in Whitstable. They'd both been born in Harrogate, in Yorkshire, to a German father. Edward's wife, Friedel, had moved to Britain from Germany a decade earlier, and had briefly become a celebrity for making a failed attempt to paddle a kayak around the coast of Britain.

Right on the Kent coast, Whitstable was a bad place for a German to be living at the start of the war. Both Edward and Friedel were immediately interned, and their two daughters whisked off to boarding school. After six months, they were released, to find their business vandalised in their absence. Even if Friedel hadn't been sympathetic to the Nazis before, she certainly was now. By the time Roberts met her in 1941, she was hoarding petrol that she planned to offer to the invaders when they arrived. Roberts's assessment of Bobby was simpler: 'rabidly pro-Nazi'.

When Dorothy asked her for help, she summoned her father.

Martin Engert was a retired pastry chef in his seventies, but when he got his daughter's message, he came at once. His willingness to travel all the way down from the north of England 'struck us as peculiar if not significant', Rothschild observed. Roberts found him to be 'an astute old man, entirely in sympathy with the Nazi regime'.

He offered 'some sound advice' to the amateur conspirators on how to avoid detection by the police and MI5. Much of this related to what they should put into writing: Engert correctly told them that the interception of letters was MI5's main weapon. Therefore they should stop discussing subversive matters by post. Dorothy was told not to sign letters as 'Annalisse', and to stop referring to the blueprint directly. They devised an endearingly transparent code: the 'tank plan' would henceforth be known as the 'picture of the T.P.'.

There remained the question of what to do with the picture of the T.P. But Dorothy had an idea. She proposed to roll it up inside a sealed container and hide it in the middle of a large jar of marmalade. It was an idea that stuck in Roberts's mind. The following year, when his friend Jimmy Dickson wrote an internal MI5 guide to searching a property, he advised that 'pots of jam, syrup, etc should be held up to a strong light'.

When he'd heard that Martin Engert travelled to advise Dorothy and 'Jack', Guy Liddell had noted in his diary that 'the Wegener case is boiling up to a climax'. This, it seemed, was going to be the moment when Roberts made a connection with a German network. But Martin, however sympathetic he might have been to the cause, had no more idea than Dorothy about how to get the blueprint to Germany. The case had, abruptly, gone off the boil.

After a year spent winning the confidence of Dorothy and her friends, the only spy that Rothschild's team had positively identified had been working for Kent Police. The tank blueprint remained in Dorothy's care, at the mercy of her preserve-focused schemes of concealment. There was, it was becoming clear, no Siemens Kriegsnetz.

To have spent the best part of a year hunting for a ring of expert spies only to realise that it didn't exist was a disappointment to Rothschild, Clay and Roberts. And while it was good news for

Britain's security, even this wasn't unalloyed. Roberts had found that while they lacked a formal network, there were certainly people at large in Britain who felt more loyalty to Germany. As MI5 was about to discover, some of them were both dangerous and determined.

8

'No organised body'

In November 1941, Liddell was summoned to an unusual meeting. He slipped into the New Public Offices on Great George Street, home to the Treasury and other government departments, and after showing his identification, climbed a set of steps. Walking past a Royal Marine on guard duty, he made his way to Staircase Fifteen, a wide set of steps that spiralled down into the basement of the building. More Marines guarded the route.

He was entering one of the most secret places in Britain: the Cabinet War Rooms, built to allow the work of government to go on even as the bombs were falling. Night and day in a poorly ventilated, cramped space, foggy with cigarette smoke, military planners and Churchill's staff worked and slept side by side.

Liddell was there to speak to the Inter-Service Committee on Invasion. This ad-hoc group had been called together under the chairmanship of Major General Dick Dewing to do one job: imagine themselves as the German General Staff and devise a plan for the invasion of Britain. Dewing had been chief of staff to the commander-in-chief of British forces in the Far East until that July, when the strain and the climate of Singapore got the better of him, and he was invalided home. This job marked his return to duty.

The imminent threat of invasion had disappeared that July after Germany's surprise attack on Russia – Hitler lacked the forces to launch an assault on Britain at the same time. The Nazis had hoped to be in Moscow by September, and for a while it seemed that might happen. But the Soviets had rallied, and the German forces were now overstretched and exhausted. Nonetheless convinced that his opponents were close to collapse, Hitler had ordered an assault on Moscow, and the Fourth Panzer Group was now advancing. Meanwhile in the Western Desert campaign in Libya, British and Commonwealth forces had spent much of the year in retreat from Erwin Rommel's Afrika Korps, and the strategically important port of Tobruk was under siege. The day that Liddell made his way into Churchill's bunker, the British Eighth Army had launched Operation Crusader, aimed at relieving Tobruk.

Dewing's committee had asked Liddell for a briefing on the state of Fifth Column operations in Britain. A year and a half after Sir Nevile Bland had terrified the government with his warnings about German parlour maids guiding in paratroops, it was time for a sober assessment. In the summer of 1940, with an invasion apparently imminent, it had been easy to believe that the German war and intelligence machine was all-powerful. But that was before MI5 started picking up the Nazi spies.

The first to arrive were four Dutchmen, who rowed ashore in two dinghies on 3 September 1940, having been brought most of the way to England's south coast in a fishing trawler. Only one of them spoke fluent English. His brief career as a Nazi spy began with him asking for a bath at the Rising Sun pub in Lydd, Kent, and ended with him paying half a crown for half a pint of beer – ten times too much. By that stage, the landlady of the Rising Sun was already certain that the stranger with the foreign accent was an enemy agent, and had summoned help. Within twenty-four hours of landing, he and his three companions had been captured. Liddell had been unimpressed. 'They were singularly badly directed,' he wrote at the time. 'To anybody with any knowledge of conditions in this country it should have been apparent that none of these people could hope to succeed.' Three of them were hanged that December, the fourth escaping execution because he persuaded the court he'd been coerced by Germany.

It was a sign of things to come. As subsequent German agents arrived – nine more that September, and another twelve in the last three months of the year – their common feature was their low quality. MI5 had advance warning of many of those who were coming, thanks to its nascent Double Cross operation. This saw captured German agents offered the chance to escape punishment if they agreed to work for the British, sending false information back to Berlin. If correctly carried through, this process was so quick that the Abwehr was unaware its agent had been turned.

But even without notice from Germany that a new agent was on the way, many were caught on arrival. Typical was one parachutist who landed near Northampton at the start of October 1940, attracted immediate suspicion from locals, and was marched to the police at the point of a pitchfork. Liddell described him as 'a poor fish who never wanted to be a spy. He joined his regiment and when a sergeant asked who spoke English he rather foolishly put up his hand. Before he knew where he was, he was an indifferent spy dropped down from the air into Northampton.'

The quality of the spies they were capturing was a puzzle to the British. Liddell noted a conversation with Major General Kenneth Strong, head of the German section of military intelligence. 'Strong has a great regard for German efficiency and cannot bring himself to believe that they could have been so stupid as to send these men over here without having schooled them properly.'

But over the year that followed, the reason for the Germans' behaviour became clear, and Liddell set it out to Dewing's committee: Germany hadn't bothered to build up a spy network in Britain in the 1930s because it didn't need one.

'I began by explaining what the pre-war set-up had been in this country and how the main effort had all been concentrated a) on propaganda through various organisations and societies to keep us out of the war and b) on estimating our industrial mobilisation capacity through the machine tool industry and other similar means,' he wrote afterwards. 'Since all these activities had been perfectly legal it had not been necessary for the Germans to establish any very deep-seated underground organisation.'

Liddell's description didn't exclude the possibility that companies like Siemens had been involved in intelligence-gathering before war broke out. In fact, it specifically included it: because it had been possible to do that kind of work within the law, there'd been no need to set up a network to work illegally.

In his analysis, German planners hadn't given much thought to the idea of invading Britain until after their successes in the Netherlands and Belgium in the summer of 1940. 'It was then that they began to take stock of the position here,' he explained. 'They probably found themselves rather badly equipped and there followed a number of hastily improvised and crude performances in the shape of parachutists and people arriving by rubber boat.'

While he allowed for the possibility that not every German spy had been caught, he didn't think they'd missed many. Finally, he turned to the idea of a Fifth Column, and here again his message was reassuring. 'From time to time we came across isolated cases or small groups of Fifth Columnists who were undoubtedly prepared to assist the enemy but never seemed to have any real plan or means of doing so,' he explained. 'We felt fairly confident that there was no organised body of the kind which was receiving direction from the Germans.'

Just because the Fifth Column panic had abated, though, it didn't mean there weren't developments to concern Liddell. In the next two weeks, two cases would illustrate the kind of problem MI5 still faced. The first involved a clandestine meeting the evening after Liddell addressed the Dewing committee, in room 513 of the Cumberland Hotel, overlooking Marble Arch in London.

The woman was in her late thirties, slim and pretty, with her dark hair brushed off her forehead. 'Good evening, John,' she said in her slight German accent, as he let her in. 'Feel that bag,' she continued, evidently pleased with herself.

The man was a little younger, with spectacles and his hair combed back. He invited her to take off her coat and make herself comfortable. Then he took her handbag, hefted it, and smiled. 'It is suspiciously heavy,' he replied in the unmistakable clipped tones of the upper classes.

The woman laughed. 'I have a present for you.'

'That is awfully nice of you. I must pay you.'

'No, no!' she protested. 'I don't want paying for them.'

'But someone must pay for them.'

The woman, Irma, again refused. She went to show him the bag's contents, but John suggested they wait until after they had been served dinner. It wouldn't do to be interrupted by the hotel staff.

'Was it difficult to get these?' he asked.

'No, I pinched the whole lot.'

As they waited for dinner to arrive, Irma chatted, describing how she'd taken her mother to dinner at a Lyons Coffee House at the weekend, and cheated the Jewish waiter out of his tip. 'I put some of those little tin medals that you get under the plate,' she explained. 'I laughed all the way home when I visualised his face when he lifted the plate.'

There was a knock at the door, and the waiter came in with room service. As he set out their dinner at the table, John and Irma made small talk. And down the corridor in room 517, three men wearing headphones put down their notebooks for a moment.

Back in room 513, as they ate their meal, John and Irma were discussing production at the small munitions factory in west London where Irma worked as a typist: 33,000 shell casings so far that week. They wondered whether the German army would reach Moscow. 'They might get there in the spring,' Irma said. 'When I heard the appeal over the wireless from Berlin to send parcels to soldiers, I sat there and cried like a child. I remember when we used to send parcels when I was a child in the last war.'

Finally, Irma announced it was time to 'settle down to business'. From her bag she pulled a tin of blackcurrant throat pastilles. 'I had them for my cold,' she explained. 'They did not do me any good.' She opened the box. There were no cough sweets inside, only small pieces of machined metal.

'This is the igniter,' Irma began. She showed him a shell casing. 'The fuse goes through there. The high explosive goes here, and it is closed here.'

The shell casing was for the ammunition for an Oerlikon 20 mm cannon, the Royal Navy's anti-aircraft weapon of choice. Irma had stolen the casing and the other parts that week, concealing them up her sleeve.

That wasn't all: she had notes of the destination of the shells, the lorry that would take them, and the locations of other factories.

'This is the goods,' John said with enthusiasm. 'This is the goods.'

The listeners in 517 had heard enough. They moved swiftly down the corridor and burst into room 513. As Irma and John stared, one of them introduced himself: Inspector William Rogers of Special Branch. 'I believe you have brought certain munitions and information about them into this room which might be of use to the enemy,' he said.

Irma was defiant. 'What will you do with that man?' she asked. John, she said, was part of a Nazi spy ring, and she had arranged the meeting to entrap him. 'I did this in order to hand them over to the police,' she said. She asked Inspector Rogers to take charge of her so that John wouldn't shoot her, and accepted her arrest calmly.

Hearing this, John made a bid to escape, but the two detective sergeants behind Rogers grabbed him. He fought desperately to get free, but he was handcuffed and dragged away.

John's struggle went on until he was out of sight, and then the sergeant undid his cuffs, and congratulated him on a job well done. He was, in reality, the Honourable John Bingham, son of the sixth Baron Clanmorris. He had been working in newspapers before the war, and had volunteered for active service. But his poor eyesight meant he wasn't allowed to fight, and so Maxwell Knight persuaded him he'd be of more use as an MI5 officer.

Irma Stapleton had been born in Saxony in 1904. She'd moved to England in 1931 with her second husband, an Irish sailor. It was an unhappy union. Irma drifted from job to job, working as a typist, and took to petty crime, picking up three theft convictions. When war came, she claimed to be Swiss, rather than German. But this didn't mean she was any less loyal to the Fatherland.

'Look at the Queen, flaunting her necklace round and shaking hands with bombed-out people,' she had told John at an earlier meeting. 'With a pearl necklace, mind you! Look at all those poor saps in the underground shelters, all these people huddled there. The big people going to America, letting the poor fish fight for themselves. It is not the same in Germany. We will break their necks.'

She hated the British. 'I am so disgusted with everything they do. Everything they do is so low. You see people enjoying themselves in night clubs. Whereas in Germany the whole nation is organised.'

In September 1941, Irma started her third job in two years, with the munitions company C G Wade's, which was busy supplying ammunition casings for the war. One of her colleagues there was a fellow German, a refugee named Helmut Husgen. In conversation with him one day she poured out her true feelings, saying repeatedly that she would do 'anything' for her country. In reply, Husgen hinted that he was in touch with the Abwehr. Stapleton was enthusiastic, and asked what information they wanted. Troop movements? Shipping movements? She was sure she could find them out.

Husgen said he would pass on her offer of help, and he was as good as his word. But unfortunately for Stapleton, the only spies he was in contact with were British ones. Husgen wrote to a man he knew in MI5.

At the start of November, Husgen took Stapleton to the Café Royal on Regent Street, to meet a man he introduced as John Brunner. This man described himself as a freelance journalist, but Irma was left in no doubt that he was a German agent.

They met again four days later, in the Cumberland Hotel. Irma told John that her marriage had been 'an absolute failure'. Her husband had 'no backbone at all'. She was unimpressed with the romancing capabilities of the average Englishman: 'He goes to pubs and takes a girl for a drink and tries to be fresh.'

She knew that people working for the German Secret Service took 'mighty risks', but thinking of the dangers faced by German soldiers, 'it is the least we can do'. She explained how she had persuaded the chaps in the drawing office to show her technical diagrams: 'I gave them the glad eye – and the rest of it.'

She suggested she could sabotage the place where she worked, slowing production a little, or even burning the whole place down.

She said it was just as well she didn't have a gun, or she would go out and shoot Jews 'wholesale'. They were 'dirty', 'slimy beasts' who were 'always fermenting trouble by trying to make money'.

As for Churchill, 'I would be willing to sacrifice my life to kill him,' she told John.

The second case came a fortnight later, when Eric Roberts took a break from fighting off Dorothy Wegener's advances to meet a soldier in Birmingham. Late on a winter evening in a dingy hotel room, he was talking to Gunner Philip Jackson of the 163rd Battery, Royal Artillery.

Jackson was committing treason. He was sick of the war, sick of the corruption, sick of 'Churchill and his rotten gang'. And the gunner had a plan he hoped would boot them out and result in a swift peace.

Jackson had first come to MI5's notice in 1936, when he applied to work for them. He was thirty years old at the time, doing casual work as a railway porter in Nottingham, when he volunteered to be an undercover agent exposing saboteurs. 'A chap like me accustomed to working men and their ways,' he wrote, 'would be much more likely to obtain facts than your agents.' He didn't get a reply, and MI5 thought no more about him until 1941, when he applied for another job. This time, it was with the Germans.

He was now a gunner in an anti-aircraft battery in the Midlands, and he hated it. So he visited the Spanish embassy in London, and then, when they refused to see him, he wrote, asking to be put in touch with Germany. 'Civilians and military personal [sic] of all services are on the verge of mutiny,' he wrote. 'It doesn't need bombing or invasion to win the war. If I could get to Germany via Eire I could tell the people the Truth over the radio and the government would soon fall.'

How exactly this letter came into MI5's possession was something the Security Service didn't wish to discuss. The official internal explanation was that a British employee of the embassy was so horrified by its contents that he had taken a copy of the letter and passed it via an intermediary to MI5. Even this was a violation of protocol, but the truth was probably far more explosive.

Diplomats and their paperwork were supposed to be off-limits for spying. But in practice the vital rule was not to get caught. MI5 had a Home Office Warrant on the Spanish embassy, enabling it to read its post before it even arrived. Meanwhile Roberts's friend Jimmy Dickson was one of those responsible for getting secrets out of embassies. One of his embassy contacts was in charge of burning sensitive paperwork. Instead, this source would put some newspaper into the furnace, and then meet Dickson in a pub and hand over the documents. At various points during the war, both diplomatic staff and servants at the Spanish embassy were listed as MI5 sources. Even the diplomatic bags were opened, with couriers being delayed and distracted while their pouches were covertly opened and the contents photographed. The sensitivity of the operation was reflected in its codename – XXX, or 'Triplex'.*

The problem was that although Jackson's letter was enough

---

* More than seven decades later, this operation remains unacknowledged by MI5. The parts of Liddell's diary that probably refer to it are censored.

to court-martial him, MI5 couldn't use it as evidence without revealing how they'd got it, an act that risked both blowing a vital source and destroying the basis on which diplomacy was conducted around the world.

There was a further issue: the letter had been copied, but not intercepted: the embassy employee had passed it to his superiors, and it was entirely possible that it had actually made its way to Germany. In that case, German intelligence might attempt to contact Jackson. Jock Whyte, the MI5 officer handling the case, proposed arresting Jackson quickly while he was away from his troop, and then seeing if anyone came looking for him.

Whyte was a punctilious man, who minuted every conversation, and was careful always to send thank-you notes. He had a poor relationship with his boss, Liddell. Whyte thought Liddell didn't make enough use of him, and Liddell thought Whyte wasn't much use. Describing Whyte's interrogation technique, Liddell wrote: 'Jock had a habit of putting all his cards on the table face up.'

Fortunately for MI5, Roberts was a rather more subtle interrogator. Under the name 'Browne', he had been corresponding with Jackson for several weeks, but this was the first time they had met. Having told Jackson to sit, Roberts got to the point: he was, he said, 'extremely suspicious' of the soldier. 'I cannot afford to take any risks,' he said.

Jackson replied that he had his own doubts about the meeting: 'I am thinking this may be a police trap.'

'There is always that risk,' Roberts replied, smiling, then jokingly opened the wardrobe to show there wasn't anyone hiding in there. He invited Jackson to look under the bed. The tension between the two men was broken.

'I don't want to be suspicious,' said Jackson apologetically, 'but I'm taking a big risk.'

'My risk is greater than yours,' Roberts told him gently.

Jackson took the plunge. 'Is it possible through your organisation for me to get across to Germany?' he asked. 'It sounds bloody silly, but I hope to get to Germany and do a broadcast instead of the fellow who is doing it at the moment.'

Roberts was silent. Jackson continued. 'There is a hell of a lot of disaffection in the army,' he said. Germany should drop its current propaganda radio star William Joyce – the fascist Roberts had reported on years before who was now known universally as Lord Haw-Haw – and 'get a fellow who has been in the army and who has seen the army in its rotten forms. It would do more good than all the bombing.'

Roberts's reply wasn't encouraging: 'Could you give us any information that would be of use to us?'

'I believe I could give you details of gun-sites,' Jackson replied reluctantly.

'That is the sort of information.'

'So that your planes could fly over and bomb them?'

'I think you had better leave that to us.'

For an hour and a half, the two men danced around the issue. Jackson wanted to be a star defector, and didn't see the point in helping the Germans bomb Britain. Roberts, in character as Browne, wanted him to be a source of intelligence.

He got his way. By the time Jackson left, he had promised to fly in a German bomber raid over England and take part in any invasion. In the shorter term, he'd agreed to locate fuel dumps and anti-aircraft gun emplacements, and to tell Germany about the ground-locating radar systems they used.

'Very, very satisfactory,' Roberts observed, and offered to walk Jackson to New Street station.

As with the Irma Stapleton case, detectives had been listening in the next room. Jackson was arrested and sentenced to death at a court martial the following year. However, he was saved from execution by a neat twist – killing him would have publicised the case, and with MI5 still uncertain whether his letter had been passed to Germany, potentially revealing Triplex, this was very much not in their interests. In 1943, he was moved to Broadmoor mental hospital.

These cases explained why Liddell continued to worry about his fellow citizens. While it was true that MI5 hadn't found any evidence of the feared Fifth Column, it did keep finding people who wanted to be Fifth Columnists. How many more such men and women were there out there that they didn't know about?

As Liddell considered this problem, a solution was emerging in the minds of Rothschild, Clay and Roberts: if the Fifth Column didn't exist, perhaps they should set it up.

9

'A masterful and somewhat masculine woman'

Guy Liddell spent Christmas 1941 at Rothschild's estate at Tring. The day was marred by the news that Hong Kong had fallen, the latest in a series of advances the Japanese had made across the Pacific in less than three weeks. Still, there were causes for hope: a year earlier, Britain had stood almost alone. Now it had powerful new allies in the USA and the USSR. Germany's advance on Moscow, which had seemed close to triumph at the start of the month, appeared to have stalled.

In January 1942, Rothschild, Clay and Roberts went to see Liddell. They felt they had taken the relationship with Dorothy Wegener far enough, but they believed that 'Jack King' still had potential. Now they were feeling their way towards a new phase of their operation, one which would allow Roberts to work on a much larger canvas.

Also present was Thomas Robertson, known to everyone in MI5 as 'Tar', for his initials. A cheerful Scot who had found his niche in MI5 after unimpressive stints in the Army and in banking, he was in charge of the Double Cross operation.

The previous November, Rothschild had helped him out of a tight spot. Double Cross was developing into an MI5 industry, with a team of German double agents transmitting information back to their masters under the watchful eyes of MI5 officers. Their activities were coordinated by the XX Committee, which was tasked with creating the correct mixture of truth and lies to convince the Abwehr of their reliability while misleading them in key areas.

Although much of this work was about choosing intelligence to send back to Germany, some of the double agents had been sent to Britain to act as saboteurs. Their credibility relied on them carrying out some sabotage. This had been the reasoning behind

Operation Guy Fawkes. In an effort to convince Germany that a half-Norwegian saboteur they'd sent was doing his job, MI5 had set about blowing up a food store in Wealdstone, north-west London.

It turned out that fake sabotage was quite hard work. The blaze had to be sufficiently impressive to get reported in newspapers, but not so big as to be dangerous. The nightwatchmen, who were sleeping on duty, had to be woken and lured away. A passing policeman on his bicycle threatened to upset the whole plan by arresting the MI5 officers, and had to be warned off by a superior officer. And that was before Scotland Yard began investigating.

The bicycling policeman had managed to put the blaze out before quite the planned level of damage was caused. That meant that part of the bomb used to start the fire survived. The police recognised it as a type used by the Special Operations Executive, Churchill's behind-the-lines sabotage organisation. Inspector Ted Greeno, the scourge of London's criminals, went to see the commandos, to ask why a device built for blowing up Nazi targets in France had been set off in a food dump in north-west London.

The Double Cross secret – that Germany's spies had all been turned by the British – was too precious to risk divulging to an ordinary detective, even one as famous as Greeno. Instead, MI5 offered him their assistance. They had a counter-sabotage section, headed by the man who was now the country's foremost expert on the subject: did the inspector want to speak to Lord Rothschild? The inspector did indeed, and may have had suspicions that something was up – according to Liddell, he asked 'some searching questions'. Rothschild, in turn, suggested that the best person to look into this act of arson was himself. The bomb the Security Service had set off would be investigated by the Security Service.

Now it was Rothschild who needed a favour from Robertson. The operation he was proposing for Roberts wasn't just a shift of focus. It was a jump in scale. The people he would be dealing with would be far more dangerous than Dorothy Wegener and her friends. And it would not be for a single meeting, as with Gunner Jackson, but for numerous meetings over months or even years. In making his pitch, Rothschild wanted allies in the room. Tar

Robertson, who was running MI5's largest long-term operation, had a valuable perspective to offer.

As Rothschild explained to the meeting, the idea for Roberts's new role was driven by a new contact he'd made, someone in whom his department sensed an exciting opportunity.

Marita Perigoe was born Mary Brahe in London in July 1914, just before the outbreak of the Great War. Rothschild described her as 'of mixed Swedish and German origin', probably because she had allowed her fascist friends to believe this, alluding vaguely to family members in Germany. In fact her mother was the Australian composer May Brahe, then famous for writing popular songs including 'Bless This House' and 'I Passed By Your Window'. The first was reported to be a favourite of President Franklin Roosevelt, and the second was sufficiently lodged in the public mind to have been adapted at the start of the war by satirists mocking the blackout.

The identity of Marita's father was a more interesting question. May married Carl Brahe in Melbourne in November 1903, a month before the birth of their first son, Alec. Another son, Douglas, was born in 1905. In 1912, May, on the advice of her publishers, travelled to London to build her career as a composer, leaving her husband and sons behind. At the start of 1914, she returned to Sydney, pregnant. Carl was apparently reconciled to her condition, because the family travelled together to London, and when Marita was born, he was named on the birth certificate as her father.

The Brahe name was well known in Australia. Carl's father had been a survivor of the 1860 Burke and Wills expedition, which travelled 2,000 miles north from Melbourne to the Gulf of Carpentaria. Of the nineteen men who set out, seven died, including both leaders. But Marita got little chance to know the man registered as her father. After war broke out, he joined up and in 1919, shortly after his return, he was killed in a motor accident.

May stayed in London and remarried in 1922, to George Morgan, an actor she'd first met years earlier, in Australia. Three years later they had a son. Marita meanwhile was developing as an artist, and at the age of seventeen she enrolled at the Slade School of Art, where she studied for two years, earning indifferent results. Perhaps realising that she wasn't going to make it as an artist in her own right, she studied picture restoration. Her mother was now earning enough in royalties to support her as she took courses at a series of London art schools.

Photograph believed to be of Marita Brahe, 1933

When the war came, May back headed to Australia with her youngest boy – her two older sons had already returned. She left her husband and daughter behind.

None of that was known to MI5. What they did know was that Marita was now a convinced fascist. In 1939, she was living with her friend Eileen Gleave, who was sufficiently closely involved in the British Union of Fascists that MI5 already had a file on her at the start of 1940. When war broke out, Marita and Eileen had debated leaving the country, but, Marita said later, 'We didn't think the British public could be so gullible.' Risking British lives to protect Poland? 'They won't fall for it,' Marita told herself. When it became clear that she'd misjudged her fellow citizens, she tried to get to Ireland, but it took too long for her to get her money together, and by then transit controls had been imposed.

Instead, in early 1940, she had married Bernard Perigoe, four years her junior, and another enthusiastic fascist. They rented a room from Gleave in Jesmond Avenue, Wembley, north-west London.

Gleave had just turned thirty, though she told people she was in her early twenties. She was a little over five feet tall, with dark, wavy hair and, according to one report, 'attractive appearance'. Estranged from her husband, she'd begun a relationship with a fellow fascist, Ron Stokes. The two couples set themselves up to oppose the war, by democratic means or otherwise.

Eileen was involved with the British Union Service Corps, a group that was, according to MI5, 'composed solely of women of the most extreme views'. At the start of 1940, it was planning demonstrations outside government meetings and 'imitating the militant suffragettes, lying down in the road to impede traffic'. It was also looking at more violent action: Gleave and Stokes were told to investigate the possibility of burning down a wooden synagogue near their home.

Much of this was just talk, but the Jesmond Avenue foursome were prepared to act on their beliefs. At the end of May 1940, as ships were lifting British troops off the beach at Dunkirk, Bernard and Ron addressed a meeting in Wembley, arguing against fighting Germany. They were arrested, and a week later appeared at Wealdstone Petty Sessions, charged with conduct likely to cause a breach of the peace. Ron was fined £10, and Bernard £2. They were ordered to pay at once, or go to prison. Eileen had the money in her handbag.

Like many wartime newlyweds, Marita and Bernard were soon forced apart, though not for the usual reason of military call-up. At the end of 1940, Bernard was interned in Brixton Prison, south London, for the political act of trying to arrange meetings in support of fascism.

Marita was growing increasingly disillusioned with the BUF. The organisation had been smashed by internment, with many leading members now languishing on the Isle of Man. Those that remained were divided about whether their duty was to their country or their politics. The main focus of activity, certainly for Gleave, was raising money to support the families of the interned men.

For the new Mrs Perigoe, this was all a waste of time. There was a war on, and she wanted to help Germany win it. In order to do this, she concluded, she needed to stay as far away from the

BUF as possible: anyone closely involved with it was bound to be under MI5 surveillance.

By February 1941, she had moved out of Gleave's house. She wrote to her friend enclosing money that was owed, and saying she wouldn't write again. At this point, her profile was low. MI5 knew Marita Perigoe's name, and believed that she, like Gleave, was putting her efforts into collecting money for BUF family members.

But Perigoe was looking for a way to do far more than that for the cause of fascism. What she needed was a secure connection to Berlin.

Roberts met her around the end of 1941, through the wife of another internee. Jeffrey Roy was 'said to have committed himself very deeply' to the cause of fascism, and in 1941 was in Brixton Prison. His wife had found a way of smuggling letters out, and was now acting as a courier for people who wanted messages to move uncensored by the authorities. That had brought her into contact with both the Perigoes and the Wegeners.

At this point, Roberts too was looking for new opportunities, and more excitement. It was becoming clear that he wasn't going to find a nest of Siemens spies, and keeping Dorothy Wegener at an appropriate distance was becoming harder and harder. He was working with her to smuggle a wireless to her brother Walter on the Isle of Man, hidden in a box of biscuits. Walter claimed he knew how to convert it from a routine receiver into a transmitter. An MI5 interception team would spend some cold, damp weeks on the island in January and February, listening for his signal and hoping it would reveal a new covert connection, but Plan Quasi-Dormouse, as it was christened, went nowhere.

Marita Perigoe made an immediate and deep impression on Roberts. She was the opposite of Dorothy. 'Not a neurotic nor feminine type,' the B1C report on her said. 'She is a masterful and somewhat masculine woman. Both in appearance and mentality she can be described as a typical arrogant Hun.' Perigoe told Roberts that she found BUF members to be too often stupid or unreliable – a view with which he had some sympathy. It wasn't clear whether she included her husband Bernard in that assessment.

It was Perigoe – 'this crafty and dangerous woman' – who was the catalyst for the January discussion with Liddell. 'A woman of this type, with so much misdirected ingenuity, might do great harm to the security and war effort of this country,' Rothschild argued, 'unless she were controlled.'

So he proposed that MI5 give her a controller.

Until now, Roberts had played Jack King as a helpless Nazi sympathiser, trailing his coat in the hope of being recruited by an established network. Liddell afterwards recorded Rothschild's plan as it had been explained to him: 'At a convenient moment, Roberts should reveal that he is an agent of the Gestapo who is contacted periodically by a man whose identity he does not know, and that his business here is to check up on the reliability of certain people whom the Germans think might be ready to assist them in time of invasion.'

It was a total switch. No one had tried to recruit Jack King, so Jack King was going to recruit others. Or rather Perigoe was going to recruit them for him; she looked like she might be rather good at that.

The kind of people Rothschild was looking for were 'persons who might give food, hiding and lodging to parachute troops'. He noted that 'the ways in which a disloyal person can be of use to invading forces have been so much publicised in the press, in books about the Fifth Column and in official publications that no tuition need, unfortunately, be given to disloyal persons who wish to help the enemy'.

One of MI5's responsibilities was the identification of people who might need to be rounded up in a hurry: the Invasion List.* Rothschild hoped that Roberts would be able to provide names

---

* What exactly MI5 or the government imagined they would do with the names on this list had the Germans invaded is an interesting question. At such a moment, with every fighting man required to push the enemy back into the sea, would they have had the capacity – or the will – to keep these people secure? It is worth noting the words of one of the Auxiliaries – men recruited to form a guerrilla resistance force within Britain if Germany landed: 'We would have killed without compunction. Our patrol might have made that decision about local people, Quislings or collaborators for example.' (McKinstry, *Operation Sealion*, 2014)

that they had previously missed. But he had another hope, too.

Roberts's conversations with Dorothy Wegener and her contacts had revealed that in the event of a German attack, many of them had no intention of sitting at home waiting to be arrested. 'It seems that certain of them already know about the invasion list and if and when the time comes they do not propose to be just where the police can find them,' Liddell wrote. 'It may therefore be a good thing to get them organised so that we know where to put our fingers on them.'

One option was to tell the Fifth Column to rendezvous at various locations in the event of invasion, where they could all be pulled in at once.

Another idea drew its inspiration from the XX Committee. Among the first schemes it had considered was the 'Blue Boot Plan'. MI5 feared that invading German troops might disguise themselves as British forces. The plan was to use this fear to their advantage, by telling Germany that, to counter such a problem, all British forces were to paint their right boots blue in the case of invasion. To add plausibility to the plan, troops were to be issued with tins of blue paint. The hope was that an undercover German would attempt to mimic this aspect of the disguise, thus revealing himself.

In the same way, Rothschild and Clay planned to issue Fifth Column members with some kind of secret badge, probably 'some innocuous object like the Union Jack', which they would start wearing when ordered. Police would then be told to round up everyone wearing the badge.

The operation was a long way off Rothschild's official brief, of investigating and then countering sabotage, but Rothschild, Clay and Roberts were keen to pursue it. The memo on the case offered an awkward justification, that 'sabotage and the security of certain very secret weapons were of special interest' to Rothschild's B1C section, and so they were 'anxious to find out to what extent disloyal persons interested themselves in such matters'. It was a shaky explanation, but Liddell was relaxed about MI5 officers roaming away from their remit, because the results could be inspired. Tar Robertson's Double Cross operation would soon go far beyond what had been originally intended.

Rothschild's plan wasn't just bold, it was elegant. He wanted, in effect, to mirror Double Cross. That involved using fake or turned agents to deceive their genuine German controllers. The 'Fifth Column' operation, as it was labelled, would see a fake controller deceiving genuine subversives. The Germans were desperate for intelligence, and there were Britons desperate to give it to them, and, in the middle – allowing both sides to believe they were in touch, while in reality keeping them apart – would be MI5.

In a way, the idea had been suggested months earlier, by Walter Wegener. Sitting in the Isle of Man camp, he had come to the same conclusion as Liddell about the Fifth Column: that it didn't exist in any useful form. Certainly he had found no evidence of it among his fellow interned fascists. According to Dorothy, he'd told her that the 'the fools entrusted with the formation of the Fifth Column had bungled their job badly'. She set out his proposal to Roberts. 'Before Germany could do a decent job in this country, a resolute organisation was needed. Walter was certain that such an organisation would be worth many thousands of parachutists and when the right moment came these men must be prepared to risk everything and to strike. He suggested that some should sabotage factories and engineering works, some concentrate on spreading rumour and defeatism, and others must be prepared to give the maximum help to the Germans at the time of invasion.'

Of those being released from internment, seven out of ten were, by Walter's estimate, still supportive of Germany. What they needed was someone to organise them, and Walter had suggested that Jack King would be the perfect man for the job.

Roberts's knack for winning people's complete trust had worked with the Wegeners. But Perigoe was a lot sharper than either of them, or Reginald Windsor, or Gunner Philip Jackson, and she was going to be asked to believe not that he was an enthusiastic fascist sympathiser, but that he was actually a cunning and dangerous Nazi agent, operating far behind enemy lines.

Roberts approached the subject carefully. For weeks, he dropped hints to Perigoe that he might have a secret. Initially, MI5 had planned to give him no proof of his claim to be a German spy 'except perhaps a draft on the Swiss Bank Corporation for several hundred pounds'. Feeling that wasn't enough, they decided to forge him some documents. Lacking the capability to do this in-house, they enlisted the help of the Secret Intelligence Service, SIS.

The small piece of paper they received back, dated March 1939, looked impressive. The script was heavy Gothic, and even those who couldn't read German couldn't mistake the words at the bottom, next to the stamp of an eagle over a swastika: 'Gestapo-Einsatzgruppe London'. Those who could understand the words would learn that Jack King was entitled to cross the border between the Reich and areas under German protection.

Jack King's faked Gestapo pass

Suitably equipped, Roberts made his pitch to Perigoe. He didn't claim to be a German – when he'd joined MI5 two years earlier, he'd said that his grasp of that language was only 'slight' – simply an Englishman who was working for the Nazis.

If Perigoe was delighted to have finally found her conduit to Berlin, she was less enthusiastic about what Roberts told her next.

'He said he was not a representative of the German Secret Service, which is concerned with the acquisition of intelligence, and he was not interested in espionage or sabotage,' according to the official report. 'His job in this country was to check up on persons who might be loyal to the Fatherland. He would relay those names to Germany for use in time of invasion, particularly from the point of view of giving food, lodging and hiding to invading forces.'

This posture was considered vital by MI5. The obvious defence for any suspect they identified through an approach like this was entrapment: that they had only done what they were doing because the agent from MI5 had encouraged them. This was the danger Roberts had had to avoid in Leeds. With Dorothy Wegener, he had consciously risked this by asking her to conceal the tank blueprint. But in that case Rothschild and Clay had already decided they wouldn't be seeking her prosecution.

The line between observer and provocateur wasn't always easy to see in practice. The previous September, one of Knight's agents, Marjorie Mackie, had been sent to Bristol to help local police investigate the Revd George Henry Dymock, rector of St Bede's church. The 62-year-old vicar was a known fascist, and Mackie, codename M/Y, approached him and proposed they write a seditious pamphlet together, for secret circulation. Dymock's response gave the police a reason to search the church premises, where they found fascist uniforms.

The police were pleased, but the Home Office was outraged. It refused to intern Dymock, and instead imposed a movement restriction on him. Officials 'took exception to the agent provocateur methods of MI5', Liddell recorded in his diary. One of them warned that Home Secretary Herbert Morrison 'would strongly disapprove of the use of agents in this way'.

Liddell was furious in return. 'If these methods cannot be employed to investigate the fifth column field we cannot be responsible for its investigation at all,' he said. 'Quite clearly the ordinary methods will lead us nowhere, and it is clearly part of our duty to find out exactly where doubtful elements would stand in time of invasion. This can only be achieved by provocation.'

Liddell's response to this problem was to limit what he told the Home Office. 'Intelligence matters were usually of such complexity that the less ministers had to do with them the better,' he later recalled. 'It was far better to get things settled, if possible, on a lower level; ministers had not really got the time to go into all the details. If therefore they were required to make a decision, it is as likely as not that it would be the wrong one!'

In particular, he didn't tell them about Rothschild's Fifth

Column operation. A year after Roberts's change of role, MI5 started sending Churchill a monthly report about its activities, in an effort to impress the prime minister. A conscious decision was taken to leave out mention of counter-subversion operations. It wasn't that they thought Churchill would necessarily disapprove, but 'the PM might speak to the Home Secretary about it, and if the latter was not also informed, we should find ourselves in trouble', Liddell wrote in his diary.*

Jack King's role as a gatherer of names rather than an organiser of espionage or sabotage might have kept Roberts on the correct side of the ethical line that Liddell had drawn, but it created operational problems. It was hard to explain. Why wouldn't the Gestapo want British people to collect intelligence? Why would it be against its supporters carrying out acts of sabotage?

One of that year's hit films was *The Next of Kin*. The Ealing Studios production was a propaganda film, but a well-made one, with battle scenes that audiences found shocking, both for their grittiness, and for their outcome. The plot was simple: German spies work to discover a British commando unit's plans for a cross-Channel raid. Liddell had enjoyed it – 'extremely well done', he wrote in his diary.

His admiration wasn't surprising: the film articulated the MI5 view of a Britain divided between large numbers of loyal citizens forever shooting their mouths off, and a small number of people who wanted a German victory and were willing to do something about it.

The movie showed no fewer than eight apparently loyal British citizens working for the Nazis. These Fifth Columnists were from all walks of life: a second-hand book dealer, a dentist, an air-raid warden. The head agent described himself as a loyal German, with a German mother. Another was forcing a third to work for her by supplying her with drugs. For the rest, their motives are unclear.

---

* It is possible that Churchill was told informally. Duff Cooper, the politician he'd appointed to oversee the Security Service, was briefed about the operation. And Churchill knew Rothschild personally. But it's also possible that the Fifth Column operation was judged to be the kind of secret you don't share with the prime minister.

But the message is clear. Encouraged by the sinister 'Number 23', a German spy played by Mervyn Johns, this network was able to establish the date and location of the commando attack, with disastrous results for the British.

For Perigoe, this kind of propaganda was an inspiration: it was exactly the role in which she saw herself. But now that she'd found her own Number 23, he was asking her to sit still. It didn't seem right. A fellow fascist in whom she confided pointed out that what Jack King had told her 'was exactly the technique that an MI5 agent would use'. This wasn't enough to scare Perigoe off, but the seed of doubt had been planted.

The other problem with Roberts's instruction to his recruits to avoid spying and sabotage was more basic: they ignored it.

10

'Somewhat melodramatic ideas'

Some men's wars took them to the jungles of Burma, or the deserts of North Africa, or up the beaches of Normandy. Eric Roberts's war took him from one end of the Marylebone Road to the other. The road serves as an informal boundary along the northern side of central London, running east–west, with Euston station at one end and Paddington at the other. Roberts's branch of the Westminster Bank had been on the north side of the thoroughfare, next to Euston. In July 1942, he temporarily established the headquarters of the Fifth Column half a mile south-west, in the basement of an antiques shop.

Marylebone High Street, which runs south from the Marylebone Road, is slightly misleadingly named. It would be about the right size for the main street in a small town, and indeed – two centuries earlier, before London overwhelmed it – that was what it had been. Now it was dwarfed by nearby city-sized thoroughfares such as Oxford Street. Although the area had been rebuilt towards the end of the previous century, the road managed to keep a lot of its neighbourhood feel, with smaller shop fronts than the vast expanses favoured in more prestigious locations. It felt like a hidden corner of the metropolis.

Denton Antiques was at the bottom of a narrow four-storey building that looked as though it had been squeezed in between its two taller neighbours. It had been an antiquarian book dealer, but was now increasingly selling chandeliers – a tricky business in wartime, with the shop window shattered at least once by a bomb blast. The basement itself was a low, dark, narrow room, without natural light, that was mainly used for storage by the shop above. The back door opened onto a tiny yard with an outside toilet.

Kenneth Denton outside his antiques shop

The choice of a location that felt hidden away was deliberate: 'the organisation has certain somewhat melodramatic ideas about Secret Service work', a note on the case reported, drily. It helped that the shop's owner, Kenneth Denton, could be relied on to be discreet. He had, like Roberts, become a Special Constable during the General Strike, and he was now working full-time for the police – more than full-time, he barely came home, sleeping instead on a camp bed at the station. He had been told that his basement was needed for meetings of a secret group, and he went along with it, periodically calling his wife Elizabeth and telling her to shut up shop early, so that the Fifth Column could meet unmolested.

A few weeks later, the base of operations shifted to more comfortable quarters, a small flat in Park West, a large modern block near Paddington. On the sixth floor, Apartment 499 had a tiny entrance area, with a cupboard, a door to a bathroom opposite and then, to the right, the door to the only other room. This was about twelve feet wide and fifteen feet long, with two windows looking out over the courtyard below. At one end, behind shutters, there was a small kitchen area. As a place to live, it would have suited a single person who didn't expect to do much entertaining, but set up as a sitting room and base of operations for an intelligence network, it was perfectly pleasant, and certainly nicer than the basement of Denton Antiques. It also, crucially, had a shared entrance that could be used without passing a doorman, allowing members of the Fifth Column to come and go unobserved. In this flat Roberts would host Perigoe and her growing army of recruits, usually alone or in pairs.

She was, it turned out, formidably effective at recruitment. At the start of July 1942, a few months into the operation, Roberts's network had already grown to an impressive size. A case summary listed seventeen of the 'more interesting' people Perigoe had brought to his attention. Many were women, and many lived near her in Wembley.

First, there was her friend Eileen Gleave. A long-time fascist, she also loathed Churchill, remembering his support for the disastrous Gallipoli adventure in the previous war. 'I lost a cousin through him,' she told Roberts, 'and I've never forgiven him.' In April 1942, Roberts filed a brief but potent report: 'Gleave would, in time of invasion, be prepared to raid the Wembley Home Guard arms depot in order to assist the enemy. She is ardently pro-Nazi and the sort of person who really would carry out what she said she would do.'

Although she was trying to keep a low profile, through her fascist connections Gleave was known to be in contact with the Duke of Bedford, a strong advocate of seeking terms with Germany. The duke was an ongoing headache for MI5, who were generally inclined to see him as a 'comparatively harmless crank' (although one 1941 report went rather further, calling him 'a sexual pervert, physical coward and a rebel against all authority'). He was a sympathiser with fascism, but the assessment was that his main obsession was a new monetary policy that he'd developed, and that he was being used by men 'much more astute and unscrupulous than himself'. There was a running debate with the Home Office about the advantages and disadvantages of interning someone who was a senior member of the aristocracy and the fourth richest man in England.

Eileen Gleave, 1947

But Gleave offered a new way to get information on him. Roberts told her that the Gestapo was interested in the duke and his associates as potential sources of disaffection, and tasked her with spying on them on his behalf.

There were also some of Perigoe's Wembley neighbours, a middle-aged couple called Edgar and Sophia Bray, who were mainly motivated by their hatred of communism – Sophia was Russian by birth. Edgar was an accountant and astrologer, who had seen in the stars that neither Britain nor Germany would win the war. He feared instead that the two sides would fight each other to exhaustion and that Russia would then overrun Europe. Sophia meanwhile had told Perigoe that she was willing to do 'anything' to help Germany – she would even 'go there and scrub the floors', if that was what was needed.

Edgar was generally viewed as an eccentric, even by Sophia, but that didn't stop him from picking up useful intelligence. In June 1942, he was out for a swim in a reservoir near his home, when he was suddenly ordered to leave the water: the Army wanted to test an amphibious vehicle. He pretended to leave, but instead climbed the banks and watched the trials. He was intrigued to see that the craft had wing floats that it used when it was in the water, and he counted thirty men getting out of it afterwards.

When he told Sophia, she was determined to pass the information on. She was aware of her friend Marita's claim to have a Gestapo contact, but having grown up in Russia, she was instinctively suspicious of secret police traps. She had questions about Jack King. If the Germans were organised enough to have someone like him operating in Britain, why did they need to drop spies in by parachute, as she kept hearing they were doing? It seemed likely to her that King was in fact an agent of MI5. In any case, hadn't he said that he wasn't there to gather intelligence? She felt that the best way to get news of these trials to Berlin was via the Spanish embassy in London. In every one of these assertions she was, of course, entirely correct.

When Perigoe reported all this to Roberts, he knew he needed to move fast. If Sophia passed the information on the amphibious trials to the Spanish embassy, it was indeed entirely possible that it would find its way to Germany. Spain was neutral in the war, but its fascist government's sympathies were all with Hitler. Rothschild spent much of his time dealing with sabotage attacks on ships passing through Gibraltar carried out by German agents based in Spain.

Apart from the immediate intelligence issue, the Fifth Column operation depended in part on Roberts being Perigoe's only channel to Germany. If Sophia found another route, there was a danger that Perigoe would start using it, too. The last thing he wanted to do was encourage her to build a network only for her to start sending its fruits somewhere else.

So he subtly shifted his position: gathering intelligence wasn't his job, but of course he could get information to Germany. He had passed Edgar's story on to his 'chief', who was suitably grateful, and had pledged to send it up the chain. There was no need for Sophia to do anything else.

He seemed to have convinced Perigoe, and she told Sophia not to worry about going to the Spaniards. But he remained unsure that he'd prevented her from sending the information anyway.

Sophia seemed to blow hot and cold on whether to trust Roberts. At the end of July 1942, she told Perigoe she was 'willing to hide German agents and give them food'. But two months later, discovering that an airfield at Burnley was a dummy, she

passed on the details only reluctantly, saying she was still inclined to write to the Spanish embassy instead. But then Sophia
found others difficult to read, too. She regarded Edgar as a
'hopeless puzzle', Roberts reported. Sophia and Perigoe thought
he was more concerned with his allotment than spying – 'a man
would not be interested in gardening and espionage at the same
time'.

Perigoe assessed which of her friends might be privy to useful
information. Hilda Leech – whom she described unkindly as 'a
fat woman of 45' – was married to a bank clerk and had served
on Harrow Council. She now worked as a clerk at the oil company Shell Mex. Perigoe persuaded her to begin providing weekly
information on the amount of petroleum stored in dumps around
the country.

Her commitment went further than this. A few months after
Leech joined the Fifth Column, Perigoe was chatting to Roberts
when she suddenly remembered something. 'I forgot to tell you,'
she said. 'I've got a contribution for you.'

Roberts was taken aback, as Perigoe handed him some cash.
'Who from?' he asked. He counted it. 'Five pounds contribution?'
That was nearly two months' wages for a British soldier.

'Yes.'

He looked at the notes again. 'Who are they from?'

'Leech.'

'Mrs Leech?'

'Yes.'

'Nonsense.' He was still bewildered. 'What for?'

'I don't know.'

'The Gestapo funds?'

'Yes.'

'Oh. Well, thanks very much.'

MI5 officers who were involved in Double Cross delighted in
seeing how much money they could persuade Germany to send
them. Roberts foresaw only trouble if he tried the same trick with
the Fifth Column. 'Now look,' he said, when he had regained his
usual composure. 'We mustn't start this sort of thing. You must
tell Mrs Leech that the Gestapo funds do not want augmentation
from outside sources. It leads to all sorts of trouble, because there
is all sorts of elementary book-keeping that would have to be

made.' It wasn't the most convincing excuse, but it was the best that the momentarily stunned Roberts could manage.

There were others on Perigoe's list: a local Roman Catholic priest was 'sincerely pro-German' but had said he had to report Fifth Column organisations to his superiors, making him an unsuitable recruit. He was passed on to another section of MI5 for investigation, as was a 'violently pro-Nazi' man who was suspected of having a wireless transmitter. Roberts tried to discourage her from recruiting one young man, whom she described to him as weak-minded. She was in turn horrified at his excess of conscience. 'Marita explained that everything should be done to help the cause, and if somebody could be useful, he should be used.'

Having set up the Park West flat as a private place where people could speak freely, there remained the question of how to collect evidence against the Fifth Column. MI5 didn't have its own bugging team. Instead, it relied on the people in the land who knew the most about the electronic transmission of the human voice: the General Post Office. As well as handling letters, the GPO was responsible for Britain's telephone network.

At MI5's request it would deploy engineers to conceal microphones. Usually, as with Irma Stapleton and Philip Jackson, at the other end of the wire would be detectives wearing headphones and taking shorthand. But that was labour-intensive. It was an acceptable way of dealing with one or two meetings which would lead to a prosecution, but for the Fifth Column operation, Rothschild took a different approach.

In the US, the FBI had just had a great success rounding up and convicting a Nazi spy ring in New York. The Abwehr had strong-armed a German-American named William Sebold to work for them. But Sebold was a bad choice: he'd gone to the US authorities. The FBI had pulled out all the stops. They set Sebold up in an office, into which they built a small room for an agent to sit behind a two-way mirror. The agent operated a film camera and a new Presto sound recording system. The technique was so novel that, when the case came to court, the recordings weren't deemed admissible. Instead the jury had to watch a silent film of one of the spies removing his secrets from where he'd stored them – in his sock – and handing them over.

MI5 couldn't run to the expense of the FBI's elaborate set-up, but Rothschild did adopt one part of it: the sound recordings. At the start of the war, the GPO had foreseen the need for better recording equipment, and had developed a machine that looked like a twin-turntable record player. It would record conversations by cutting grooves onto 12-inch cellulose discs, spinning at 50 revolutions per minute, which needed to be changed about every ten minutes. After each meeting of the Fifth Column, the recordings were transcribed and compared with Roberts's own report. And if they wanted to, Rothschild and Clay could listen to the recordings themselves, and experience the feeling of being inside the room as Roberts did his work.

A Post Office twin-turntable portable disc recorder

What they heard in the early days of the operation was an atmosphere of constant distrust.

'All disloyal persons are extremely suspicious of so-called members of the German Secret Service or Gestapo as they are well aware that this technique is used by all security services to find out who is loyal and who is not,' a July 1942 case summary read. 'It would not be an exaggeration to say that during thirty per cent of Jack's time with the fifth column, members firmly believe that he is in MI5.'

Roberts tried to assuage Perigoe's doubts by turning them into a joke. 'Look at Marita, she looks at you with half-closed eyes,' he laughed to Gleave, after Perigoe had questioned who he was really working for. She was, he said, 'so terribly suspicious'.

Perigoe was defensive: 'Well, I haven't asked you if you were working for anything for some time, so I thought I'd better.'

'You asked me about MI5 on Saturday,' Roberts pointed out.

'Did I?'

'Yes.'

'Well, I have to do that fairly regularly, don't I?'

Roberts even made a joke out of the idea that they were being bugged, when that was precisely what was happening. The first time he invited Perigoe and Gleave to the Park West flat, he stepped out of the room, calling casually back: 'Oh, Marita, whilst I'm out of the room, you can amuse yourself with the microphone.'

She replied in the same spirit: 'I've looked for them already.'

But this was only partly a joke. In the months to come, when she was left alone, Perigoe would launch genuine searches for a bug. Was it under the carpet? Behind the photograph of Churchill? In the vents, high up on the wall, that let in air from outside?

For Roberts, humour was a way to ease tension, making difficult situations into the subject of shared jokes. He teased Perigoe about her 'threats to bump me off', suggesting that she would stab him with a penknife, or poison him. She joked in turn about how she would dispose of his corpse, saying she'd drop him down a coal hole in London's clubland. And like the microphones in the flat, this was a joke with an edge: by August 1942, Perigoe had talked about killing him at least once. Afterwards, she denied it had happened, and then tried to laugh it off. But Roberts had seen the 'virulent' look on her face. He knew that if she concluded he was deceiving her, his life would be at risk. This operation was a far more serious business than hiding blueprints in marmalade with Dorothy Wegener.

As Roberts tried to assess how much Perigoe really suspected him, he was also worrying about other threats to his safety. He continued to be concerned that his colleagues at MI5 were too complacent about the possibility of German penetration. MI5's confidence in this area was based on the success of the Double Cross operation. German communications, decrypted by Britain's codebreakers at Bletchley Park, suggested their reports were being believed.

But if MI5 was capable of hoaxing the Abwehr, it was possible that the Abwehr was capable of playing an even larger hoax back to Britain. If Germany had realised its spies had been turned, there was great value in not revealing this: a report that is intended to mislead can reveal the truth, if you know that the person who sent it to you is lying.

There were a very small number of people in the Office that Roberts really didn't trust. Not that he simply disliked, but that he felt might not be entirely what they seemed. But he wasn't sure, and he knew that he was doing a job that made men doubt everyone. He was uncertain what to do with his suspicions.

Some traitors are driven by a desire for revenge, some by a desire for money, and some by ideology. Perigoe fell into the final camp, but, after Roberts suggested it several times, she did agree to be paid expenses by what she thought was the Third Reich. Every Thursday evening, a letter would be posted from a different part of London, containing another envelope, which in turn contained two pound notes. 'She feels secure because the money is in a double envelope, so that if any curious person at the GPO were to hold the letter up to the light, he would not see the pound notes inside.' Thanks to inflation, it was worth around the same as Knight had offered Roberts eight years earlier when he'd sent him into the BUF.

Just because she was taking money from him, though, Perigoe didn't feel obliged to obey Roberts's instructions. In particular, now that she had found a conduit to Germany, she was determined to prove her worth as a spy. 'It has been found impossible to control her,' a note in her file read. 'On more than one occasion she has spontaneously committed acts of espionage, involving considerable ingenuity, against our instructions.'

There wasn't much call for picture restoration in 1942 – most of Britain's art treasures were in storage, far from where bombs might fall – so Perigoe worked as a secretary at the Fortiphone company, which made hearing aids ('the amazing FOCUSSED Golden-Tone transmits all sounds', the newspaper ads promised). This wasn't at first glance an auspicious position for a secret agent, but she saw opportunity everywhere. One of the managers was a keen officer in the Home Guard, who did his dictation for that job while at work. In April 1942, he was busy preparing for a weekend overnight war game, in which he was responsible for transporting troops and ammunition. Perigoe noticed that his secretary, who was typing up his orders, was using fresh carbon paper in her typewriter, and knew this was her chance. Once his secretary had finished typing, Perigoe popped her head round the door and asked if she could borrow some carbon paper. As she'd hoped, she was handed the closest ones, which now bore a negative imprint of the manager's Home Guard memo, something that she took great delight in pointing out to Roberts when she handed them over.

The incident and the intelligence involved were trivial, but Maxwell Knight, among others, was impressed. He commented that he 'would very much like to have her as one of his own agents', to which the reply came that she was already working for MI5, even if she didn't know it.

Knight had a strong belief in the secretary as spy, and he would always try to secure such roles for his agents. 'No official or other single individual ever has the same opportunity for obtaining information covering a wide area,' he wrote. 'If it were possible for any business magnate or government official to be able to see into the mind of his secretary, he would be astounded at the amount of knowledge concerning the general affairs of the business or department.'

The ideal, he believed, was for a spy to become 'a piece of the furniture' so that visitors to an office 'do not consciously notice whether the agent is there or not'. This approach made Knight unusually forward-thinking in his use of women; because they were so likely to be overlooked, and to occupy apparently unimportant secretarial roles, he had used them with great success to penetrate the communists in the 1930s. Properly directed by an agency that wanted to use her, Perigoe could have been just as effective. She had a 'remarkable aptitude' for espionage, Rothschild and Clay concluded. But Roberts's job was to divert her talents in other directions.

For fifteen years, Roberts had been an agent. Now he was an agent-runner. According to the man from whom he'd learned his craft, Knight, this was a harder task than simply being an agent – a role Roberts was, of course, also still playing. The runner, Knight wrote, 'will have to be continually adapting himself to agents who vary very much in character and personality'.

The ideal agent-runner, in Knight's mind, was 'a man of very wide understanding of human nature; one who can get on with and understand all types and all classes'. The Fifth Column operation didn't test that very hard: most of its recruits were drawn from the English lower middle class: administrative staff, salesmen, skilled tradesmen. They were people who felt that they worked hard but saw little fruit from it. Many had reason to believe that they had been held back from what they wanted by the snobbery of others. They saw themselves in G. K. Chesterton's *The Secret People*, which talked of a quietly resentful English population, ruled over by a series of masters, from the Norman conquerors, to Oliver Cromwell's roundheads, to the twentieth-century bureaucrat, none of whom understood the people they governed, 'For we are the people of England, that never have spoken yet.'

Britain's current rulers, according to Chesterton, were

Lords without anger or honour, who dare not carry their swords.
They fight by shuffling papers; they have bright dead alien eyes;
They look at our labour and laughter as a tired man looks at flies.

It was a view with which Roberts could empathise. At MI5 he was surrounded by university dons, lawyers, former Army officers. He was simply a clerk, on loan from the Westminster Bank. Like Chesterton's silent English heroes, he preferred ale to wine. 'I still pin my faith to English beer,' he said. 'And, I could add, to English beef and Yorkshire pud.'* His colleagues looked down on him, he said, because he had 'plebeian tendencies – not the Officer type'.

He was getting on no better with Edward Blanshard Stamp, who made little attempt to conceal his contempt for Roberts. Class often made its way into their rows. When Roberts tore one of his shirts in the course of his duties, he asked the office for help replacing it. Stamp refused the claim. For Roberts, it was more than the question of the seven shillings and sixpence that it would

---

* One of the poem's other themes, that the English preferred the pub to revolution – 'a few men talked of freedom, while England talked of ale' – could also have been written for Roberts, whose years undercover had left him with a contempt for political extremism on both wings; communists, he said, were 'deadly boring', and 'even bloodier than the fascists'.

cost to buy a new shirt. Clothing rationing had been introduced in 1941, and coupons were scarce. To the wealthier classes, this was merely an irritation: they had large wardrobes to fall back on. But Roberts owned only three shirts. He had to appeal to Curry – and, in a sign of how difficult his relationship with Stamp had become, offer to resign – to get the five ration coupons he needed for a replacement.

Fascism had offered Perigoe's recruits a political programme that would have protected them from the forces they felt were making their lives more difficult. It promised to recreate the greatness of the British Empire, building a country that acted in its own interests, not the interests of foreigners or money men. And it offered an enemy, who also featured in Chesterton's poem: the 'cringing Jew'.

Whatever they differed on, Perigoe's recruits were united in their anti-Semitism. Special Branch reported that her friend Gleave 'remains violently anti-Semitic and complains of the number of Jews residing in her block of flats'. Edgar Bray cancelled his subscription to an astrological newsletter, suggesting its editor was under the influence of Jews and freemasons. Hilda Leech was 'violently anti-Semitic'.

'There are few, if any, of these people who are not anti-Semites,' an internal MI5 report concluded, 'and it matters little if they became admirers of Nazi Germany and fell for its anti-Semitic propaganda, or whether they admire Germany solely because of her treatment of the Jewish problem. The result is the same.'

While a suspicion of Jews continued to run widely through British society, the war meant that it was less acceptable to admit to such thoughts in polite society. Newspapers had toned down their anti-Semitic language. But, even in wartime, fascists had their own news sources. One of Maxwell Knight's agents, reporting on a different group of former British Union members, noted that 'all, without exception, listen in to the German news bulletins, believe them and consider the BBC broadcasts as "democratic lying propaganda". Their only hope seems to be that Hitler will kindly oblige by giving Britain her own National Socialist Government when he has won the war against the democrats and the Jews, and to that end they believe in a German victory.'

As Roberts was learning, those beliefs were held by the most unexpected people.

On a Saturday afternoon at the end of August 1942, Roberts met up with Perigoe, and together they made their way to Piccadilly.

The papers that day carried news from Stalingrad, where the Russians were clinging on as Hitler threw men and machines into battle in an attempt to make a breakthrough. The war had now been raging for three years, and it was not at all clear that it was going Britain's way. For much of the year, the news from the Western Desert had been of British retreats and defeats at the hands of Rommel. At home there were signs of weariness. In Scotland, 2,000 miners were out on strike in a row that started when three of their number were arrested for non-payment of a fine.

The *Daily Mirror* carried a light story on its front page about how a telegram from the Admiralty telling a mother that her son was missing in action had been opened by the young man himself, who had arrived home an hour earlier. It was less amusing than it was made to sound. The sailor had taken part in the disastrous raid on the French port of Dieppe a week earlier. Poorly planned and executed, driven by political rather than strategic needs, the raid had left most of the largely Canadian attacking force dead, wounded or captured.

For Roberts, 1942 was proving to be a good year personally as well as professionally. A daughter, Crista, had arrived at the start of the year. She was named for a German friend that Audrey and Eric had made on their honeymoon. He tried to get home as much as he could – his son Max, now six, noticed how Audrey would brighten when he did. After hearing the family's news, Eric would disappear into his study. Through the door, Max could hear his father's typewriter clicking away over a recording of Sibelius on the gramophone player, a sound he grew to hate, because it meant his father couldn't be disturbed. Work aside, these visits were a happy time for the family. At weekends they would walk over Epsom Downs, along the old Roman trail, and have a picnic near Headley Court mansion.

Even on these walks, the family couldn't escape the war. Max delighted in watching the planes flying overhead, and finding bomb fins to add to his shrapnel collection. Their long garden was dug up so that Audrey could grow her own vegetables, and keep chickens and ducks. At the bottom of the garden was a railway cutting, where Max and his little brother Peter watched injured soldiers being unloaded from carriages with red crosses painted on top – the Canadian Army had a hospital nearby. And when the sirens sounded while Eric was away, it fell to Max to lead Peter down into the air-raid shelter, while his mother carried the baby.

Peter and Max Roberts

As Roberts and Perigoe walked in to the Piccadilly outlet of the upmarket Slaters restaurant chain, he knew he was being taken to meet another prospective Fifth Columnist. They found Perigoe's friend Eileen Gleave at a table with a fresh-faced young woman. She introduced her as Nancy Brown, up from Brighton, on the south coast, where she worked for the council. The pair had known each other before the war. Gleave gave Roberts a look. 'We have been having a long discussion on old times,' she said meaningfully. That was the signal she had agreed with him beforehand that Brown was willing to join their group.

Brown wasn't the sort of recruit Roberts was used to. She was young and attractive and full of verve. Frankly, she looked a picture of health, and after three years of rationing, that wasn't to be taken for granted. 'I found it almost impossible to believe that she would form suitable material as a Gestapo agent,' he reported afterwards. 'There was humour and decency written on her countenance.'

Whatever his doubts, Eileen had given him the nod, so Roberts suggested they go somewhere more private, and the little group made their way to the Park West flat. They avoided the grand art deco reception area and went into a smaller entrance opposite, where there were stairs and two lifts. Coming out of the lift, Apartment 499 was on the left, one of four flats at the end of a short corridor.

They got there just before five – the perfect time to serve drinks. When everyone was settled, Roberts got down to business. 'Well,' he said. 'I hear you are more or less of our way of thinking.'

Brown met his gaze. 'Yes I am,' she said. 'Not more or less, it's definite.' This was greeted with appreciative noises from Gleave. Brown went on. 'I've always had to play for safety, because I live with my parents, and my father's retired, and they haven't much money to live on.'

Roberts nodded understandingly, and she continued. 'Of course, I have to go to work, and he's pretty nervous. So even right at the beginning of the war I had to be pretty careful. But the more Eileen's told me this afternoon, I think I would like to start now.'

Seventeen years inside subversive groups hadn't blunted Roberts's capacity for surprise. He had only just met Nancy Brown, yet she was pledging loyalty to him in the belief he was a Nazi spy. Her only request was that he keep her address out of his records until it was time for Germany to invade.

Brown, it emerged, had long loved both Germany and fascism. She had been involved with the British Union before the war – which was how Eileen knew her – and also The Link. This group had been set up in 1937 to promote good relations with Hitler's Germany. By the middle of 1939 it had had more than 4,000 members, opposed to Britain joining what one called 'a Jewish war of revenge'. The Link's founder, Admiral Sir Barry Domvile, the former director of Naval Intelligence, was a regular speaker at public meetings, where he operated on the assumption that all awkward questions came from Jews.

But although Brown had been a committed supporter, she was

sure her name wasn't on any of the government's lists of fascists. 'I once called at the local headquarters of the fascists a long time before the war, but I never joined them there,' she explained.

Gleave reassured her that, if the government had her down as a supporter of The Link, she would have been questioned by now. 'They've made enquiries about all those that they knew,' she said. 'You know Stella? They came and searched Stella's place.' Gleave was right about this: Brown's name wasn't on the list of Link members that MI5 had.

But there was one place it did appear: at the top of an article in the August 1939 edition of The Link's magazine, the *Anglo-German Review*. In the article, headlined 'Rhineland Holiday', Brown enthused about the 'physical perfection' of a party of schoolchildren that she watched on a hiking expedition in Germany.

'One bright-eyed boy was playing his accordion, and as he played the shining plaits of the little girls around him gleamed in the sunlight like neat braids of gold,' she sighed.

Fortunately, Gleave had a suggestion for how Brown could answer any awkward questions about that piece. There was, she pointed out, another Nancy Brown, who had worked for John Beckett, a fascist politician who had split with Oswald Mosley in the late thirties. 'Nancy Brown was secretary of that other business,' she said. 'Did you put your address in that *Review*?'

'No.'

'Well, Nancy Brown was the secretary of that business Beckett was in. Spelt exactly the same way. You can always put that down to her.'*

Brown's Rhineland holiday had been only one of a series of visits she'd made to Germany in 1938 and 1939, where she'd made a number of friends, including one young man in particular. 'When war was declared – or rather, a week before – I wrote to him and said, "It looks pretty bad,"' she told Roberts. 'I had a card from him written in the train. It said, "I hope we won't struggle. You will hear from me again." And of course I never did. He was going to be a teacher.'

---

* There was also a Nancy Brown among the names of members of Captain Ramsay's Right Club. That list didn't specify which of the fascist Nancy Browns this was.

Could 'Jack King' get word of him? 'I'd very much like to hear what happened to him,' Brown explained.

'May take a little time, but I could find out,' Roberts assured her.

Now Brown wanted to know how she could help Roberts. 'Very often one hears what one thinks is gossip, don't you?' she said. 'You don't know whether it's really true or not.'

'Gossip is valuable,' Roberts told her.

'Is it?' Brown asked.

Gleave insisted it was, 'even if it sounds crazy'.

'Um . . .' Brown prepared to give her first intelligence report. 'Last week they said that the Brighton hospitals were full of the Dieppe dead and wounded. They were all lying about. I didn't get in the hospitals to see whether they were or not, but I should think it's highly probable.'

'Yes,' said Roberts, coaxing her for more.

'That sort of thing, you mean?' Brown asked, uncertain that anything she had to say could really be of interest to the German high command.

'That's the sort of thing we're very interested in, yes,' Roberts reassured her.

Brown carried on, encouraged. 'Eileen said something about gun positions. I know where, definitely where there are some at the moment, they're in the Brighton Grammar School grounds.'

'Do you know what sort of anti-aircraft guns?' Roberts gently pushed her. 'Heavy, or . . .?'

'Heavy, pretty heavy, yes,' Brown replied, then laughed. This wasn't as hard as she'd thought it might be. 'I know a lot of local civil defence stuff. That's not so interesting, of course.'

'Well, they're quite interested in that,' said Roberts, using 'quite' to mean 'very', as only an Englishman can. 'You might have special instructions about invasion.'

Brown wasn't sure about that. 'I don't see anything about the invasion plans,' she said.

Gleave piped up: 'But then, of course, you haven't really been trying to find out.'

'No, that's true. No, I haven't thought about it really.'

Gleave explained the transformation that Nancy was about to

undergo: 'Once one becomes conscious, one becomes sort of . . . brighter.'

Brown thought that if she'd been approached a year earlier, she'd probably have refused. But she had now been at war for three years, and there was no prospect of either side winning, and she was 'fed up'. War was miserable for a woman. At least the men could run around with guns. For women, war meant endless shortages, of food, of tobacco, of clothes, of make-up. Nancy Brown was supposed to be at a carefree age, but instead she was being urged to dig for victory, to make do and mend, to consider whether her journey was really necessary. Even the colour had gone out of life. There was no light in the evenings. US soldiers embarking for Britain were warned not to be shocked at the drabness of the place. 'Britain may look a little shop-worn and grimy to you,' a guide to the country for servicemen read. 'The houses haven't been painted because factories are not making paint – they're making planes. The famous English gardens and parks are either unkempt because there are no men to take care of them, or they are being used to grow needed vegetables.'

The more she thought about it, the more excited Brown became at the prospect of being able to help Germany. 'I want to do anything to hasten on the end now,' she explained. Her great fear, she confided, was that Hitler wouldn't invade – 'That would be awful,' Gleave agreed.

'The majority of our people, honestly, are such fools that they're really worth nothing,' Brown explained. What the country needed was to be ruled by the Germans. 'They'd make a better race of us.'

For Roberts, the conversation wasn't getting any less astonishing. Brown and Gleave were now fantasising about life under Hitler. They asked him to reserve some nice blond SS men for them. Brown said she much preferred them to the American and Canadian soldiers that other young women swooned over – 'Germans have far better manners.'

It was a relief for Brown to be able to say what she really thought for once. Usually, she had to pretend to be enthusiastic when someone told her of an Allied victory, or a German plane being shot down. 'Very hard sometimes, but I try my best,' she laughed.

Others in her family weren't as good at concealing their feelings about the war. 'Mother says she doesn't know how I can do it,' Brown said. 'We have to keep her away from people, otherwise she'd spill the beans. She'd shout at the top of her voice and tell them where they got off.'

They began to discuss bombing targets. Brown described the location of a nautical instrument factory – 'it is beautifully cam-ouflaged'. And she told Roberts about a hotel on Brighton seafront where pilots were sent to recuperate.

'Well, we will try and hasten their recuperation,' Roberts said, acting his part with appropriate menace. Brown said she thought the Luftwaffe had tried to hit it before, 'but they weren't quite good enough'.

She paused briefly to consider the fates of these young airmen. Gleave was philosophical. 'By probably having a few of them killed we are saving a lot in the long run,' she said. Brown agreed.

That morning, she said, she'd had no idea that Gleave was going to suggest anything like this, still less that she might find herself a signed-up German spy before dinnertime.

'I must say, you've taken it very calmly,' Roberts told her.

'I think when I come to get in the train tonight and think it over, I shall probably be a bit alarmed for a bit,' Brown replied. 'But you can depend on me.'

Gleave offered her the advice of someone who had now been a conscious Nazi agent for several months. 'You'll feel much better when you find that you survive, that the weeks go on, and you're still alive.'

It was time for Brown to head back to Brighton. They discussed which bus she should get to Victoria for the train home, and whether there was anywhere else in Brighton that the Luftwaffe ought to be bombing. She thought mainly the guns at the grammar school. 'I wouldn't mind if they got hit at all,' she said. 'Because just opposite to them is the National Fire Service. I wouldn't mind if they got bombed at all. They're awful people.'

'Well,' said Roberts. 'We'll do our best to oblige.'

Afterwards, he recorded his disbelief at the afternoon's events. 'So far as I could tell here was a citizen of responsible character, capable of forming a sane and balanced judgement on her coun-try's affairs and of no ill will towards those who are doing their best to carry out their duty,' he wrote. 'However within the space of an hour, without the offer of any financial or other inducement, nor pressure of any description, Nancy Brown was doing her best to tell a man she supposed to be a German agent what little she knew of the disposition of armed forces, war factories, etc in the Brighton area. The fact that the items of information volunteered might have resulted in the deaths of many people counted for nothing.'

Brown was as good as her word. At the start of that November, she handed Roberts four hand-drawn maps showing the location of targets in Brighton that she'd picked out for the Luftwaffe. They included the fire station, ammunition dumps, places where tanks were concealed, and the Army Records Office – where 600 women worked, according to Brown.

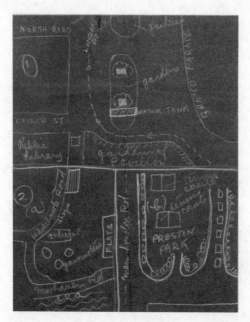

Nancy Brown's sketches of targets for the Luftwaffe in Brighton

Had Roberts genuinely been a German agent, he could have looked with satisfaction on the fruits of his first six months as a Gestapo man: he had some strange recruits, it was true, but he also had some who were enthusiastic and able and who could be directed into positions where they could be truly effective. From the perspective of an MI5 man, the results were more worrying, but the operation was still proving effective, and identifying people who were prepared to take serious risks for Germany – any of them could have been arrested for saying the things they'd said to him.

But not everyone was so pleased with the Fifth Column.

11

'Such methods were necessary'

'The whole of the Rothschild family is engaged in collecting something or other,' Victor once observed. 'They seem to have got a collecting gene. Some of them collect fans, some of them collect Limoges enamel. They collect everything.'

Victor had the bug, too. Before the war he had collected books, acquiring thousands of eighteenth-century editions. It was an elite passion, the kind that only people with an abundance of time and money could pursue.

Now he was beginning the ultimate collection, one that no one else in the world was in the position to build up, one that enjoyed a Top Secret classification. Victor Rothschild was collecting fascists.

He pursued his new hobby with the same rigour that his father and uncle had devoted to their butterflies. His small department, B1C, had its own card index of targets, with its own coding system, separate to MI5's. Roberts's reports were split up into paragraphs on each member of the Fifth Column, and these were then rewritten to remove clues to their origin and put into each person's file in the official MI5 registry, referring simply to 'Source SR' – the codename Roberts was using now that his days as Maxwell Knight's man inside the BUF were behind him.

The people in Rothschild's files fell broadly into two categories. First, there was the small group of conscious agents, who knew – or thought they knew – Jack King's true allegiance. They not only gathered information themselves but passed on information from and about the second, much larger group – a network of unconscious agents judged by the Fifth Column to be likely to be useful to Germany.

Right from the start of Roberts's formal employment with MI5 in 1940, he had faced the question of whether his undercover work amounted to provocation. With the Leeds fascists, the matter had been simplified when Windsor confessed to the arson attempt on Dawson's shop, which took place before he had ever met Roberts. With Gunner Philip Jackson, his letter to the Spanish embassy, even if it couldn't be used directly, showed that he had made the first move. But as 'Jack King', Roberts was swimming in murkier waters.

Had there been a Siemens spy ring to pick up his trailed coat and recruit him, his actions with Dorothy Wegener and the tank blueprint would have been entirely justifiable as a way to identify it. But instead, Roberts had found himself setting up his own spy ring.

Summarising the case in July 1942, Rothschild referred obliquely to 'certain unfortunate events in another case' which had had 'bad psychological effects' on MI5 agents. This may have been a reference to the Ben Greene case, whose ripples were still being felt across the service.

Ben Greene, cousin of the novelist Graham Greene, was an ardent pacifist who had found himself drawn into fascist circles by his opposition to the war. In 1940, Maxwell Knight had been asked to investigate him, and had sent one of his agents, Harold Kurtz, to speak to him.

Kurtz was the man who would trap Molly Hiscox and Norah Briscoe the next year, but his actions in Greene's case were less clear-cut. He reported that the pacifist had made a series of treasonous remarks, and, this being the height of the invasion scare, Greene was arrested and interned.

Unlike many of those who were locked up, Greene had friends and resources to fight his corner, and a plausible argument that he had been framed. His case became a cause célèbre for those who viewed internment as a step too far for a democratic state, even one fighting a war such as this. In 1941, his brother Edward tricked Kurtz into going to a meeting with his lawyer, who proceeded to grill him on his previous statements. The answers he gave were evasive, and serious doubts were cast on the case against Greene. At the start of 1942, Greene was released, amid criticism of Kurtz's evidence. MI5 stood by their man and their argument that Greene had been a danger, but the case threw a shadow over Knight.

Eric Roberts was a much more circumspect and reliable agent

than Harold Kurtz, but he was also doing a much more difficult job. Though Rothschild blithely asserted in July 1942 that the way the Fifth Column operation was being run would 'obviate any possibility' of Roberts being accused of being a provocateur, other officers inside MI5 had severe doubts.

The leading initial critic was Edward Blanshard Stamp, Roberts's adversary from their days together at Blenheim. F3, the section of MI5 that Stamp was in, was supposed to be in charge of monitoring fascists, so when Rothschild wrote up the progress of the Fifth Column operation in July 1942, he was copied in. His response was to try to tear the operation to pieces. He was deeply sceptical of Rothschild's plan, and knowing that it relied on Roberts's good judgement did nothing to ease his doubts. He suggested it should be shut down at once.

Worried that their masters would agree with Stamp, Rothschild and Clay went to Liddell to plead their case. Liddell had been back in Britain for just under three weeks, having spent June in the USA and Canada. Most of the trip had been work, liaising with his counterpart agencies. He had also taken a week's holiday: his four children now lived in California with Calypso, his ex-wife, and her stepbrother.

But Liddell kept his turmoil private. His job was to harness the competing egos of the Security Service to create an effective force. Much of that involved listening to complaints from his officers and then offering them guidance. After hearing Rothschild out, he agreed that the Fifth Column operation should continue, but asked Curry to look over the case history and provide a formal briefing.

It wasn't simply the ethics of the operation that bothered people in MI5. The 'spectacular' nature of Roberts's reports was also troubling. Could they really be true? Could it be this easy to find people who actively wanted to help Germany win? That didn't have to mean Roberts was fabricating or embellishing – though that was always a risk in intelligence – but what if he were being taken in, if the people reporting to him were, either maliciously or out of a desire to please or simply because they were deluded, misreading the level of support they had among friends and neighbours?

Stamp wasn't the only doubter in F3, and its officers set about checking out Roberts's reports. Their motives may not have been wholly noble: these were the people who were supposed to be the experts on underground groups, and Roberts was revealing increasing numbers of people of whom they were unaware.

But if they had hoped to humiliate Roberts and to push Rothschild back to his counter-sabotage work, they did the opposite. Time and again, the parts of Roberts's reports that could be checked were found to be accurate.

Rothschild was able to point to positive benefits from the operation. When he'd passed Edgar Bray's intelligence about the amphibious vehicle trials to the War Office, the Director of Armoured Fighting Vehicles, Major General A. W. C. Richardson, had confirmed that the information was accurate and that he was shocked it had leaked out. 'We certainly do not want it in the wrong hands,' he told Rothschild.

But that was nothing to what Hilda Leech – Perigoe's 'fat woman of 45' – had delivered. Roberts's initial impression of her wasn't promising. 'I have rarely heard such a lot of tripe talked within an hour and a half,' he reported after their first meeting. 'I do not, however, think that she is harmless, as she seems to believe in what she is saying and gives you the impression that she is willing to be made a martyr of. How she combines her expressed love for her country with her present espionage is beyond me, except that I do not think it has actually dawned on her that what she is doing is called by such an ugly name.'

On this basis, MI5 paid little attention to Leech at first, but in July 1942 that changed. She told Roberts a story she'd heard from a friend of hers who worked at the aircraft-maker Handley Page: 'experiments were going on on a new type of tail-less aeroplane which ran on low-grade fuel'. This meant nothing to her or to Roberts, but Rothschild, with his classified scientific contacts, realised she was talking about the top secret project to develop a jet engine. 'This is a good example of the need for paying attention even to a woman of this type, as there is no doubt that the enemy would be extremely interested to hear of these experiments, which are in the "most secret" category,' he wrote.

Curry's memo, when it arrived in August, certainly satisfied Liddell. He said it put 'the whole question in its proper perspective'. In Liddell's view, much of the counter-fascist work within

MI5 was 'moribund' and in need of stimulation. It was true that the immediate threat of German invasion had receded after the summer of 1940. Operation Sealion, Hitler's plan for an amphibious assault, had been abandoned after it became clear that the Luftwaffe wasn't able to achieve command of Britain's skies. Hitler's decision to invade Russia in 1941 meant that he simply didn't have the necessary forces to attack Britain at the moment. But Liddell feared this situation could suddenly change. Stalin might be beaten, or driven to surrender, and Spain might enter the war on Germany's side.

'We must I think regard the whole situation in the light of a collapse on the Russian front, ourselves driven out of the Mediterranean and 200 German divisions brought back to the West,' he wrote in his diary. 'In such an eventuality, how should we be feeling about the 60,000 enemy aliens at large in this country and other subversive bodies?'

Curry proposed that the Fifth Columnists being unearthed by Roberts should be added to the Invasion List, the set of names of people to be arrested in the event of a German attack on Britain. He also suggested that the ethical questions around the operation could be addressed by taking it to the Home Secretary for approval. On this, Liddell disagreed. He suspected he knew what the Home Office would think if they learned about the Fifth Column operation.

After the turmoil of 1940, MI5 had undergone a reorganisation in 1941. Jasper Harker was judged not to be up to the job of running the service, and had been replaced by Sir David Petrie, a veteran of the Indian Police, who had taken the title of director-general. Harker stayed on as his deputy, an arrangement that, surprisingly, seemed to work.

Petrie wanted some sort of oversight of the Fifth Column. He passed Curry's note to Duff Cooper, a Member of Parliament and former information minister who had recently been appointed by Churchill to oversee the Security Service. Cooper, a close friend of Rothschild's, was unlikely to be too critical of the operation.

Others were very far from happy. Roger Fulford, the head of F4, which looked at pacifist groups and 'new politico-social and revolutionary movements', now waded in.

A vicar's son, Fulford was a journalist and historian who had trained as a lawyer but never practised. He was another of the clever types corralled into MI5 during the great recruiting drive of 1940. One of his passions was Liberal politics: he had tried to get elected for the party in East Suffolk in 1929, and still harboured political ambitions. Another was English history. Neither of these led him to feel comfortable in an outfit that specialised in locking people up without trial, on the basis of secret evidence.

By 1942, he was miserable with MI5 all round. He felt it had neglected fascism before the war, and was now going too far in the other direction. A man who was quite happy picking fights with colleagues, he was furious about the Fifth Column operation, which he felt trespassed on his turf and offended his Liberal values. He wrote Rothschild a memo telling him as much.

'Fulford profoundly disagrees with everything' about the operation, Liddell sighed into his diary. He also objected to Curry's case summary being sent to Cooper without his agreement. He suspected Rothschild of trying to bounce the operation past him, and responded by saying he wanted to go over the details of the way Dorothy Wegener had been handled.

Rothschild wasn't used to being criticised, and he didn't enjoy it. He was inclined to fire straight back at those who were doing it.

It fell to Liddell to calm matters. He sat Fulford down, and joked that he'd half-expected to see him advancing up St James's 'on a white charger, brandishing a sword'.

Liddell couldn't quite tell whether the younger man wanted the operation closed down or simply transferred to his control. But after Fulford said he thought the evidence on which the investigation was based was 'flimsy', Liddell had had enough. He thought Fulford was 'rather complacent'. It wasn't Rothschild's evidence that was 'flimsy', he replied, but the evidence that had been gathered by the people in MI5 who were supposed to be tracking Fifth Columnists.

In Liddell's view, MI5 was 'only scratching the surface' of pro-Nazi sentiment in Britain, and simply didn't know the feelings of many of the people who lived there and might reasonably be expected to have mixed loyalties. He set out his scenario for a renewed invasion threat, accompanied by wireless broadcasts from Germany designed to unsettle people, and a fresh wave of spies being parachuted in. This, he said, combined with a few small acts of sabotage, 'would be quite sufficient to start a spy psychosis'.

In those circumstances, it would be easy to imagine the sort of people that Roberts was uncovering becoming more active. This was why it was so important to know who they were.

Fulford replied that he simply didn't like provocation, but Liddell wasn't finished. 'I replied that it was no good tackling a job like this with Liberal kid gloves,' he reported afterwards. 'We might not like anything that savoured of agents provocateurs but such methods were necessary in times of crisis. Information was obtained which could not be used for purposes of prosecutions but we should at least learn where we stood.'

Liddell said he didn't agree with everything Curry had written – in particular he didn't think they needed to get the Home Office involved. But, he told Fulford, he could forget any ideas of taking over the operation himself. 'Rothschild had handled the case very successfully . . . and it would be folly at this stage to move such a complex matter from his direction.'

The discussion, as far as Liddell was concerned, was at an end. He concluded that Fulford had been 'rather shaken' by it. He left MI5 soon afterwards.

Liddell, too, had been shaken by the Fifth Column operation, but in a different way. If one agent, simply by announcing he represented Germany and was ready to listen, had been able to find a significant number of people who were willing to risk their necks to help Hitler win, how many more such people were out there? Were Perigoe's contacts exceptional, or were they the visible signs of a much broader mass of people?

He set out his thoughts on the question of provocation in a more measured way later in the year. Addressing MI5 officers from around the country, he talked in general terms about the problem of identifying Fifth Columnists. His concern, he said, was that after three years of war, they still didn't know much about what many British people were thinking. Even those identified as potentially seditious at the start of the war had been subject to only a cursory and 'haphazard' investigation.

He repeated the argument he had made to Fulford, that in

the event of a Russian collapse and renewed German interest in Britain, they would suddenly be very concerned about all these people. 'Would not certain people at this stage perhaps come out of their holes and did we know exactly who they would be?' he wrote afterwards, in a summary of his talk.

He alluded to Roberts's work, saying that an existing investigation indicated that 'certain people whose cases had never been investigated were of a highly dangerous kind'. Without giving details, he said the case involved unusual investigation techniques, in particular the use of agents. He asked his audience to consider whether this should be more widespread.

'Ought we perhaps to change our method of investigation? We knew the man who waved a swastika flag in the street, the man who waved it in his back garden and was seen by his neighbours, but did we know one who waved it inside his own house?'

Four centuries earlier, facing external invaders and internal sedition, Elizabeth I had declared that she nevertheless didn't want to open 'windows into men's souls'. So long as her people obeyed the law, she would not enquire into their private beliefs. This was one of the principles that set democracies apart from totalitarian states. It had already been suspended in the case of those who had been locked up for their nationality or their fascist sympathies. But Liddell was making the case for a further shift: to defeat Nazism, should Britain be prepared to use the kind of secret police tactics more commonly associated with the Nazis?

12

'You bomb them, and blow the lot'

In June 1942, Perigoe mentioned an unusual possible recruit to Roberts. With the exception of the Russian-born Sophia Bray, the Fifth Column was so far a British group. Now Perigoe suggested they approach a German. She'd known the man in question, Hans Kohout, before the war, when she said he'd been a committed Nazi, but she wasn't sure about his attitude now. Roberts suggested she cautiously sound him out.

She reported back a fortnight later: Kohout 'would be willing to do anything to damage England'. If Roberts wondered how much damage someone that Perigoe had described as 'a highly paid tinfoil expert' was capable of doing, he would find out when they met.

Kohout was, it turned out, Austrian by birth. As a teenager, he had been an early member of the Nazi Party, joining it in his home town of Hofstetten-Grünau in 1924. As a young man, he'd moved first to Belgium and then in 1929 to Britain, becoming an expert in aluminium foil manufacture. Five years later, that skill had won him a job at a mill in Britain, and he'd settled in Wembley. He had escaped internment at the start of the war partly because he was no longer Austrian. Six years before Roberts met him, Hans Kohout had taken British citizenship.

After Perigoe mentioned his name to Roberts, Theresa Clay began researching him. With Rothschild occupied by protecting British targets from sabotage, not just at home but in Gibraltar and the Middle East as well, she was to take an increasing role in running the case. She was amply paid for it, apparently. Her companion Richard Meinertzhagen wrote to a friend that she was 'very high up and drawing a huge salary'. And internally, she did have some status, increasingly signing memos under her own name. But not always. Notes further afield, including to the police, were in the name of 'Lord Rothschild', without his signature.

A young Hans Kohout

Clay was an unusual woman, a member of the upper classes who even before the war was used to being taken seriously as a scientist, and was content to be the subject of gossip around her unconventional private life.

She was respected by Liddell, and they discussed the running of the Fifth Column operation in Rothschild's absence. She was not the only woman in MI5 to be doing a job traditionally reserved for men, but whatever Maxwell Knight's views about the value of women as agents, the Security Service was very far from a bastion of equality. For a start, it didn't have any women officers. There had been one, Jane Archer, but Harker had sacked her in 1940 after she denounced him as incompetent. Clay was one of more than fifty women who were designated 'assistant officers' – doing officers' jobs without officer rank.

As she looked into Kohout's background, she found that in June 1940, MI5 had received a letter warning them that he should be investigated. It was one of the thousands of such letters pouring in to MI5 from people newly suspicious of their neighbours, especially if, like Kohout, they had heavy Austrian accents. A month earlier, another neighbour had told the police they should look at him.

A local police sergeant had been sent to make 'discreet inquiries'.

His employer spoke well of him, and aside from the two who had made the reports, no one else had a bad word to say about him. He was given a clean bill of health, and no more thought was given to him for the next two years.

Whether or not Kohout was aware of these investigations, he knew that the British authorities needed little more than suspicion to lock him up, and was appropriately wary. He worried about the Germans, too. When Perigoe told him that she was in touch with a Gestapo man who was checking the loyalty of people in Britain, he was keen to explain that he had only changed his citizenship as 'a matter of expediency'.

In 1938, he explained, he had wanted to rejoin the Nazi Party – 'in order to avoid unpleasantness when that body took over control in England', according to Roberts – but had been forbidden because he was no longer a citizen of the Reich. Instead, he said, he'd been instructed to join 'the English equivalent', Mosley's British Union.

That hadn't been his only attempt to serve the Nazi cause. The same year, he had approached the German government and offered to be a spy in Britain. After an interview in Vienna, he had been turned down.

But now he had a chance to prove his worth. Aluminium foil, and the related materials Kohout's factory produced, had military applications that few people appreciated. In one of their first meetings in July 1942, Kohout told Roberts that his company had just supplied one of the Admiralty's laboratories with ten thousand yards of paper coated with magnesia dioxide. This was cut into small squares that were then compressed into tubes to make batteries.

Rothschild sent a note to his friend Alan Lang-Brown, the Admiralty's senior scientific officer, asking if that meant anything to him. The reply was immediate: 'There has been a serious leakage,' Lang-Brown wrote back. 'This report would be of very great value to the enemy.'

The one comfort, he noted, was that Kohout had misunderstood the paper's purpose. He had told Roberts the batteries were for submarines. In fact they were Zamboni Piles, a high-voltage, low-current cell designed to power a top secret project: a night vision system.

The units that Kohout's batteries would power were known as 'Tabby' receivers – because tabby cats can see in the dark. Weighing around three pounds, and designed to look like a British Army water bottle in the hope they might escape German notice, they were most useful when used with an infra-red torch, either for illumination or for signalling.

Theresa Clay, continuing to act as Rothschild's deputy, visited the Admiralty to reassure the anxious Lang-Brown that the information hadn't been sent to Germany, and then set about investigating their new recruit's finances.

Kohout, she learned, was an entrepreneur in his spare time, always on the lookout for ways to make a bit of extra cash. He was investing his earnings in houses that he rented out. According to Perigoe, he had also been involved in an enterprise to sell black market meat. Kohout approached espionage in a similarly industrious spirit.

At the start of August, Group Captain Joe Archer, the husband of the sacked Jane Archer, and the man responsible for liaison between the RAF and MI5, briefed Guy Liddell on the Air Force's latest weapon, the De Havilland Mosquito fighter-bomber. Made entirely of wood, it was far faster than any other bomber the RAF had – 'probably the fastest thing in the air,' Liddell recorded afterwards – and could fly higher. It was a machine that would enable more accurate and effective bombing of Germany, and give a decisive advantage to the RAF over the Luftwaffe. Four weeks after Liddell was briefed, Roberts received the same information in the Park West apartment – from Kohout.

Nancy Brown, thrilled at her new secret life, had just left Perigoe and Roberts in the flat. Minutes later, Kohout came up to fill them both in on his latest intelligence-gathering activities.

Roberts handed round cigarettes, and then he began. 'How did you get on?'

'Quite good,' replied Kohout. He had met a man from Smiths, the engineering firm. 'They make instruments for the instrument board, clocks and that kind of thing, for aeroplanes.'

After a couple of drinks, the Smiths employee had a loose tongue. 'I heard about a dive-bomber, it is still on the secret list, named a Mosquito.'

Roberts began to take notes, and Kohout went through his

information. 'Two engines, 15 to 16 hundred horsepower. It can be used for four different purposes, first of all dive-bombing, fighter-bomber and bomber and another one.'

'Reconnaissance?' Roberts suggested.

'No, not reconnaissance. Something with fighting or bombing.'

'Fighter? Purely and simply?'

'Yes.'

'What was its fighting speed, do you know?'

Kohout didn't know that. But he did know that you only heard it nine seconds after it had passed. And he knew other things.

'What would you call them things that would go under the wings?' he asked, in his heavily accented English.

'They're elevators, aren't they?' Perigoe offered. 'They're the things that press up and down.'

'If you open them,' Kohout tried to explain, 'the aeroplanes can roll continuously, like that. Now the aeroplane is very small, amazingly small. A hundred have been built for experimental purposes.'

He apologised for not being able to tell them about its armaments, but offered other information instead: the location of an aircraft factory. He had more, too. 'Have you heard about a rocket plane?' he asked. 'It goes about 600 miles per hour.'

'Six hundred miles per hour?' Roberts repeated.

'But she is useless, she is useless for anything, because they can't steer her.'

Roberts was incredulous. Kohout was pleased with the response. 'I know things, yes? I find out things, yes?'

'You do, yes,' Roberts assured him. 'Who's making this aeroplane then, or experimenting with it?'

'I only know Smiths of Cricklewood is making the instruments.'

Perigoe tried to get some more detail: 'Do you know anything about that plane at all?'

'All I know is that it goes up to 600 miles per hour and it's useless for war, fighting and bombing, because they can't steer the blooming thing.'

'Do you know what makes it go?'

'Some kind of explosions. The idea comes from Germany,' he said. 'It goes in a tube.'

Roberts and Perigoe made appreciative noises, and Kohout revealed one of the problems with his method of espionage. 'I would tell you more, but I was half tight, you see.'

Perigoe disapproved: 'You shouldn't get tight.'

'I can't help it, I can't take all these whiskies half the night long!'

Roberts, who liked a drink himself, was more understanding: 'No, no, no,' he reassured Kohout as he tried to recall more about the aircraft design.

'In the middle of the plane, somewhere near the cockpit, there is a tube,' he explained. 'A big opening where the wind flows through.'

Roberts decided it would be best to give the impression of having many sources of information, of whom Kohout was just one, if a valued one. 'That's quite enough to go on,' he said. 'This 600 miles per hour, that's damned good. The speed of that plane was of great interest to us, it was a complete mystery. Now we know.'

Much of Kohout's information was wrong: the Gloster E.28/39, the prototype British jet that had flown a year earlier, could be steered, and it didn't go close to 600 miles per hour – he or his source may have misunderstood a kilometres per hour speed. But enough of what he said was correct. It would have been plenty for a real spy ring to go on.

If that had been all that Kohout had brought with him, it would have been an impressive haul. But he had more. He had a potential recruit, Mr Crump, a mechanic who, though married, was in love with an Austrian woman who had been interned. He might, Kohout said, be prepared to work for them if he was promised German citizenship. 'He's definitely a Nazi,' Kohout assured Roberts.

'He's Aryan, is he?' Roberts replied, as if considering the citizenship question.

'Yes.'

'You're sure of that?' Roberts checked, before giving his answer. 'If he's prepared to help us, of course we should be prepared to help him.'

He suggested a way in which Crump, a man who travelled, might be able to assist. 'We should very much like to learn something about the defences in Sussex, if he can help us in that way.'

Kohout had news on that front, as well, if not actually in Sussex. He produced a map of Hertfordshire, on which he'd marked both defences and targets. He explained the key: 'Number one – what do you call it – *strassesperren?*'

'Street? Blocks?' Roberts searched for a translation.

'Street blocks. Number two is pill boxes. Number three, minefields.' Roberts repeated each one after him. 'Number four, searchlights, number five anti-aircraft guns. Number six, camouflaged factories. Number seven, explosive factories . . .'

'Gosh, you've been busy.' Roberts could barely keep up. 'Explosive factories!'

'Number eight is the places where the Army and Air Force is stationed. Number nine, aircraft factories, and nought – just a plain nought – is tank traps. And a cross if wireless stations.'

Perigoe and Roberts tried to process it all, but Kohout had more. 'And a triangle . . .'

'A triangle?'

'Airfield.'

Perigoe examined the map. 'Oh, you've only got one of those. Oh no – two – no, one.'

'Only one,' Kohout said. 'I haven't been everywhere.' He was defensive. 'It's hard work, you know.'

He had a final mark: 'Gas cylinders. You bomb them, and blow the lot up!'

He complained that the scale of the map was too small for precise marking of locations. Roberts promised to get him a large scale one, but said he was worried about Kohout's safety. 'If anyone finds it on you, it's too dangerous.'

Kohout had already worked out a plan: he would lay a piece of paper on top of the map and mark that. He would hide the paper in his tie, and if anyone found it, 'it gives nothing away – he doesn't know what's what'.

Kohout had finally run out of things to tell Roberts. He looked at his handler. 'What do you think?'

Roberts had to balance the expectations of his recruits with his instructions from MI5 to discourage spying. 'Actually,' he said, 'the department does not do much in the way of espionage proper, do you see? That's the job for the Abwehr, but our job is to . . . we're the forerunners, you see. We have to find out our friends and our enemies.'

Kohout was clearly frustrated that his heroic efforts for the Fatherland weren't being met with more enthusiasm. Roberts tried to mollify him. 'All this is passed on,' he assured him. 'I shall pass it on tonight myself.'

'I get the credit?'

'You'll get the credit for this, it's very good work. I'm very pleased with you, and I'll get you a bigger map. You've got plenty of brains. The idea of pinning it in your tie is perhaps the best bit of work I've seen for a long while. My chief will be very amused at that.'

Had Roberts's chief really existed – or at least, had he existed and worked for German, rather than British intelligence – he would have been more than amused. An untrained agent, who had only been working for them for two months, had provided intelligence on three different technologies, two of which related to aircraft, an area of particular interest for the Germans, as MI5 knew from the requests that were sent to the double agents it controlled. Hans Kohout was the best spy that Germany had in Britain in August 1942. The only problem was that his reports went no further than MI5 headquarters in St James's.

Marita Perigoe was less than delighted to find that she had introduced someone to the group whose ability to deliver intelligence might exceed her own. She set about trying to diminish her rival in Roberts's eyes. The Friday after Kohout's star turn, Roberts, Gleave and Perigoe assembled at 499 Park West. Gleave was wet from the rain, and flushed with exertion.

Roberts offered to go out to buy sandwiches, and asked the women to see to the blackout curtains in his absence. It was eight in the evening, at the start of September, and despite the country operating on 'Double Summertime' – putting the clocks forward onto European time so as to save energy at the end of the day – the nights were starting to draw in.

In his absence, Perigoe decided to have a proper hunt for microphones. She explained to Gleave that it was possible to detect whether something had an electric current by touching it, which she demonstrated using an ironing board. Just as the pair of them were trying to lift the carpet, Roberts returned.

He took in the scene, guessed what they had been doing, and also that they had been unsuccessful. These moments required nerve from him. What if one day they did work out where the listening device was? After all, it was right in front of them.

While Perigoe hunted on the floor, she was ignoring a clearly visible wire that came into the flat next to the front door, ran around the wall, across the floor, up onto the table, and then connected to a microphone. All Perigoe saw was a telephone, and she never gave it a second thought. But telephones were the electronic devices that the GPO understood best of all. Which explained why, when Roberts had a phone line installed in the hall of his home in Epsom, he forbade his children from talking about him near it.

But even if Perigoe didn't suspect the phone, Roberts knew that she suspected him. The best way for him to win her trust was to show he trusted her. Nothing would have been more suspicious than refusing to leave her alone in the flat. He decided to stick to his strategy of making a joke of it.

'How far did you get?' he asked.

'We decided to give it up,' Gleave answered, laughing.

As they ate, Gleave showed him how she'd spent her afternoon. She'd been cycling round Watford, attempting to verify the details identified by Kohout on his map the previous week. He'd told Roberts that one location was a military base, but Gleave was doubtful.

'Going along here, and there's the entrance, and there's a civilian at the entrance, not a soldier,' she said, pointing.

'And no soldiers dotted round the place at all?' Perigoe asked, leading her witness.

'I didn't see any soldiers at all.'

'But there must be some there,' Perigoe said.

'Kohout said there'd be about forty there,' Roberts added, taking Perigoe's point.

'Well, there weren't,' Gleave replied. She gave more details of what she'd seen. It didn't, Roberts observed, fit with Kohout's account at all. 'I'll wring Kohout's neck for him, if he's not more accurate than that.'

This was the effect Perigoe was aiming for, and Gleave had more. She disputed that Kohout could have seen some of the things he claimed. 'There's heaps of places where you can't see at all, there's only three or four spots where you can get a good view of it,' she said of one of the Austrian's supposed observations. 'I went round and round, you know.'

'Well, it looks to me as if Kohout's led us up the garden over that place,' Roberts mused. 'I wonder why.'

'It might not be deliberate,' said Gleave.

'Well, of course you have to bear in mind that the chap has great difficulty in making himself understood,' Roberts said. He congratulated Gleave on her work. 'Well, thank you very much indeed, it's excellent.'

'Beautiful,' said Perigoe, with feeling. 'It's lovely.'

'And do you feel better for that ride?' Roberts asked.

'No.' Gleave's main feeling was exhaustion. Perigoe, sympathising, said she must have covered twenty miles. Gleave put the figure above thirty.

Roberts, on behalf of the German government, offered her some comfort. 'When you hear of that place being wiped out later on,' he said, 'you'll be able to pat yourself on the back and say, "Well, I had a hand in that."'

The pleasing thought of having helped direct the Luftwaffe's bombs led the group into a discussion of how their fellow spy might have gone wrong.

'I don't think it will be wise to let Kohout know that you've checked up on him,' Roberts cautioned.

'Oh no, of course,' said Gleave. 'He's very funny.'

'You're telling me,' offered Perigoe. She wished she could be there when Roberts confronted him. 'Shall I bring my microphone along and put it in the bathroom and listen?' she joked.

Kohout had told Roberts that an airfield he'd looked at could be captured by one hundred men. After handing round some plums, Roberts put that suggestion to Gleave. She thought the idea unlikely. 'One hundred men would lose their lives,' Roberts mused.

'A very un-German attitude, I must say,' Perigoe observed. 'I mean, the German method is to be prepared and to see that you jolly well don't miss it.'

Roberts replied that Kohout was a 'silly ass'. The conversation turned briefly to films and Perigoe gave a scathing series of reviews of recent anti-Nazi propaganda films she'd sat through – 'Marita is worth two of James Agate,' the person transcribing the conversation observed, comparing her to a leading critic of the day. The party broke up shortly afterwards, with Perigoe confident that her work was done: Kohout was going to have a strip torn off him at his next meeting.

But when Kohout arrived at 499 Park West two weeks later, Roberts was all concern. He poured him a drink, and offered him some dinner. 'Are you finding life pretty lonely nowadays?' he asked the Austrian.

'Sometimes,' Kohout replied.

'You are very happily married, are you?' Roberts asked.

'Oh yes, very,' Kohout assured him. 'Why do you ask?'

'Well, we always take a kindly interest in the domestic affairs of our agents,' Roberts, an agent-runner in the image of Maxwell Knight, replied.

As Roberts knew, Kohout hadn't seen his wife and son in three years. They had been separated by an accident of war. In 1934, he had fallen in love with Auguste Frenzel, a 16-year-old Austrian who was visiting Britain. The following year they had married. A son, Ernest, followed in 1937. With her husband busy at work, Auguste opted to spend the summer months at home with her parents in Austria. At the start of July 1939 she and Ernest had travelled there as usual. Kohout had joined them for a fortnight and then travelled back to England to work. If either of them had worried about the possibility of war breaking out, they didn't act on these fears, and in September Auguste found herself trapped in Austria, and unable to travel back to her adopted home. Her only means of communication with her husband was through letters passed by the Red Cross.

Since then, Kohout told Roberts, he had written to his wife and son 'dozens of times,' and had tried to send photographs, but these were always returned by the postal censors.

Turning back to business, Kohout said he'd brought some more information. He had discovered his error over the Zamboni Piles: they weren't batteries for submarines. 'You remember when I spoke to you about that black paper?' he asked. 'For the Admiralty?'

'Yes.'

'The Admiralty intends to extend the use of that particular material also for the signals,' Kohout said, in his stumbling English. 'That means the little flash lamps, you know, they start moving about?'

The piles were electrical accumulators, 'that run a long, long, time – some say it's indefinite, but I don't believe that,' Kohout said.

In fact his sources on this, as on so much else, were quite correct. The top secret 'Tabby' receiver used so little power that its batteries were indeed intended to last the lifetime of the unit.

Kohout offered to get some samples of the paper. If it was urgent, he could pass them to Perigoe? Roberts thought that would be a bad idea. 'You needn't bother Mrs Perigoe,' he said. From now on, he was going to need to keep them apart, especially if Kohout was bringing in more triumphs.

One of the tricks Roberts had learned in his years undercover was to be a mirror. With Kohout, he was another chap, a concerned husband and father, trying to do his best in a difficult situation. With Perigoe and Gleave he was playful and snide, as much one of the girls as a married father of three in his thirties could be.

Perigoe disliked Kohout, was jealous of his successes, so in his meetings with her Roberts reflected that back at her and encouraged it. He pondered aloud whether it was suspicious that Kohout could remember insignificant details, but not important ones. 'I thought he looked a singularly evil little man on that Saturday night when that lightning was flashing across his face, didn't you?' he commented. 'Something spidery about him. Little eyes sort of flickering back from you to me, me to you.'

'He has nothing to him at all, except a kind of nasty cunning,' Perigoe replied. 'I don't like people with just cunning. It's a Jewish trait.'

'Yes,' Roberts said. 'You must make it your special duty to keep your eye on him, and keep it on him well.'

'Crumbs. I can imagine a pleasanter object to keep one's eye on.'

'If you allow people like that enough rope,' Roberts explained, 'they inevitably come to the point where they put the rope around their own neck.'

'Vermin,' Perigoe said. 'He ought to be exterminated. Such people shouldn't live.'

'We'll exterminate him in due course,' Roberts promised her. 'I shall take great personal pleasure in seeing him put out of action.'

If Perigoe was hostile to Kohout, Roberts decided, it wouldn't hurt to encourage some reciprocal hostility, the better to play them off against one another. He was pushing at an open door: Kohout had disliked Perigoe since he first met her in their British Union days. He'd found the local group 'a washout', led by a man who 'had no personality – he could not speak or dress.' Perigoe and Gleave, meanwhile, had stoked the internal rivalries in the branch, leading Kohout to leave it.

So when the men met at the start of October, Roberts poured Kohout a drink, lit him a cigarette and took him into his confidence.

'Mrs Perigoe has been rather curious about you lately, wants to know how you are getting on,' he told Kohout, conspiratorially. 'I said that you had been very unsatisfactory.'

Then he had a further thought for Kohout. 'She's never been friendly with any police officials, I suppose?'

'I don't know.' Kohout was silent for a moment. 'I remember one incident,' he began, recalling how Marita had threated to 'get the police on' someone she was arguing with.

'Well,' Roberts said, moving the conversation on. 'She is very useful to us because of the knowledge she's got of the BU movement.' He had sown his seed of doubt in Kohout's mind about Perigoe's loyalty to their cause. He gave the man another cigarette, and the conversation moved on.

Kohout's discovery of secrets around the Tabby receiver had been worrying to the Admiralty, but his next scoop related to one of the greatest secrets of the war in the air, a development that it was hoped would save the lives of air crews flying the highly dangerous bombing missions over Germany.

The development of radar before the start of the war had been vital in winning the Battle of Britain, enabling the RAF to locate and intercept German bombers efficiently. But by 1943, the same technology was being used by the Luftwaffe to attack Bomber Command's planes. As raids over Germany increased, so did the numbers of Air Force casualties – close to 10,000 in 1942.

Air crews would be much safer if the Germans could be deceived about the location of incoming attacks, so that fighters were mis-deployed and the wrong gun crews alerted. And British scientists had known for years about a way that, in theory, radar could be deceived. The problem was that they couldn't agree on whether to use it.

This row had been raging since the start of the war. If they deployed it, would the Germans use it against them in return? The argument wasn't simply about judging the wisest course. On opposing sides were two members of the military scientific community who had been arguing with each other for years. Sir Robert Watson-Watt had been behind the development of Britain's radar. He was nearly fifty, a small, chubby Scot, whose verbosity was among a number of qualities that made him tricky to deal with. He was very protective of his brainchild, to the point of resenting any proposal that might threaten the reputation of radar.

Arguing against him was the 31-year-old Reginald Jones, who as a boy in south London had become fascinated by the emerging technology of the era, wireless. He had won a scholarship to Oxford to study physics, and began to research infrared radiation. The son of a Grenadier Guards sergeant, Jones was a patriot who in the 1930s abandoned his promising academic career to join the Air Ministry staff, applying his research to the question of whether infrared detectors could be used to locate aircraft. There he had been on the losing end of an argument with the more senior Watson-Watt, which had resulted in him being moved from his post. At the start of the war he was appointed MI6's tame scientist, with access to top secret intelligence material that he used to understand the military technology Germany was developing.

While Watson-Watt's contribution to the defence of Britain was well known, Jones's was still highly classified. In early 1940, he had concluded that the Germans were using radio to guide bombers to their targets at night, and set about defeating them. An inveterate practical joker, he decided that better than simply jamming the German signals would be spoofing them.

Over the coming months, the 'Battle of the Beams' saw German scientists improving their systems only for Jones to develop his own countermeasures. In the end, he won out, disrupting the German signals sufficiently for the Luftwaffe to conclude that radio navigation was inaccurate, but he wasn't always fast enough: at the start of November 1940, Coventry was heavily and accurately bombed while he was still trying to understand the new German system.

The battle had won Jones the ear of Churchill, who referred to him as 'the man who broke the bloody beam'. The young scientist, already unburdened by any false modesty, was impatient with those he saw as letting their own pride or intellectual weakness get in the way of decision-making.

Jones had seen the way that radar could be fooled almost as soon as Watson-Watt's system was explained to him in 1937. One of the scientists involved boasted that their radio waves could detect a wire hanging from a balloon at forty miles. 'All one might therefore need to do to render the system useless would be to attach wires to balloons or parachutes at intervals of half a mile or a mile, and the whole radar screen would be so full of echoes that it would be impossible to see the extra echo arising from an aircraft,' he wrote later.

By 1942, research had shown that a few hundred strips of foil just under a foot long and an inch wide would give the same reflection to the German radar as a Lancaster bomber. These were light enough that they wouldn't need a balloon to hold them up: thrown from a plane, they would simply float to the ground slowly. The system was given a codename: Window. But the row about whether to use it went on for all of that year.

Kohout knew none of this, but he got one of the first signs that Jones was winning his argument when, in March 1943, his company was approached by the Air Ministry. Could they make foil strips to precise specifications? Naturally they turned to their aluminium foil expert, Hans Kohout, the man who was secretly trying to bring about Britain's defeat.

He wasn't told what the strips were for, but he could tell that they were important to the Air Ministry. His first proposal to Roberts, in a meeting at his home, was that he could sabotage the work, holding it up for weeks. He would be able to get away with it without it being traced back to him, he assured his handler. The proposal was exactly the kind of thing that those within MI5 who opposed the Fifth Column operation had warned of: that far from being controlled, potential saboteurs would end up being emboldened.

Roberts didn't know what the foil was for either, but if it was important to the war effort, then he wanted Kohout to use his skill to make sure it was done as well and as quickly as possible. He was firm with him on the idea of creating a delay. 'I told Kohout that he was not to consider any such thing and that when we wanted him to commit sabotage, we would ask him.'

Kohout said that in that case, he would at least give Germany access to the same weapon. He wrote out for Roberts the Air Ministry's specifications, adding for good measure a list of German companies that he believed would be up to the job of making the strips.

Roberts passed the information back to Rothschild, but Window was so secret that Rothschild couldn't work out what Kohout was talking about. An investigation revealed no evidence of any Air Ministry contracts with Kohout's company. What on earth could the strips of aluminium foil be for?

At the start of April 1943, the committee to discuss the use of Window met again, with the chief of the air staff, Sir Charles Portal, in the chair. Jones had calculated that 12 tonnes of foil would be needed to deceive German radar. Other Air Ministry scientists offered estimates of 48 tonnes or 84 tonnes. Watson-Watt declared that all of these were too low, and that around 240 tonnes would be necessary. In his desire to protect the reputation of radar, Watson-Watt had overreached himself, and Portal realised this. He announced he'd ask Churchill to approve Window's deployment as soon as possible.

Days after that meeting, MI5 got a further clue as to what was going on. 'There's a thing going out, a thing like a search light,' Kohout explained to Roberts. 'That works if the beam touches metal.' Roberts had no idea what he was talking about. Despite thirteen years living in Britain, Kohout still struggled to make himself understood.

What he did know about, though, was aluminium foil. He

explained that the aircrews were supposed to throw bundles of these bits of metallic paper out of the plane as they flew and let them float to the ground. But if the metal strips were cut in the wrong way, they would stick together and fall to the ground in a single bundle.

'Here, take this book!' he told Roberts, full of enthusiasm at his demonstration. He showed how, because of the way the paper was cut, the pages stayed together and the book stayed closed as it dropped to the ground. This wasn't what the Air Ministry wanted. Their specification was for strips of foil that would scatter when released into the air, not fall in lumps. 'It has to be this idea you see of cutting it against the grain. Just let it go and the whole thing separates. And if you take it in the other way, the whole parcel may separate into big wads.'

Even with these clues – the paper had to be thrown from an aircraft, it had to separate and flutter downwards, and, while doing this, it had some effect on search beams – it was more than a month before Rothschild found out what Kohout had got his hands on. Finally, at the start of May, a contact who was working on radar explained it to him.

Rothschild, keen to show the value of the Fifth Column operation, didn't hesitate to talk the discovery up.

'Kohout has hit upon something which is considered to be of the most secret and hush-hush devices so far developed in the UK,' he recorded in a note stamped 'MOST SECRET'. His contact considered it 'far more secret than H2S' – the ground-directed radar system that Bomber Command had recently started using. Unlike most radar systems, 'this one could be copied by the enemy almost overnight. Something like H2S might take over a year to introduce into aircraft. It is obvious that the slightest leakage of it to the Germans would put them in a very strong position.'

What no one in Britain knew was the Germans had in fact developed their own version of Window in 1942, and had opted not to use it for exactly the same reasons as the Allies – fear that it would be immediately copied and turned back against them. Hermann Goering, the head of the Luftwaffe, had been so horrified by its effect on German radar during trials that he had ordered the destruction of the reports, in case the Allies learned of the technology.

Kohout meanwhile may not have understood the precise purpose of the pieces of foil that he'd handed to Roberts, but judging from the behaviour of the Air Ministry staff he'd dealt with at the factory, he knew that the secret he'd hit on was a big one. It was also one in which he had a personal stake. The planes that were carrying Window were dropping bombs not just on Germany but on Austria, too, where his wife and son lived. By passing his information to Roberts, he hoped to tilt the balance a little in favour of their defenders.

The information stopped, of course, with Rothschild and his colleagues at MI5. At the end of June, Churchill chaired the final meeting on whether to use the new technology. Told that the benefit to Britain's bombers outweighed the potential benefit to Germany's, the prime minister was enthusiastic. 'Let us open the Window!' he declared.

The secret weapon was finally used on 24 July 1943, in a raid on Hamburg. Out of 791 aircraft sent in the attack, only twelve didn't come back, a quarter of the usual losses on that run. The following evening, during a raid on Essen, Jones listened as German fighter controllers tried to direct pilots to intercept bombers that weren't there, fooled by a trick that owed a small part of its success to the manufacturing expertise of a man who believed himself to be a Nazi agent.

In April 1943, Roberts and Kohout had a heart-to-heart. After a year of working for the Gestapo, Kohout was a star and he knew it. 'He surmised that some agents might pass their lives without getting the "scoops" that he had been fortunate enough to get,' Roberts reported afterwards. The Austrian recalled with delight how an Air Ministry official visiting the factory had urgently warned paper manufacturers of the dangers of any information leaking out. He'd had no idea as he talked about spies, Kohout mused, 'that one was within ten feet of him'.

As he looked at the man who was both his agent and his enemy, whom he was betraying even as he congratulated him, Roberts found himself in an interesting position. 'I felt a certain sympathy,' he wrote. 'I knew that if positions had been reversed, and I had been in Germany, I would have been every bit as thrilled.'

It wasn't such a fanciful transposition. Roberts and Kohout had a lot in common. They were a similar age, both with young families. Both came from inauspicious backgrounds, and had achieved success in their fields through skill and hard work. Both had been attracted to fascism as young men, and both wanted to serve their countries. More than that, while many men dreamed of being secret agents, Roberts and Kohout had crossed the threshold from dreams to action, and found that they enjoyed the thrill.

If Roberts was struck by his fellow feeling for Kohout, the other man's thoughts about their relationship were ones of pure relief. 'Kohout said that he sometimes shuddered to think of what might have happened if he had not contacted me,' Roberts said. 'I asked him what he meant, and he replied that he could not have kept quiet with information in his possession of the type given during the last month or so.'

Kohout said that he would probably have made a 'last effort' to get the information to Germany through a neutral embassy – Spain was of course the obvious one. 'He knew that he would in all probability have been caught in the attempt but he said that he was certain that he would have made the effort.'

As it happened, he wasn't the only man trying to get the Window secret out of the country. A secretary at the Air Ministry, Olive Sheehan, had given the details to Douglas Springhall, the national organiser of Britain's Communist Party, who had attempted to pass it to the Russians. Sheehan's flatmate had realised what was happening and reported her, and Springhall was sentenced to seven years in prison.

Springhall could at least argue that he had only been trying to help an ally. Kohout believed he was passing intelligence to Britain's enemy. He had been recorded discussing how to help Germany, and MI5 had evidence of him repeatedly acting to do so. Roberts might have felt he had a lot in common with Kohout, but he also knew that he was putting a noose around his neck.

13

'A twinge of uneasiness'

If Roberts had reached a point of total trust with Kohout, he was nowhere near that stage with Perigoe, as he learned in November 1942. In the wider war, the British had finally had some good news. British forces in the Western Desert had won the second battle of El Alamein, and Axis forces were in retreat. Meanwhile a second Allied army had landed in North Africa, and was advancing eastward.

In London, Perigoe was eating a meal with the man she knew as 'Jack King' when she suddenly asked a question: was his name really Roberts?

There was no clue as to what was behind the question, but it was easy to guess. For the vast bulk of his career as an agent, Roberts had been working under his own name. He had used it to penetrate the Leeds British Union cell two years earlier. Reg Windsor and Michael Gannon had known it when they were arrested and interned, though Windsor at least at first didn't believe Roberts had been the man who had turned them in. But the pair had now spent close to two years on the Isle of Man, comparing notes with other fascists, many of whom had known Roberts before the war.

There was, for instance, Bernard Porter, the district leader for Epsom, where Roberts lived. Porter had been interned, and must surely have found it odd that Roberts, who outranked him in the organisation, hadn't. It was hardly as if Roberts was a peripheral figure: he had been an enthusiastic fascist, joining every group he could. If the internees were trying to work out who had put them behind barbed wire, Eric Roberts was bound to be near the top of the list of suspects.

And once they had reached that conclusion, it wouldn't have been difficult to get word back to London. Roberts had first met Perigoe, after all, because she knew how to smuggle messages to and from the Isle of Man. Perhaps his past was beginning to catch up with him.

Or there was another possibility, even closer to home. Roberts had never discussed his work in front of his children, he thought. But Max was a sharp lad, and had begun to suspect that his father had a secret. Finally, goaded by other boys, he yelled that his dad wasn't, as he'd previously claimed, a conscientious objector. He was a spy. Eric and Audrey had been horrified when they heard this, and Max was sent back to the boys to say that he had lied. Probably his friends hadn't believed him in the first place – it was exactly the kind of lie a child would make up. But what if they had nevertheless repeated it to their parents? Not every fascist in Epsom had been locked up.

Roberts thought fast. He knew that Perigoe saw herself as a German agent, deep behind enemy lines. She didn't speak with the melodrama of some of the other recruits, but she was all the more dangerous for her cooler take on the world. It was only a few months since she'd joked about stabbing him with a penknife. He was certain that she was capable of violence, even murder, if she believed she had been betrayed. And if she did believe that, killing him might be her best chance. Like Kohout, she had said and done quite enough to earn a death sentence, but her capture and trial might depend on Roberts being alive to identify her. For all her talk of microphones, she couldn't know that her voice was in Rothschild's archives.

All this he weighed in a moment as Perigoe watched him for a flinch, a twitch, a sign that he knew he'd been found out. And then, without looking up from his food, Roberts gave his reply: 'Yes.'

Perigoe was wrong-footed. She had almost certainly expected a denial, and was poised to judge its plausibility. Roberts's response wasn't the one expected from a guilty man. Its insouciance left open a range of possibilities. Was this another of Jack's jokes, like his remarks about microphones in the Park West flat? Or was Roberts actually his name? And if it was, what did that mean? It was a fairly common name, after all. Could there be two men named Roberts inside British fascism, one working for the Gestapo and the other working for MI5? Her moment of challenge passed, and she was uncertain what she had achieved.

*

Thinking about the episode later, Roberts took the view that
Perigoe didn't really believe he was an MI5 man. Even if word
had come back from the Isle of Man that Eric Roberts was not to
be trusted, it was unlikely to have come with a photograph. What
would a description say? Tall man in his late thirties, starting to
lose his hair? That was a fairly wide field. There was the scar on
his face, of course. Those were rather less common, even in this
time of war. But if Perigoe genuinely thought he was this Roberts
person, would she have come to meet him?

The more troubling possibility was that the information about
his name had come not from the Isle of Man but from within MI5.
Roberts had long had his doubts about whether the organisation
was as secure as it ought to be.

Not long after he began working for Rothschild, he had been
walking past Charing Cross station, next to Trafalgar Square,
when he ran into an MI5 colleague, Dick Brooman-White,
who dealt with Spanish espionage. He was five years younger
than Roberts, and had joined MI5 after Eton, Cambridge and
a career in journalism. Despite those disadvantages, he had
an abundance of charm which had won Roberts over easily.
He had delighted in teasing Roberts and Dickson in the early
days of the war, and his default tone was that of exaggerated
conspiracy.

Brooman-White greeted Roberts and begged him to keep silent
about their encounter: he had skipped out of the office to meet a
'personal friend' who had not shown up. As they were both there,
would Roberts like to go for a coffee?

Roberts would have preferred a beer, but he agreed to go to
the Lyons Corner House across the road from the station. A
vast multi-storey restaurant, staffed by waitresses too busy to pry
into anyone's business, it was a suitably anonymous location for
two intelligence men to talk shop without being overheard. On
typical form, Brooman-White asked Roberts if he had brought the
Watchers – MI5's network of surveillance experts – along with
him. As they sipped their drinks, Brooman-White asked a tricky
question.

'Robbie, you have the art of never wearing your heart on your
sleeve,' he started. 'Your pal Jimmy regards me as through the

eyes of a civil servant, slightly eccentric or mildly crazy. What is your opinion?'

Roberts was usually too careful to give a frank answer to a question like that, but this time he was flattered. If Dickson had given him the civil servant's view, he would give him the secret agent's.

'I said that in my own private mind I often attached tags to the people with whom I was dealing and in his case, it was "Agent Plus",' Roberts recorded later. 'I thought him wasted as an officer, he should have been an agent.'

To Roberts, the field man who hated the office, there was no higher praise to offer, but as soon as he had said it, he worried he'd given offence. Instead, Brooman-White laughed. But what he said next was troubling. He alluded to a line from a report that Roberts had sent to Rothschild a couple of days earlier. How did he know that? Those reports were copied to Maxwell Knight, under an agreement he'd reached with Rothschild, and Roberts guessed that either Knight himself or someone on his staff must have mentioned it to Brooman-White.

Despite the light mood of their conversation, Roberts felt 'a twinge of uneasiness'. How many people were reading these reports, he wondered. 'Being in the limelight could be disastrous. I avoided it as far as possible.'

Brooman-White changed the subject a little, asking about Rothschild, and whether he ever discussed his friends. Wondering what lay behind the question, Roberts replied that they didn't have those kinds of conversations. His unease continued. He knew Brooman-White to be very right-wing. Could he also be a little anti-Semitic?

But there was something about Brooman-White that invited confidences. Perhaps it was this quality – the same one that Roberts himself had in abundance – that had earned him the label 'Agent Plus'. He had another question: did Roberts think it was possible that the Office had been penetrated?

If the question was a surprise, the fact that Roberts answered it was even more of one, even to himself. Yes, he said, he believed it was. And as he unburdened himself of the thought that had been troubling him for months, he went further. He identified two men he suspected might be working for the Abwehr. One was in Knight's department, and the other was a man with access to some of MI5's greatest secrets. But as soon as the words were out of Roberts's mouth, he knew he'd made a mistake in speaking. Brooman-White didn't believe the Office could have a traitor inside it – certainly not the second chap Roberts had named, who'd been to a good school and university. He had been pulling Roberts's leg, and had got a better result than he could have hoped for.

'Robbie,' Brooman-White laughed. 'You will be suspecting Vic Rothschild next!'

Roberts had made a fool of himself. Humiliated, he resolved to keep his thoughts to himself from then on. But he also did something else: he went to Rothschild and Clay and asked them to take Knight off the circulation list for his reports. He might feel stupid making his accusations, but he would feel even more foolish if the Fifth Column found out who he was. The fewer people who knew what he was up to, the fewer people could spill the secret.

It would be a quarter of a century before the truth emerged.

Turning back to Perigoe's accusation, though Roberts was confident he had seen off her suspicions at least for the moment, he took her question about his name seriously, and reported it back to Clay. She, in turn, thought it was sufficiently important to refer up the tree to Liddell. He asked her to prepare a short briefing note on the case as it stood.

Liddell was one of the few supporters of the operation at the higher levels of the Security Service. Petrie, the director-general, had asked Harker, his deputy, to look into it again. Harker sat down with Liddell, his deputy Dick White, and Jack Curry. Liddell and Curry argued that the case showed the need for further investigation into Germans and their sympathisers living in Britain. After all, a single agent, simply by identifying himself as a Gestapo agent, had managed to unearth dozens of people who were apparently willing to help Germany. How many more might be out there?

Petrie, Harker told them, did not think it was 'necessary or desirable' to find out. He also opposed using Roberts's intelligence to widen the Invasion List. 'He thought that the Fifth Column aspect was rather out of date,' Liddell recorded in his diary. 'Both Curry and I were in disagreement with this view.' It was a stalemate. 'Obviously nothing is going to be done,' wrote a frustrated Liddell.

Perigoe soon had a number of problems to distract her from the question of Jack King's true identity. Her husband was proving a difficulty, too. Internment, with little end in sight, had apparently left Bernard bitter towards all sides in the war. Now that he knew of Marita's connection to the Gestapo, he saw an opportunity.

He proposed blackmailing the organisation. His wife was already being paid, but Bernard was the one who had to suffer imprisonment. Why shouldn't he get some compensation, too? And if the Gestapo wasn't willing to come up with the goods, well, the British authorities would be grateful to learn of a German operation under their noses. And perhaps he would be released as a result.

As blackmail ideas go, it was an unconvincing one: Bernard would have been threatening to expose his own wife as a spy, and potentially send her to the gallows. But if the possibility of exposure worried Marita for one reason, it worried Roberts for another. When she told him her husband's thinking, he realised he had to be stopped before things went any further. If Bernard reported the Fifth Column to the police, then MI5 would have to decide whether to order the arrest of its members. If they arrested them, the operation would be over, his role would be revealed, and the Home Office was likely to demand an explanation. But if there was no investigation, then Marita would surely smell a rat. Either way, if Bernard opened his mouth, the operation was in danger.

To try to persuade Bernard to stay silent, Marita enlisted his parents. Charles and Emma Perigoe had moved away from Wembley at the start of the war, to Hastings in east Sussex. On one of the stretches of England's south coast closest to France, the name of this fishing port was synonymous with invasion – William the Conqueror landed a little way down the coast in 1066. In 1940, when it had seemed Hitler might come at any moment, the town had been transformed, with gun emplacements, tank traps, and barbed wire along the beach. Pipes were installed to pump oil out into the sea – if the Germans tried to land, the British hoped to set fire to the water as they arrived.

Marita didn't enjoy the company of her in-laws, but she knew they were loyal to fascism and angry about their son's continued imprisonment. The hostility they'd suffered from neighbours over these things had only turned them further against Britain.

When Marita first told Roberts she had persuaded them to join the Fifth Column, his private response was sympathy. 'I feel sorry indeed for these parents,' he wrote. 'But it is a good example of how fascist propaganda over a long period can undermine the loyalty of ordinary decent citizens. The Perigoe seniors are not dangerous in the same sense as the younger BU members, but I maintain that their sense of duty to their country has been seriously affected.'

This was putting it mildly. Marita had handed him statements signed by each of them, pledging their loyalty to the Nazi 'cause'. Charles had asked if he could become a full-time agent. Emma went further still. Marita returned from a visit to Hastings in May 1943 with a map her mother-in-law had drawn, with the aim of helping attackers. Emma had come up with a cover for their reconnaissance trip: a visit to the cemetery, carrying flowers to lay on relatives' graves, provided a fine chance to scout defences. She 'showed an excellent capacity for memorising gun positions and other items of military interest', Roberts reported. 'Marita remarked that Mrs Emma Perigoe felt very happy to think that she had done something of a concrete nature to help the German Secret Service.'

Emma and Charles were very worried by Bernard's threats of blackmail. At the start of 1943, he was temporarily moved from the Isle of Man back to Brixton Prison, making it easier for them to visit him. Charles believed his son's character had altered as a result of his treatment by the government. Emma tried to suggest to Marita that Bernard might have been joking, but Marita knew she didn't really believe it.

By deciding to join the Fifth Column, though, they had given Marita a card to play back at Bernard. If he went to the authorities, not just his wife but also his parents now faced treason charges. That would mean imprisonment and even hanging. Roberts might not have been a real Gestapo man, but his chief operative was using Gestapo tactics.

Whether it was this threat or the gentler persuasion of his

parents that won him round, Bernard had a gift for Marita when she next visited him. In his characteristically extreme style, he had written a five-page signed statement in which he agreed to obey the orders of the Gestapo without question. As he observed himself, it would be enough to get him a death sentence.

His conversion to the cause seemed genuine, though. When he was sent back to the Isle of Man, he began providing Marita with a steady supply of information on internees. He had, unwittingly, become MI5's source on the island. This was an important function: the Home Office, typically squeamish about intelligence-gathering, had forbidden the use of paid informants in the camps, and MI5 knew it couldn't trust those who volunteered information, either out of spite or to ingratiate themselves. Bernard's status as an unconscious informant made him more reliable. It also meant that Roberts was once again passing on information on the people he'd been monitoring before the war, people who had probably identified him as a spy and who would be liable to take revenge if they ever met him.

Those fascists who hadn't been interned also posed a threat to Roberts, which was why he had told Perigoe to steer clear of past members of the British Union. She treated this instruction as she'd treated his order not to engage in espionage – she ignored it.

In March 1943 she presented him with two potential recruits, Lizbeth Raven Thomson and her friend, a Miss Scott. This was a problem. Lizbeth was the wife of Alexander Raven Thomson, the former director of policy of the BU – someone on whom Roberts had been filing reports as far back as 1935. Lizbeth was just the kind of person who might point out that Jack King, Gestapo agent, had, until 1940, been Eric Roberts, bank clerk.

Roberts told Perigoe that the two women were unsuitable recruits: Raven Thomson was likely to be under police surveillance. He reproved Perigoe. It was 'unwise' of her to have become mixed up with them.

Perigoe hit back. 'She asked me what we meant by constantly discouraging initiative,' Roberts reported. 'It was obvious that the people in question were genuinely Nazi. She alleged that I had adopted a completely incomprehensible attitude towards these people.'

When Roberts repeated that Raven Thomson was probably

being followed by police, he was met with scorn. 'Marita replied that I was so scared that it was a wonder anything was done at all. I protested that it was for her own safety. Marita said it was a curious thing that no objection was raised to an approach where non-Fascists were concerned.' This was true. Roberts had slipped up.

Perigoe's suspicions clearly still lingered. She now mentioned that she believed there was an MI5 man named 'Roberts' active who was responsible for interning fascists. It was because of re- marks like this that MI5 was increasingly concerned for its agent's safety. But an agent who had spent so long operating unofficially wasn't going to leave his and his family's safety up to others. Roberts had his own plan.

Marita had told him of another rumour among the internees, of a German agent who was operating in Britain. The truth of this was a matter for another section of MI5, but Roberts didn't want her trying to make contact with anyone else. He decided to turn his two problems into one solution.

He expressed his doubts about the German agent rumour. It sounded like the kind of ruse that MI5 might dream up in order to trap people like her. As they discussed it, Perigoe began to wonder: was it possible that the German agent was in fact the MI5 man 'Roberts'? That was certainly possible, he told her. Having one of their people pretend to be a German spy in order to lure out unsuspecting fascists was exactly the sort of thing MI5 might do. It might be best to steer well clear.

In Hastings, meanwhile, Perigoe's mother-in-law Emma was finding working for the Gestapo rather invigorating. She was particularly pleased by the effects of German bombing. 'She keeps on telling me how funny it is the way things work out,' Marita remarked. 'All those people [who] were so nasty to her – they've all been bumped off in raids. She spends all day recounting to me all the horrible things they did to her. You've only got to dislike someone well enough, I suppose, and the Luftwaffe annihilates them.'

Roberts considered this, then responded as best he could: 'Do you feel like some tea?'

'Very much,' Marita replied.

Emma Perigoe was far from alone in taking pleasure in the bombing of her home town. Marita Perigoe and Eileen Gleave had also discussed with Roberts where the bombs should be directed to in their own neighbourhoods. 'You think Harrow and Wembley would be two good districts to bomb?' Roberts had asked.

'Oh yes,' Gleave had replied. Perigoe gave a more considered response. 'It depends what part of Wembley,' she said, explaining that in one district morale was low, and a few more bombs might push people into revolt against the government. 'They are all working people, labourers, working very hard on a very low food ration. And they don't like it at all.'

Kohout, too, was frustrated that bombing in his area hadn't been more concentrated. Roberts assured him it soon would be: 'I think it is about time Watford had a little attention,' he said, doing his best impersonation of a menacing Nazi.

But for Roberts, the most shocking example came one Sunday afternoon in April 1943, when Perigoe, Gleave and Nancy Brown came to the Park West flat. After chiding him over the state of the flat – Gleave said the bathroom was ghastly, and Perigoe urged him to get a charwoman in to clean – Brown gave Roberts the name of a Margaret Doyle in Wales who was a likely recruit – 'a terrific Jew-hater'. They then got on to discussing the news from Brighton. Brown excitedly described a Luftwaffe attack.

'They were watching the RAF doing their exercises by the Aquarium,' she said. 'And someone said "Oh, look at those planes," and they looked out to sea and saw some big black planes flying in over the top of the water – couldn't hear a sound – and just as they got to the end of the pier they seemed to turn their engines on and they flew straight up like that, branched out and started machine-gunning and cannon-firing and dropped a lot of bombs! You know, it was almost cruel, they were such very good near misses. One of them, you remember my telling you about the guns on top of Telephone House?'

Roberts said he did.

'Well, one large bomb fell two houses to the right, to the north of it, demolishing a block of flats and a Baptist church! Oh it was marvellous, it really was a near miss.'

The source of Brown's delight became clear as she went on. 'One bomb fell in the municipal market, and that made me quite

sure it must be because I – from what I said.' She was laughing. 'Because do you remember my telling you about the ARP
headquarters?'

'Yes.'

'Well, you see, there was a very near miss there because the
bomb fell on the corner of the municipal market, which is bang
next door to the ARP HQ.'

She came to the question of injuries. 'A greengrocer had his
head blown off, and umpteen casualties through cut glass and
things.'

Another bomb had fallen on a school clinic. 'It killed a clerk
there and badly injured two of the girls, and killed one expectant
mother and about two children.'

Even the fact that she had been caught up in the raid herself
didn't dampen Brown's enthusiasm. 'I'd no sooner sat down in
Ward's to have my coffee when suddenly: "Crack! Crack! Crack!"
And everybody dived to the back of the shop because they felt
quite sure the bullets were coming in at the windows and we
were all huddled together. And then "Boomp!"' – she banged the
table – '"Boomp! Boomp!" And the windows blew in and out and
the doors blew in and out. And when we came out we could see
great columns of smoke coming up.'

Roberts watched the women. 'I looked in vain at the faces
of these three women for any signs of contrition,' he reported
afterwards. 'Nancy Brown looked a fine, healthy specimen of an
Englishwoman, but it was obvious that the deaths of these people
meant absolutely nothing to her. I thought of the excellent impression that this woman would make on an Advisory Committee
or the Home Office or a jury. She sat there pleased and happy to
think that the news she had given me resulted in the deaths and
damage of that last raid.'

There was a benefit to Roberts of her delight, though. One of
the problems of a deception operation was trying to convince the
person being deceived that their work was having an effect. The
Double Cross team put great effort into making German intelligence believe that its agents in Britain were carrying out sabotage
operations – hence the midnight detonations of empty sheds. The
Fifth Column group discovered they didn't need to go to such
lengths. Their recruits reported information, and within a few

months, the Luftwaffe bombed somewhere close to the location of the report. The minds of the Fifth Columnists connected these attacks, and proved the value of their work.

For Emma Perigoe and Nancy Brown, there was little incentive to doubt the link – quite the reverse. The excitement of a bombing raid was only increased by the thought that these huge explosions, the destruction and the death, might in some way be their own doing.

Nancy completed her report: 'It was a very successful raid.'

14

'Oozing with gratitude'

When Marita Perigoe had first suggested Kohout as a recruit, she had identified his friend Adolf Herzig, a German who worked in the same factory, as well. And Kohout too had thought that Herzig would want to join. But although he was sympathetic to their goals, Herzig remained reluctant at first. Perigoe had more success with his wife, Luise.

Shortly after the Fifth Column began operating in 1942, Luise worried that she was pregnant. She had two daughters already and did not want any more, so she consulted Perigoe, a woman of the world. Perigoe told Roberts that she'd given Luise some 'very simple advice' about dealing with an unwanted pregnancy. Abortion was illegal, although it was far from uncommon, either through expensive clinics or, at the lower end of the market, back street operators.

'You don't think you took too much of a risk?' Roberts asked.

'Good gracious no. Why should it be a risk?'

'If anything goes wrong, what is your position?'

Perigoe assured him it would be fine. Roberts relaxed. 'Do you think she'll be grateful to you for it?'

'I should think she'd be oozing with gratitude.'

And so, it seemed, she was. Luise Herzig began to pass information to Marita about the German Club. This group met in the German Catholic Church on Adler Street in Whitechapel, after the Sunday service. It was supposed to be a social and non-political group for people to socialise with others who shared their homeland. Before the war, it had had close to 400 members. Now it was less than half that number – many people felt that attendance might be misunderstood as sympathy for Germany.

The police were assured that the club's activities were innocent, but neither they nor MI5 had anyone on the inside. Nor would it be easy to put someone in. Its membership was small, and anyone trying to join would be likely to face scepticism. To attempt to recruit one of the existing members would risk revealing their interest. In Luise Herzig, Roberts had found the answer. She didn't need to win people's trust, because she already had it. She didn't need to feign enthusiasm for the Nazis, because she already felt it. And she couldn't reveal she was spying for MI5, because she didn't know it.

By the start of 1943, Herzig was supplying reports directly to Roberts. She thought she was carrying out the work the Gestapo wanted: identifying men and women who might be helpful to Germany in the event of an invasion. There were several in the club. Mrs Rutzler, for instance, was furious about the bombing of Germany. 'She swore that Britain would get it back tenfold if it was the last thing the Nazis did,' Roberts wrote, passing on what Luise had told him. 'Mrs Rutzler expressed admiration for the Nazi regime and bitterly attacked the Jews responsible for British policy.'

There was 'a sister from a Hendon convent who expressed strong pro-Nazi sentiments and rebuked a young German girl who claimed that German propaganda was a tissue of lies.' And Herr Spiegelhalter, a watchmaker. 'He contends that Britain engineered this war on behalf of the Jews.'

Luise had also helped to persuade her husband to come on board. In June, Kohout brought his friend to meet Roberts. Adolf Herzig 'is now working wholeheartedly for us', an MI5 note on the operation read. 'Herzig came to the conclusion that in the event of a second front in Western Europe, information regarding communications would be of great value to the enemy. He is therefore doing a series of maps of communications in the Watford district. This is of a much higher grade than anything we have had before.'

Roberts was again struck by the gap between his recruits' apparent nature and their true character. 'Herzig looks honest and decent and nobody would suspect a naturalised citizen of Herzig's type of encouraging any subversive activity,' he reported. 'If he had been interned, he would have been released within a short time. He represents the best type of open, honest, sincere German, a useful citizen, a devoted father and an ardent Civil Defence worker.'

Luise Herzig's recruitment drive didn't stop with her husband. She suggested a friend, Mrs Wynne – 'she's very keen' – who lived in Wallasey, a town just outside Liverpool on the north-west coast of England. Conveniently, her house overlooked the River Mersey, where convoys of ships would assemble to make the dangerous run across the Atlantic to America.

'She says the very thing what people want, she can see from her window,' Herzig reported in her flawed English. 'She can see some of the army ships getting ready, and sometimes she saw even the destroyers come along.'

Mrs Wynne was around seventy. 'She is a very old woman,' Kohout explained to Roberts, 'but very well educated. Well, my personal opinion is that if anybody approaches her she will kiss him. That is my personal opinion. I have met her dozens of times, and she always said, "If I could do something to make the finish of the war . . ."'

After her initial enthusiasm, Mrs Wynne got cold feet. When Luisa visited her in June 1943, her report led Clay to tell Rothschild that Wynne had 'more or less backed out'. But there was still cause for optimism: Mrs Wynne's husband Fred took Luise for a drink, and explained that he had been deliberately muddling orders at his shipping firm, in an effort to damage the British war effort. Clay's report on him also said he and 'two trusty friends' had spent the past year engaged in an unspecified 'anti-Semitic campaign'.

Other recruits also had second thoughts. One, Harry Knott, was initially keen when Eileen Gleave approached him, until his wife caught him marking military targets on his Bartholemew's half-inch map of Hertfordshire and Buckinghamshire. When he told her that he was trying to help the Germans, Mrs Knott called him a 'dirty traitor', and threatened to leave with their children if he didn't cut off all connection with the Fifth Column immediately.

'Oh, I was furious,' Gleave told Roberts and Perigoe. 'I told him off. I said, "Can't you stand on your own feet? Do you have to do exactly as your wife tells you all the time?"'

'But why did he have to mess around with these things while she was there?' Perigoe asked, exasperated.

'She's there all the time,' Gleave complained. 'I told him what

I thought of him when he came round, I don't mind telling you. I said: "No wonder the British Union didn't get anywhere with the people that have been in it."'

Knott had carried out one small act of rebellion against his wife: he gave Gleave the map, and a list of military bases to finish marking on it.

Roberts generally took a forgiving view of people who backed out, something else that made Perigoe suspicious of him. 'Marita remarked that she sometimes wondered how I came to occupy the position I held as I was so humane to people,' he reported in May 1943. 'She had noticed that where it was possible to make an excuse for a person, I generally did so. If things were left to her, she would be genuinely ruthless. It did not pay to be soft.'

Roberts defended himself, saying his policy was to make allowances for foibles. Besides, he explained, it wasn't their job to make converts. They were looking for willing volunteers, who showed initiative.

His approach to the potential recruits who were brought to him was certainly gentle. 'I'm compelled to be quite frank with you, and I think it's the best way,' he told one man. 'Well, I'm a German agent.' His job was to identify people who would cooperate with the Nazis, 'so that in the event of an occupation, we shall know who to leave alone and who not to leave alone. Well, if you would like to help us in any way at all, I shall be very grateful to you. There's no pressure.'

But Perigoe's criticisms worried Roberts. The following month, Kohout proudly produced a revolver, which he'd bought illegally. The last thing Roberts wanted was an armed Fifth Columnist. It was one thing for Perigoe to talk about poisoning him or killing him with a penknife, but how hard would it be to pull a trigger? Roberts persuaded Kohout to sell him the pistol.

Perigoe could only approach people that she knew and trusted. That inevitably gave the Fifth Column a local feel, with many of its members living within walking distance of each other, in Wembley. This suburb of north-west London had been transformed over the previous decades, as developers built street upon street of reasonably priced homes for those who worked in the capital but wanted to escape its slums. Much of the building took place along the route of the Metropolitan Line of the London Under-ground. In the 1920s, the line's owners had given the places that were now within commuting distance of the city the collective label 'Metro-Land', and built tens of thousands of family homes there.

Although these housing estates were the summit of modern suburban living, their mock-Tudor style tried to evoke the rural houses of a bygone era, with black beams and dormer windows that suggested these semi-detached three-bedroom homes were places with which Elizabeth I or Sir Francis Drake might have felt familiar. At a time when Britons suspected their nation's place in the world might be declining, their architecture dwelt on an earlier century when its star had been on the rise.

Metro-Land was for the newly middle class, for those who were making their way in the world, and the Metro-Land spies that Perigoe recruited were drawn from these circles: people who had to work for a living, but who were clear that they weren't working class. Perigoe herself was a picture-restorer. Edgar Bray was an accountant. Hilda Leech was a bank clerk, as Roberts had been. They shared a resentment that many of their 'betters' owed their stations in life to accidents of birth, rather than merit.

And while Perigoe looked down her nose at him, Kohout was the ultimate Metro-Land aspirational spy. Not only was he an expert in the modern material of tin foil, he had set himself up as a landlord, with a portfolio of five houses in the area.

The Fifth Column weren't the only spies in Metro-Land. A few minutes' drive away, in Hendon, on the other side of the Brent Reservoir, where Edgar Bray had watched the amphibious tank trials, lived the Abwehr's apparently most prolific agent. Juan Pujol Garcia was a Spaniard who had volunteered his services to German intelligence in 1941. He was given the codename 'Agent Arabel', and told that if he could get himself to London, Berlin would take him seriously.

By the end of that year, Pujol was sending to Berlin not only his own reports of Britain's situation, but those of three other agents he had recruited. If his progress delighted the Germans, it was causing some concern to MI5. Just as they had concluded that there were no German spies in Britain, intercepted transmissions, decoded at Bletchley Park, showed that there was an entire network. But on closer examination, a lot of the information seemed either ridiculous or wrong. The reports were understandably confused by Britain's pre-decimal currency system of pounds, shillings and pence, but they also suggested that in Glasgow there were men 'who would do anything for a litre of wine'. And there were descriptions of a tank that didn't exist. The MI5 investigation concluded that whoever these spies were, they were either mad or fraudulent.

What neither MI5 nor the Abwehr considered was that Agent Arabel might not even be in Britain, and his network might be entirely inside his head. At this point, Pujol was living in Lisbon, filing imaginary dispatches based on what he could learn from tourist guides to Britain. Meanwhile, he was repeatedly failing in the next stage of his plan: to get recruited by British intelligence as well. He had realised that having a German agent working for them might be a good thing for the British. To his frustration, he couldn't find anyone from Britain who agreed: the MI6 officers at the embassy in Lisbon showed no interest.

Even when Pujol's wife Araceli went to the American embassy, and persuaded them to reach out to their British counterparts, progress was slow. It was only a chance conversation in early 1942 between Tar Robertson and one of MI6's men in Lisbon that led to the realisation that Pujol was running his own fake agent operation, and had the Germans fooled. MI5 rapidly decided it would be best if he worked for them, so they brought him to Britain and set him up with his young family in Hendon.

There, he was given a British codename, 'Garbo', after the screen goddess Greta Garbo, in tribute to his skill at inhabiting different roles. By 1943, his 'network' consisted of seven imaginary agents, including a Portuguese salesman who lived in South Wales, and a Gibraltarian waiter in London. They were spread from North Africa to Canada, supplying information to Germany selected by the XX Committee and turned into messages by Pujol and his case officer, Tommy Harris.

The case was going swimmingly. Pujol and Harris created personalities and life stories for each of their spies, sending them on missions and even killing off one who was notionally based in Liverpool when they realised it would be impossible for him to explain how he'd failed to warn of the sailing of large numbers of troopships towards North Africa in November 1942.

The problem was at home. Fearing that his wife would accidentally reveal what he was doing, Pujol had forbidden Araceli much contact with fellow Spaniards. As she spoke little English, this left her with few people to talk to. A couple of years earlier, she had been a partner in his spying adventure. Now she was stuck caring for two small children in a suburban home in a foreign country, with little adult companionship. She begged to be allowed to go back to Spain, but was refused – there would be no way of monitoring her activities or protecting her from unwanted attention from Germany.

In June 1943, she had had enough. Araceli told her husband that she was going to go to the Spanish embassy in London and reveal what he had been doing. She then telephoned Harris and repeated the threat. MI5 went into a flap. Mrs Pujol was a Spanish citizen, and they had no power to stop her from asking to see her consul. If she revealed the extent of her husband's fraud upon the Abwehr, it was bound to lead to an investigation into their other British agents, whose reports synchronised with his. Araceli could destroy the entire Double Cross operation, and MI5 had no power to stop her.

Liddell, Robertson, Harris and MI5's legal adviser, Major Edward Cussen, held a crisis meeting. 'She ought really to be locked up and kept incommunicado, but in the state of the law here nothing of the kind is possible,' Liddell complained afterwards. They considered other options: warning the Spanish embassy that a mad woman fitting Araceli's description planned to kill the ambassador. 'This would, we hope, ensure her being flung out,' Liddell considered. 'It would, however, result in the police being called in, which would be a bore.'

The coincidence of geography that made the three miles around Wembley Park station the base of so many of the spies that MI5 was controlling suggested another possibility. If Araceli wanted something to do, perhaps they should give her an agent to run. Obviously they wouldn't trust her with a real spy, or even one of her husband's imaginary ones, but they already had a fake agent working in Metro-Land.

'It has also been suggested, to give her an interest in life, that she would be shown a bogus message indicating that a Gestapo agent here has some instructions to make contact with Garbo,' Liddell recorded. 'We would then put in Jack and let her run his case.'

Araceli would be told that she must meet this Gestapo man and, at all costs, keep him away from the truth about her husband's work. Roberts would play the inquisitive agent of Germany, scaling his activities to keep Araceli busy. It would be a deception wrapped in another deception to protect a third deception. 'This will of course be an added complication to the already complicated Garbo case,' Liddell observed.

It would be an added complication to the already complicated Fifth Column operation, too. Roberts would not only have to be a fake agent-runner, he would have to be a fake agent as well. It was a measure of Liddell's confidence in Roberts's powers of deception that he was considering it.

In the end, the plan was rejected in favour of Pujol's own proposal – a cold-blooded deception of the mother of his children. Araceli was told her husband had been arrested, and that Harris was himself being disciplined for his handling of the case. Mrs Pujol was initially distraught, and then sceptical. She called another MI5 man, Charles Haines, and asked him to come round. When he arrived, he found Araceli sitting in her kitchen, with all the gas taps turned on. Haines was unconvinced that this was a real suicide attempt, but with the Pujol children in the house, feared an accident. He consulted Harris, who sent his wife round to sit with Araceli.

It was Mrs Harris who persuaded Araceli of Pujol's ruse. She so convincingly played the worried wife of a man who was in disgrace that by the morning, the other woman was convinced the situation was serious. Then came the coup de grâce: Araceli was driven, blindfolded, to Camp 020, MI5's detention centre in Richmond, south-west London. There her husband was brought out to her, dressed in prison clothes and unshaven. Mrs Pujol was broken. 'She promised him that if only he were released from prison, she would help him in every way to continue his work with even greater zeal than before,' Harris reported. 'She would never again ask to go to Spain.'

Pujol was back in business, and Roberts was free to get on with running his own branch of Metro-Land's intelligence community.

15

'A National Socialist atmosphere'

If the residents of Metro-Land dreamed of a more rural existence than their urban occupations allowed, Ronald and Rita Creasy lived one.

Their farm was 75 miles north-east of London, in what they advertised to potential paying guests as 'the quiet of the real Suffolk country'. It was a world away from Metro-Land, with its rows of suburban houses a brisk walk from the station. The closest railway stop to the Creasys was seven miles away.

Ronald Creasy also occupied a quite different position in Britain's social strata from the Metro-Land Fifth Columnists. The son of a substantial landowner, he was no petit-bourgeois – he had been educated by a private tutor. The Creasys, he said, could trace their line back to Norman times, when they'd held a lordship situated between Dieppe and Rouen. They'd owned land in the neighbouring county of Norfolk since the thirteenth century. By 1930, they had stakes in over eighty farms in the two counties. When he turned 21 that year, he was given the management of one of them.

But Ronald wasn't content to follow the path of his ancestors and take his place at the top of the local social order. On visits to London and Paris, he was troubled by the plight of destitute people he saw. Closer to home, he was acutely aware of the difficulties facing agriculture. Both his father and their tenants had been hit by cheaper imports that had pushed down grain prices. Men had been forced out of work, and good land lay dormant, because it was uneconomic to plant it.

And if suburban dwellers harked back to a mythical bygone age, the farmers of Suffolk had begun the 1930s with a protest against one particular ancient tradition. Under the 'tithe' system, which dated from a time when people were expected to support their local priest, many farmers were legally required to pay money to the Church of England, or in some cases the colleges of Oxford and Cambridge universities, which had once been religious houses. The law that required this was obscure, and the deeds of the land often made no mention that it carried this obligation. The tax had once been supposed to be calculated based on the value of the crop, but as wheat prices fell, the amount demanded didn't.

The young Ronald Creasy

Ronald was furious with the church. He saw farmers driven to despair and even suicide by their plight. Meanwhile, in church on Sunday he noted that his family, as the leading one in the area, had a reserved pew at the front, while lesser families were expected to sit behind them. 'I could see our privileges and their lack of privileges,' he later recalled. Orthodox religion, he concluded, 'was always for those who have against those who have not'. He rejected the faith of his family in favour of pantheism.

A young man angry with the government and with the injustice of the social order might easily have pursued either communism or fascism in the early 1930s. But communism held no appeal for Ronald. For one thing, he saw himself as a patriot, and for another, his desire to overturn the social order didn't extend all the way to giving up his own place in it. Rather, he saw himself as a Mosley-like figure, a member of the upper classes who would use his position to help the ordinary people.

'The fascist idea suited me remarkably well,' he said later, 'because fascism means leadership and I was prepared to be a leader. I was born to leadership. That also encouraged me to leave the old behind and, for the sake of the people, to go into the BUF, but as a leader.'

He met Mosley and said that he would join the BUF – but only in a position commensurate with his status. Mosley, quite comfortable with snobbery, agreed, and Creasy was duly appointed the District Leader for his new local branch. Rita, his wife, was named Women's District Leader.

Ronald saw the tithe as a means of engaging his fellow farmers. For several years now, they had been protesting about it. Some were nonconformists, and didn't see why they should help fund a church to which they didn't even belong. Others were newcomers who had bought their farms without understanding the tax. Meanwhile the church commissioners insisted upon their dues, and sent in bailiffs to collect the money.

Creasy persuaded Mosley to deploy Blackshirts to Suffolk to defend those who were refusing to pay. The 'Tithe Wars', as they became known, were an ideal cause for the British Union of Fascists, which combined nostalgia for a mythical past with attacks on those who had traditionally held power. This was a battle between downtrodden, honest British yeomen and the forces of the government, the police and the Church of England, a body that many identified with the Conservative Party. The farmers had been made poor by free trade and financial manipulation. Their fortunes would be restored by a government that would act in their interests. Beyond that, it was a straightforwardly popular local cause, the ideal thing for any insurgent party to attach itself to.

Mosley's campaign against tithes was popular with farmers

The Blackshirt intervention made a difference. One stand-off with bailiffs and police in Ringshall, near Stowmarket in Suffolk, ended with the tithe receiver, in this case King's College, Cambridge, giving way. At another farm near Wortham, twenty miles away, the Blackshirts fortified the entrance with trenches, and prepared to do battle with the bailiffs. They remained there for more than two weeks, until fifty policemen arrived from London and arrested nineteen of them. BUF membership across the region swelled, approaching 2,000 in 1934. Even though it fell away quickly after that, it remained popular enough for Ronald to be elected to the local council in 1938 as the British Union candidate.

But when war came, his association with fascism was less popular locally. He was attacked in the local pub when he tried to distribute leaflets advocating peace with Germany. A local journalist wrote confidentially to MI5 saying he suspected Ronald would be willing to help the enemy if he could. And in June 1940, he was rounded up and interned along with other BU leaders.

Ronald found prison hard. He was used to spending his days roaming across fields, accorded respect by those around him. Now he was stuck in a cell in Liverpool. The train there had stopped at every station to pick up more men like him. His particular fury was provoked by the one thing left for him in his cell: a Bible. This was Christian mercy, to lock a man up for his political beliefs?

Back in Suffolk, Rita was trying to manage the farm, as well as look after their five-year-old son. It wasn't easy. The time was approaching when seeds needed to be sown. Ronald understood that – what should be planted where, and when.

Rita Creasy

By the time Ronald's case was reviewed in September, he was in a sorry state. When the Advisory Committee questioned him about his views, he kept talking about his desire to return to the soil. As he rambled on about his love for his country, the committee chairman became increasingly frustrated. As Ronald began another speech, he interrupted: 'Oh for God's sake don't quote Shakespeare to me.'

The committee struggled to decide whether Ronald was deliberately trying to lie to them, or whether he was simply in the midst of a breakdown. In the end, they decided it was the latter. 'This man is clearly interested in agriculture and nothing else in the world,' they concluded, ignoring that, a year earlier, Ronald had described himself in the census as a politician and writer. 'His attachment to the British Union arose from what may be described as his agricultural obsession; he is an agricultural fanatic and has no fanaticism for or interest in anything else.' In the face of the protests of both MI5 and his local police force, they urged his immediate release.

In Ronald's absence, Rita had moved back in with her mother, where she was rumoured to be hosting parties late into the night for local troops. Afterwards, she was reported to be spending hours scribbling furious notes. But these reports weren't taken terribly seriously by the Security Service, who noted there had also been rumours that Rita's mother had a wireless transmitter, and these had proved to be groundless.

Neighbours also claimed that the couple's son, Karl, had been heard to say that Hitler was 'a good man'. Whether this was true or not, it was certainly his father's view. Ronald had visited Germany a couple of years earlier and been deeply impressed. 'The happiness, the contentment, the wealth, the prosperity,' he recalled. As for the Führer himself, 'What a man! From poverty, from nothing, he built up a great nation.' He received the 'worship' of the people, and Ronald thought he deserved it.

Even after war had broken out, he and Rita were advertising their farm in the BUF paper as a place where people could come and stay in a 'National Socialist atmosphere'. The Advisory Committee, it seemed, had underestimated Ronald's enthusiasm for non-agricultural activity.

But after he returned from internment in November 1940, he and Rita opted to lie low. Whatever his private views, Ronald had no desire to go back to prison.

In September 1942, Perigoe mentioned the Creasys to Roberts. Their son had been staying with the Herzigs during the harvest. Rita felt unable to leave Ronald with crops still in the field, so the seven-year-old was due to travel back from north London to Suffolk by train on his own. 'Please tell him what a big man he is to travel alone,' Rita wrote sadly to Luise. 'It will help to give him confidence.'

The Creasys had been having a hard time of it since Ronald's release. The local shops refused them service, and occasionally villagers were sufficiently emboldened – or inebriated – to hurl abuse or even clods of earth at Ronald. But Perigoe reported that despite or perhaps because of this hostility, the Creasys remained loyal to Germany. They could, she said, be relied upon to do all they could to help an invasion.

Roberts was initially wary of allowing their recruitment to the Fifth Column. They broke his rule of keeping former BUF members at a distance. But Kohout weighed in on their behalf. They were close to the coast, he said, ideally placed to assist invaders. From Roberts's perspective, they were sufficiently distant from London that he had never met them during his own time in the British Union. Also Ronald's internment had been brief, and hadn't overlapped with Reg Windsor's. Perhaps it would be safe to allow the Creasys into the group.

In early 1943, Kohout visited the Creasys to sound them out. He came back with excellent news. First, Ronald and Rita had lost none of their zeal for the cause. 'They knew if Hitler lost then Mosley would also lose,' Roberts noted, after Kohout had reported back. 'They were not proposing to become Nazis but they were British Union members and would do anything likely to bring Mosley into power. By helping Germany, they thought this could be effected.'

The couple had Italian prisoners of war working on the farm – Churchill's government, having in 1940 decided that British-Italians were too dangerous to be allowed to stay in the country, had in 1941 realised it needed workers, and begun importing captured Italian soldiers as a labour force – and were in the habit of exchanging fascist salutes with them: 'Viva Mosley, Viva Il Duce!'

The Creasys claimed local soldiers had told them about the previous year's attack on Dieppe three days in advance. Ronald promised Kohout that if they got more such information, he would send Rita with it to London at once.

And Rita was more than a helper in her husband's cause: Kohout said he thought Rita easily the more pro-Nazi of the two, 'and by far the more dangerous to the British'. This was a view that the police and MI5 seemed to share. She was tall, with dark hair and eyes – there was a report she was half-Spanish – and wore lipstick and colourful clothes. According to one MI5 case summary, she was clearly 'pretty immoral', though the evidence for this seemed to be the gossip about the parties she'd held while Ronald had been interned.

The Creasys' devotion to the fascist cause was serious, but it didn't completely blunt their self-interest. They told Kohout that they would be willing to shelter German agents, but not for free: they proposed taking them in as 'paying guests'.

Kohout wasn't completely positive. He told Roberts that Ronald had the air of a 'political lunatic'. But he felt the advantages of recruiting the couple outweighed the dangers. The Creasys were put onto the Fifth Column's books.

It didn't take Rita Creasy long to put the operation into jeopardy. Within a month of Kohout's visit, she had told a friend that she was collecting intelligence for Germany. That friend told another friend, who in turn told someone else, who reported the conversation to the local police sergeant. He told his chief constable.

As with Roberts's earlier manoeuvres with Dorothy Wegener, any activity that provoked a police investigation was a threat to the Fifth Column. If they questioned Rita, and she named Kohout or the Herzigs, it would be hard to explain why they weren't immediately rounded up.

Fortunately, the chief constable of East Suffolk followed his chain of command, and informed MI5 of the tip-off. He was, in any case, doubtful about Rita's story. Whether out of a belated sense of concern for security, or to give her tale a more romantic edge, she had told her friend that she made her reports to a Czech woman who lived in a rectory close to an airfield outside Ipswich. In a final, improbable, touch, she claimed that this agent of Nazi Germany, who was sending weekly reports back to Berlin, was Jewish.

If the police thought this tale 'too fantastic' to be believed, MI5's local man, Major Hughes, didn't. He began a fruitless search for the 'Czech Jewess', something that, given the numerous clues, should not have taken long: there were only eleven Czech women registered in all of East Suffolk, and initial research revealed half of them had since moved away.

A fortnight later, the police reported that Rita had been talking again. On a trip to the cinema, she'd told her companion more about the supposed German spy. The woman was now reported to be working as a maid at a rectory.

The immediate question was whether the German spy that Rita

was talking about was a clumsily disguised 'Jack King', or someone else. The possibility, even a remote one, of an unknown agent
operating in Britain was enough to justify a check not just on the
Creasys' post but also on their phone. In the following months,
MI5's listeners were introduced to aspects of agricultural management that had previously passed them by, such as the complexities
of wire netting and the sexing of hens' eggs, conversations that
were probably innocent, but might have been an elaborate code.

Meanwhile the police were tasked with finding out about Rita's
contacts. In some cases, their reports revealed more about them
than their subjects. Dennis Rudd, a clergyman, 'acted in a most
peculiar manner for a curate', they reported. 'He walked about
in daylight with his arms around his wife's waist, and would kiss
her.'

Other reports were little more than village gossip. Rita had
been seen in a pub with an American sergeant who was stationed
nearby. But of the Czech maid, there was no sign. 'I fear that this
report does not carry us any further,' sighed Hughes.

He had now been searching for his spy for two months, and
was coming to the conclusion that she was probably fictitious.
The listeners were told they could stop their check on the Creasys'
telephone.

In June 1943, Kohout visited the Creasys again. Ronald and
Rita, he reported afterwards, were more determined than ever
to help the Fifth Column. During his stay, Ronald had brought
out from its hiding place a record of the Nazi anthem, the 'Horst
Wessel Song', and listened with tears in his eyes. The cause of the
British Union and National Socialism were one, he told Kohout
afterwards. He had a suggestion, too. He'd heard that the nearby
American airfields used radio signals to guide their bombers.
Couldn't the Fifth Column sabotage a local power station, to
disrupt these signals 'at a critical moment'?

Rita, meanwhile, busied herself distributing a leaflet to Polish
soldiers stationed nearby. It began in an arresting style:

HIS MAJESTY WLADYSLAW THE FIFTH, BY THE
GRACE OF GOD KING OF POLAND, HUNGARY AND
BOHEMIA, GRAND DUKE OF LITHUANIA, SILESIA

AND THE UKRAINE, HOSPODAR OF MOLDAVIA,
ETC. ETC. ETC. HIGH PRIEST OF THE SUN.

Proclamation to the English, the Poles, the Germans and the jews.

The author, a New Zealand poet named Geoffrey Potocki who
now laid claim to Poland's throne, took an expansionist view of
what his country's rightful territory should be, proposing a realm
stretching from the Gulf of Riga in the north to the Black Sea
and the Adriatic in the south. At the bottom of the pamphlet, his
address gave a clue as to the distance of his dreams from reality:
'Half Moon Cottage, Little Bookham, Surrey'.

The leaflet was anti-Semitic in tone, and naive about Germany.
But the reason for Rita's interest was its astonishing claim that
one of Britain's allies, the Soviet Union, had carried out a war
crime against another, Poland, killing thousands of prisoners in
cold blood.

The pamphlet's opening lines made it clear that it was written
by someone who was, at the very least, highly eccentric. (Potocki's
other claim to fame was his jailing, a decade earlier, over an
attempt to publish an obscene poem titled 'Lament for Sir John
Penis'.) Which made it all the more remarkable that the leaflet's
central allegation was completely accurate.

In April 1943, Germany had announced to the world that its
army in Russia had found mass graves in the Katyn forest near
Smolensk. There were 4,400 corpses, their hands wired behind
their backs, each killed by a shot to the back of the head. Their
uniforms revealed them to be some of more than 20,000 missing
Polish officers who had been captured by the Soviet Union in
1939, when Hitler and Stalin had been dividing up Poland between them. The Germans claimed their discovery was evidence
of a Soviet massacre. The Polish government in exile demanded
answers. The Russians blamed the Germans. The Germans suggested the Red Cross should come and investigate.

For Britain, it was a difficult moment. Poland had been one
of the reasons Britain went to war in the first place, and then a
vital ally, supplying pilots to fight in the Battle of Britain, and
cryptographic intelligence to help break the German Enigma code.
But the war was no longer about Poland, and the USSR was

now a more important ally, laying down millions of lives on the Eastern Front as it pushed the German army back. On the Western Front, it was to the USA that Churchill now looked for troops and supplies. The Poles had become a side issue. It wasn't worth antagonising Stalin to get justice for them. The British and American governments pretended to believe the Russians. Their newspapers largely followed this line.

But the Nazis and their supporters saw a wedge they could drive between the Allies. Potocki was passed the information by Poles who had serious doubts about whether their allies could be trusted any more. He in turn argued that they were fighting the wrong enemy. 'It is high time for a negotiated peace,' he wrote, 'in which we hope the Germans will be persuaded to display a proper regard for the rights of Poland.' Given the events of 1939, this was hardly a realistic proposal, but it was in line with his call for the return of the Tsars to Russia and the monarchy to France. Potocki anyway had a high regard for Hitler. Reports of mass killings by Germany were, he said, 'mythical'.

Rita's view of Potocki's claims was nuanced. She told Kohout she thought she'd been 'rather silly' to distribute the leaflet, but she was bored, 'and she wanted to do something to help fascism whether the people concerned were British fascists or not'. Besides, she argued, the leaflets wouldn't have been published if they were illegal.

This point was in fact at the centre of some debate within MI5 and the British government. At the end of June, MI5 was looking into prosecuting Potocki, with Rita standing trial as an accessory. When she heard about it, Clay moved swiftly. Up to then, she had been letting Major Hughes worry about the Creasys, in collaboration with Miss Burke, a Blenheim-based woman who like her was designated an 'assistant officer'. Now she was worried the pair were throwing the whole operation into jeopardy.

A police investigation into the Creasys would be likely to scare the rest of the Fifth Column into hiding, she feared. Worse, a police search of the Creasy house might turn up something that pointed to Ronald and Rita's contacts with Kohout or Herzig or even Roberts himself. Even if it didn't, the Creasys were aware of a Gestapo man named Jack King operating in London. What if they tried to denounce him to the police in exchange for better treatment? 'It should be considered whether it is worthwhile losing a useful source of intelligence regarding subversive people in this country for the doubtful success in prosecuting Mrs Creasy for an offence for which she may merely receive a caution or a small fine,' Clay wrote.

This was the paradox of the Fifth Column operation: because the Creasys were working, albeit unconsciously, for MI5, MI5 had an incentive to protect them.

MI5's legal adviser, Edward Cussen, meanwhile, advised against prosecuting Potocki. Someone styling himself 'High Priest of the Sun' was unlikely to be taken seriously, and a court case would only have drawn attention to him. Although he wasn't completely safe. In October, he was sentenced to two months' hard labour for breaking the blackout. His response to the court was defiant: 'I call upon God to punish you. Heil Hitler!'

In July, Roberts finally got to meet the Creasys for himself, accompanied by Kohout and Luise Herzig. The farmer set out to ingratiate himself to the Gestapo man, telling him that he was himself a vegetarian, like Hitler. Keen for some affirmation in return, he asked if the Führer was, like him, a pantheist. Roberts knew a thing or two about pleasing his audience as well. He was, he said meaningfully, not allowed to give an 'official' answer to this question, because the Reich was anxious not to offend those with other religious sensibilities. Ronald heard what he wanted, and replied that he had always suspected he shared his beliefs with the leader, and was glad to know this was true.

Ronald wasn't a physically impressive man: average height, slim, a ginger moustache across his thin face. He told Roberts at some length about his experience appealing against his internment to the Advisory Committee, which he embellished somewhat, claiming among other things that they had warned him he would be lucky not to be shot if they saw him again.

'I listened in patience, examining Creasy closely,' Roberts reported. 'I knew that the man was telling lies, but after a time I came to the conclusion that he really did believe in what he told me. Creasy had a way of putting over his story that was extraordinarily convincing.'

As Ronald continued to speak, Roberts saw why Mosley had been sufficiently impressed to appoint him a BUF District Leader.

'The man has a wonderful grasp of the English language and despite his political fanaticism, he can hold the attention by his ability to make use of the beauty of words,' read his report. 'His theme was the nobility of the fascist creed. The man is a semi-lunatic, but after a while I noticed that Kohout and Mrs Herzig were listening with rapt attention, not grasping much of what was being said, but visibly moved by the sounds of the cascade. He eventually turned to the Jews. Creasy certainly knew his subject. His style might not appeal to farmers, but it would make a wonderful appeal to hooligan elements of the BU type.'

Ronald's feelings about working with Roberts were mixed. He clearly found the prospect attractive – he'd gone to the meeting, after all – but he was also nervous about the risk he ran of being sent back to internment. 'He had not now the courage for propaganda work,' Roberts wrote. 'Creasy hoped to save himself for activities after the war. The returning soldiers would be fed up with the Yids and more wide awake than the local farmers. He could see that fascism stood a good chance. I advised Creasy to save himself for his leader, who would be in want of idealists like himself.'

In the coming months, Ronald continued to try to have it both ways. He told the Herzigs his observations of the operations of the nearby US airfield, but tried to make light of them. 'Creasy intimated that the information was to be regarded as gossip from himself and not a deliberate attempt to help the enemy, although he knew the destination of the information,' Roberts wrote. 'Typical BU man.'

The farmer had long been frustrated by his inability to convince the farmers of Suffolk of the wickedness of the Jews. But he now had a fresh plan for stirring up local anger. In 1941, the US Army Air Force had begun taking over large parts of East Anglia to build airfields. It was currently on course to build an average of one every eight miles – 100,000 acres in Norfolk. And each of these bases had hundreds or even thousands of airmen and ground staff on them. These troops were brash, and tended to thrown their money around. Some of them were also quite different from anyone the people of Suffolk had ever seen before.

'The presence of coloured troops in the neighbourhood of Eye had led to a certain amount of friction with the villagers,' Roberts reported. 'Creasy was keeping an eye on this development and would seize any opportunity of stirring up trouble. The villagers and farmers were not Jew conscious, but they were rapidly becoming colour conscious.'

The Creasys' hatred of Jews didn't, however, override their desire to make money. As Christmas 1943 approached, Ronald was conscious that the 200 turkeys he'd reared were in high demand – the Ministry of Food estimated only one family in ten would get a bird that year. He offered them to Kohout at four pounds ten shillings apiece, arguing he'd be able to sell them on in London, but Kohout turned him down. It was with some pleasure that Ronald later reported he'd got twice that from a Jewish black marketeer who supplied London's hotels. 'Ronald had never made any secret out of the fact that it was quite fair to make money out of the Jews and that this would not affect one's attitude towards them when the time arrived for a general "beating-up",' Roberts wrote. The farmer took a similarly flexible attitude to paying off public officials: 'Creasy said it was against his high principles to give bribes, but it worked wonders.'

Clay was becoming concerned that too much information was being shared about the Fifth Column operation. She attributed this to Burke's habit of sharing excerpts from reports with MI5's regional officers, who then passed them on to the local police. At the bottom of all Roberts's reports, typed in red and underlined, were the words: 'NO ACTION WITHOUT REFERENCE TO BIC LORD ROTHSCHILD'. In practice, that often turned out to mean Clay, working on the correct assumption that her boss's name and title were more likely to impress strangers. But this warning was getting lost as the reports were passed on. Even though Burke was careful always to describe the information as coming from a 'delicate source', the police were inclined to act on it.

And in a rural area like Suffolk, it was hard to keep secrets. In August 1943, Rita was taken aside by an American officer with whom she had become friendly. His commanding officer had told him to stop seeing her. She and Ronald were viewed as 'dangerous people', he said. More than that, they were under observation by the authorities, and had been for the past decade (this wasn't true, at least as far as MI5 were concerned: its file only went back as far as 1939). Rita was doubtful about this – given some of the things she'd said and done that year, she should surely already be under arrest – but the American was insistent. He explained that the authorities were content to let subversives roam freely, so long as they knew who they were.

Rita reported this back to Kohout, who reported it to Roberts. The Austrian added that the last piece of information had been troubling to his contacts: what if MI5 was watching them all the time, and waiting to pounce? Given that this was precisely the situation, it was even more troubling to Roberts. One reason why the Fifth Columnists trusted him was that they had all by now incriminated themselves to him, and not been arrested. If they started to think that they were deliberately being left alone, it wouldn't be long before they suspected he was playing them false.

Clay now put her colleagues on a tighter leash, urging Burke to be more circumspect in her enquiries. Burke, writing to Hughes a fortnight later, said she'd been told he could communicate discreetly with the local police, but must instruct them not to share information with the Americans.

A year into the Fifth Column operation, Marita Perigoe's natural aptitude for espionage, combined with her industrious approach and her commitment to the Nazi cause, meant it was proving more successful than Rothschild and Clay could have hoped. Her MI5 file grew thicker at the rate of a volume a month. Just as Liddell had suggested, they were finding fascists that other searches had missed, and gathering evidence that these people were truly hostile to Britain. But that created a new problem: what to do with them all?

16

'The more violent it was, the better'

By the summer of 1943 it was becoming clear that a German invasion of Britain was no longer a real concern. Two thousand miles away, on Germany's Eastern Front, Nazi forces had begun the year with defeat at Stalingrad. The initiative was now with Russia's generals, who were slowly pushing the invaders out.

Meanwhile in the Mediterranean, British and US forces successfully landed on Sicily. Three years after Hitler's armies swept across Europe and seemed on the brink of taking Britain next, they were retreating everywhere.

The Fifth Column felt the effects of these German defeats deeply. 'The recent Allied successes have had a profound effect upon the group and its numbers are beginning to realise that Germany may lose the war,' an MI5 report of August 1943 read. 'As a result, they vary between the deepest depression and efforts to readjust themselves to the idea of a post-war world which will not be dominated by a victorious Germany. They are therefore beginning to formulate tentative plans to enable them to make the best of what to them is a major tragedy.'

Kohout and Adolf Herzig had already started thinking about the next war. Kohout explained to Roberts that in two decades, Germany would be ready to fight again, and at that point would need spies. His own experience had shown how effective a man inside the right industrial sector could be, but it also showed the importance of implanting them early. 'Kohout's scheme, which he is working out in considerable detail, deals with industrial espionage and plans to penetrate industry with Germans,' the report said. 'Herzig's ideas are similar, and he has suggested organising the Germans in this country on a secret basis.'

Neither had much time for the British fascist movement, but they saw that its members could be exploited for Germany's purposes.

The British members of the Fifth Column had come to fairly similar conclusions. In hindsight, it was clear that it had been a mistake for Mosley to seek election to Parliament, and that he would have done much better to organise the British Union as 'a secret rebel association with the objective of grabbing power by force'.

This informed their planning for the future. 'Eileen Gleave would join any movement that was intelligently planned to gain power ultimately by force,' Roberts wrote. 'Marita thought that the pro-Nazis and convinced National Socialists, unknown to us and probably to the authorities, would undergo a reaction similar to Eileen Gleave and search for some outlet.' Eileen herself told Roberts that 'if Germany lost the war, it was her intention to join the first movement with "guts" and the more violent it was, the better'.

Perigoe felt that the first objective of any subversive group they formed should be 'the penetration of the Home Office. She did not think it would be very difficult.'

While they waited for signs that people were ready to join them, the Fifth Columnists agreed that the best way of encouraging the British people to rise against their government was to identify a common target for hatred. And they knew who that target should be.

'Hilda Leech had lent Marita Perigoe a book by Arnold Leese dealing with Jewish ritual murder, and stated that it would open Marita's eyes to the type of people these Jews were,' Roberts reported. 'Marita thought the book a trifle exaggerated but pointed out that the circulation did a lot of good stirring up trouble and suspicion about the Jews, especially among the uneducated.'

Fred Wynne, Luise Herzig's friend in Wallasey, 'said that it was necessary for every sensible person to refrain from doing anything at the moment that would bring them to the attention of the police. He alleged that he and several friends were systematically spreading anti-Semitic propaganda, and he hoped that their efforts would bear fruit when the war finished.'

These feelings weren't just voiced by subversives. Sir William Strang, one of Britain's most senior diplomats, had got to know one of the Fifth Columnists, and begun voicing his private opinions to her. 'Strang said that he personally hated the Jews and regarded the Bolshevists and the Jews as the two great enemies of all that was decent,' Roberts reported, adding six days later: 'Strang alleged that the Bethnal Green tube disaster was caused by a Jewish pickpocket gang, the ringleader of which netted £200.'

This was an astonishing statement. In March 1943, 173 people, 62 of them children, had been crushed to death as they tried to get into the east London underground station to take shelter from an expected bombing raid. Fearing the damage to morale, the government had suppressed news of the disaster as much as it could. The actual cause was some combination of a woman tripping as she went down stairs wet from the rain and a rush from above as the crowds trying to get into the station were spooked by the unexpected sound of a new type of anti-aircraft battery firing from a nearby park.

There was talk in the aftermath that it was the work of fascists, or Jews, according to the taste of the person spreading the rumour. But the blame for the tragedy, if it lay anywhere, rested with the authorities, for failing to ensure the safety of a shelter that was being used by hundreds of people. Strang, as a senior civil servant, was in a position to know this. Instead it seemed he was passing on a classic anti-Semitic tale – the scheming Jew, plotting and profiting from the death of Gentiles. Rothschild's response to this behaviour, from a man who was responsible for relations with the governments-in-exile of occupied Europe, was less outrage than a weary sigh.

'The members of the Fifth Column are well aware of how to exploit economic disorganisation and the present growing anti-Semitism,' he wrote. 'These facts are unfortunately not apparent to many people in responsible positions who spread anti-Semitism, not realising they are playing into the hands of this type of British National Socialist.'

What worried Rothschild and Clay was that the Fifth Column might be right about the undercurrents of change coming in British society. It was easy to see why. Fascism had risen partly in response to communism. Britain's alliance with the Soviet Union was rehabilitating communism. Might this not inspire exactly the reaction that Perigoe and her friends hoped for?

'There is likely to be a turn to the Left after the war, and this will intensify fascist sympathies, not only amongst toughs and disgruntled people, but also among industrialists who can supply the money and thus produce a situation similar to that which brought Hitler into power,' Rothschild and Clay wrote.

As well as making plans for post-war activism, Eileen Gleave was trying to get her domestic arrangements under control. She had broken things off with Ron Stokes, and given up a tentative bid to reconcile with her husband. She now wanted a divorce, to allow her to marry a serviceman, Cyril, with whom she'd become involved. Special Branch, in one of their periodic updates of her situation, thought the man in question was unaware of her political views 'and would not hesitate to break with Gleave if he became aware of her connection with fascism'.

That didn't stop her from trying to do some spying on the side when she went to visit her fiancé's family in South Wales. On the way, she gossiped with a sailor about his next convoy and with a soldier about his posting, enjoying the fact that she was doing so under a poster that warned 'Careless Talk Costs Lives'. She noted that the iron and steelworks at Port Talbot would be a 'lovely target' and that there was a big works next to the railway station at Neath.

In May 1943, Sir David Petrie, the director-general of MI5, demanded to be brought up to date on the case. He wanted to see what Roberts was bringing in. Rothschild became defensive. It was, he replied, 'exceedingly difficult' to pick out individual reports. 'So many of the hundreds we have contain interesting nuances,' he wrote. 'These, however, are difficult to appreciate without a vast amount of reading.' His fear was that Petrie would weigh in behind those who thought the case a large political risk for a trivial intelligence gain.

Rothschild set out to prove four things: the 'total disloyalty' of the Fifth Column members; Roberts's care never to push someone who was 'on the fence' into joining; the value of the intelligence; and the usefulness of keeping the Fifth Columnists busy. Reports featured Kohout, Brown, and Perigoe and her in-laws.

He was helped by a piece of intelligence that Perigoe had just brought in. She'd been to visit friends in Derby, and knowing that her host was a senior man at Rolls-Royce, had gone through his desk. His company's contribution to the war was the Merlin engine, which powered Spitfires and Hurricanes as well as Lancaster bombers, so she hoped he might have some intelligence to share.

To Perigoe's delight, there was an envelope marked 'Secret', containing the minutes of a meeting of the government's Aeronautical Research Council. Pulling out the invisible ink that Roberts had given to her, Perigoe copied down the entire report, including, Roberts noted, 'exact experimental results and details arrived at by the research sections of each of the aero-engine manufacturing firms in this country'. Neither Perigoe nor Roberts could make much out of the report, which he said 'appeared to be about contra-rotary screws or blades'.

Rothschild and Clay had their own thoughts about the future of the Fifth Column. They saw two options. The first was to prosecute as many members as they could, once it was clear that victory in the war was imminent. The goal would be to expose the extent of the treachery of British fascism, and to discredit the movement. The second option was rather more ambitious.

MI5 had filled the demand for a Fifth Column by creating one, Rothschild reasoned, so why couldn't it fill a demand for a new fascist party as well? He suggested running a rival to the British Union, which would 'absorb the majority of ex-BU members and the fanatical anti-Semites and anti-Communists'. This party could, he then argued, be broken up at the point it became dangerous.

There was a practical problem with this. The operation was currently run around Roberts, 'whose genius at this type of work has made it possible'. Once the war was over, though, many of his old BU contacts would be released from internment, and would immediately point out that he was Eric Roberts, not Jack King. The only way Rothschild and Clay could see their idea working would be for Roberts to use others as fronts, and to stay in the background himself, perhaps posing 'as an agent of an underground German Nazi Party'.

The idea certainly didn't lack ambition, but for MI5 to have actually run a subversive political party that it was also supposed to have been monitoring would have taken the Security Service well beyond the bounds of what any of its political masters would ever have accepted. Even for a supporter of the operation like

Liddell, who took the view that 'there is nothing to which exception can be taken in war time', the rules were different during peace. The idea was vetoed. Meanwhile, the internal pressure to end the operation immediately hadn't gone away. Dick White, Liddell's deputy, favoured prosecution.

But Liddell couldn't see the advantage in prosecuting. The Fifth Column operation cheaply and efficiently rendered harmless people who might otherwise be dangerous to the country, while keeping MI5 informed about their activities. As an alternative to any of the suggestions he'd been offered, he proposed putting more agents into the group, ones who, unlike Roberts, would be able to drift alongside Perigoe, Gleave and the others into whatever new fascist body emerged.

'I am quite sure that after the war we shall have a good deal of trouble from both the left and the right,' Liddell mused, 'and somebody should be thinking about putting in agents at the bottom and writing them off for a year or two when they may rise to a position of some importance or to the post of secretary to some important leader.'

White's problem, Liddell thought, was that he missed the point of the operation. 'Dick I think has still got a general impression that the case is not of much importance and that we are dealing with a pack of hysterical women,' he wrote, recording a remark that was a reminder of the way many men in MI5 viewed the opposite sex. 'Personally I think there is more to it than that. The basic ideas of the people we are dealing with are Fascist and they are working with the tools of anti-Semitism, and anti-communism, both of which may have a considerable appeal. I feel that if we just liquidate this case without putting in some straight agents, we may be losing an opportunity.'

Roger Hollis, in charge of monitoring subversive groups, including fascists, also wanted to shut the operation down. 'He cannot get out of his liberal mind that this is a serious form of provocation,' Liddell recorded. 'In a very mild sense it is, but in the absence of other methods, I do think it is desirable to ascertain something about evilly-intentioned persons.' Hollis's position on his fellow Britons was simultaneously cynical and optimistic. 'Roger's view is that the country is full of evilly-intentioned persons, but that there is no necessity to drag them out of their holes. They had much better be left to rot in obscurity, and will be swamped by the common sense of the community as a whole.'

As the operation continued, so did the debate within MI5 about its future.

On a Tuesday evening in January 1944, Clay, Rothschild and Liddell talked over the situation. Although, or perhaps because, Roberts was the central MI5 officer in the case, he wasn't present. Rothschild was partly preoccupied by a wave of fires on troop ships and transports at ports down Britain's west coast. An officer from B5, the Security Service's investigative branch, had been sent to establish if these were coincidence or malicious – the locations of the fires suggested Irish Republicans might be to blame. A suspect device left after one of the fires was on its way to London for Rothschild to study. In the wider war, Allied forces had landed at Anzio, near Rome, and seemed to threaten the city.

The question facing the group that evening was what to do with the names that Roberts was collecting? In a note to Liddell, Rothschild complained that the case was operating in a 'false atmosphere', with Hollis and MI5's director-general David Petrie doubtful about its value. He set out a defence of the operation against their criticisms.

Was MI5 guilty of encouraging and equipping subversives? 'Yes, to a limited extent, but it is known that these people would have started reorganising and becoming interested in subversive matters in any case.'

Weren't the people they were looking at 'unimportant or un-balanced'? Perhaps, but the question was whether they provided useful information. Hilda Leech, who was both of these things, had nevertheless been invited to join the inner council of the Imperial Fascist League, a group that was supposed to be defunct. She would now be supplying information about it to MI5 without knowing it.

Rothschild proposed that the operation should continue after the war, and that he and Clay should continue running it. His motives were partly personal. He'd been bitten by the intelligence bug, and he knew there was unlikely to be much call for the defusing of Nazi bombs once the war was over. An ongoing operation would give him a reason to stay involved. 'We do not consider that Jack would work satisfactorily for any case officers other than Miss Clay and myself,' he argued. 'This is not said through any spirit of egotism. It is a commonplace for agents to become attached to persons who have been running them for a number of years and to resent any transfer, and we are fairly certain from general but not specific conversations on this subject with Jack that any transfer would be impracticable.'

Whatever the motives, this view of Roberts's feelings wasn't wrong. He hadn't lost his suspicion that the Office had been penetrated, and Rothschild, Clay and Liddell were among the only people in the building that he fully trusted.

In particular, he had lost faith in Maxwell Knight, his first mentor in espionage. Knight had long insisted on running his section from his flat in Dolphin Square. This had merely been eccentric in the 1930s, but now that MI5 was a large bureaucracy, it had left him out of touch. Meanwhile the man who had been a master agent-runner was proving to be a poor manager.

Nearly twenty years after he had been entranced by Knight as a teenager, Roberts was now a grown man, with a successful espionage career in his own right. He had married and started a family. Knight, by comparison, seemed stunted, his second marriage ended. The Tyler Kent intelligence coup was now a long time ago. Looking back, Roberts believed he had been deceived by Knight's 'personal magnetism', only to discover that he 'proved to be an egg shell of a man'.

In his meeting with Liddell to discuss the Fifth Column, Rothschild set out a third course between prosecution and continuity: humiliation. Kohout and the Herzigs could have their British citizenships revoked, and other key figures such as Marita would be called in and told the truth: that far from being cunning Nazi spies, they had been dupes of MI5. But he didn't favour this option. It would, he argued, only push the fascists further underground.

Rothschild was far more wedded to continuation. He pointed out the possibilities. Some of the Fifth Column had said they planned to go to Germany or Spain after the war, and Rothschild proposed helping them to do that: they could provide information about fascist groups there.

Liddell, more cautious, wasn't about to approve MI5 running an international fascist-hunting operation once the war was over.

He simply agreed that it should continue 'for the present'.

In the meantime, Rothschild was so pleased with the Fifth Column that he wanted to take Marita on full-time, and increase her pay to five pounds a week. Not a vast sum, but it was paid in cash and it was tax-free.*

As far as Roberts was concerned, she was already working quite hard enough. At the end of February 1944, she spent six hours briefing him on a visit to internees on the Isle of Man. At the end of his twelve-page write-up of the meeting, he closed, drily: 'I left Marita at six pm. She said that she had more to report. I asked for mercy.'

The pair had met Marita that Friday lunchtime in a pub in St James's, round the corner from MI5's headquarters, and Roberts had been surprised to find her 'not only cold but almost hostile'. The reason for her irritation with him, she revealed, was that she had been certain he had been killed in an air raid two days earlier, and was annoyed to find her intuition had been wrong.

She had been caught in a raid on the Wednesday night and the following morning had gone to see the damage. 'When looking at the devastation, Marita's mind was troubled by a vivid memory of the panelled room of which she had once had a dream, in which she had seen Gestapo members poring over index cards taken from a box,' Roberts explained. 'The conviction gripped her that this room was in one of the flats in King Street which had been destroyed and although she fought hard against this idea, it had filled her mind by the afternoon and her fears had become a certainty. She knew that the room had gone and that several of the Gestapo had been killed, including myself.'

Apparently disappointed in herself more than she was relieved that Roberts was alive, Marita vowed never to trust her intuition again. That wasn't a response which Roberts wanted to encourage – he felt intuition could be a useful sense in an agent. In an effort to encourage her, he told her that their headquarters had indeed been damaged, and his chief slightly injured.

As it happened, there was a grain of truth in this: that month,

---

* In this respect, Marita, an unconscious MI5 employee, was in the same situation as other, conscious MI5 staff, who were paid, untaxed, in cash until after the end of the war.

Roberts's boss had been bombed out of his flat in St James's. It was the closest Roberts had come to telling one of Britain's most industrious fascists that she was working for the country's leading Jew, Victor Rothschild.

17

'Carrying on the struggle'

The early months of 1944 saw two armies in southern England preparing to invade France: a real one and a fake one. While US forces built up along the western end of the coast, and British and Canadian forces in the centre, in Kent, at the point where the Channel was narrowest, the First US Army Group amassed. FUSAG faced a problem unique in the history of mechanised warfare: unless they were tied down, its tank-carrying landing craft tended to blow away in high winds.

As part of Operation Fortitude, the plan to deceive Germany about Allied intentions for D-Day, a vast imaginary force was created that appeared poised to invade Calais. General George S. Patton was announced to be in command of FUSAG. Mobile wireless vans drove around broadcasting to each other, to create the impression of the kind of traffic a real force would create. Tar Robertson's Double Cross agents reported on the activities of this army. At the start of May, one of Pujol's fictional agents reported sighting the US 6th Armored Division in Ipswich. Meanwhile the real spies near Ipswich, Ronald and Rita Creasy, were told that, as known fascists, they had to stay away from coastal areas. Robertson was '98 per cent confident' that he controlled all the German spies in Britain, but the planners were taking no chances.

With most of the Fifth Column, it would be impossible to impose similar bans without revealing that they were suspects. The hope was that the only person they were passing information to was Roberts.

In a country completely mobilised for war, even people in unimportant occupations had access to useful information. Eileen Gleave's work in a laundry had meant she dealt with large amounts of troop kit, and had to send it after them when they were redeployed across the country. Bernard Perigoe's parents in

Hastings were well placed to assess the number of troops in their area, as was Nancy Brown in Brighton.

Hilda Leech meanwhile was becoming increasingly anxious. In April, she called Roberts and asked him to meet her that evening. She was sure that she was being watched. The previous November, she had found herself talking to a smart man who was courting a young friend of hers. She had detected fascist leanings in him, and had begun to reveal her own sympathies when her friend mentioned that he was a police detective. Struggling not to collapse, Leech had asked which bit of London he covered. 'The Edgware Road area,' she had been told – that meant the Park West flat was right on his patch. Leech had refused to believe it was a coincidence and – unsuccessfully – urged Perigoe to stop going to the apartment.

Now she had intelligence that she said was so urgent that she had to risk the phone. Roberts met her at Marylebone station and took her to a nearby pub. She'd learned from her son that the Home Guard were to have special duties when the regular army invaded Europe, and had now been on standby for some time. Meanwhile Home Guards on the east and north coasts had been warned the Germans might try to stage a counter-invasion.

'Mrs Leech thought the news of sufficient importance to warrant the use of the telephone,' Roberts reported. 'She was certain that her mail was being opened and her telephone tapped. I asked her why she was so certain but she could not give me a satisfactory reason apart from a conviction which to use her own words suddenly swept over her.'

It was, Roberts said, 'useless arguing about it' and so he asked instead what precautions she was taking. Leech replied she was 'telephoning everybody she could think of and talking at great length' in the hope that 'the listeners would become so bored that they would report that her conversations were not worth checking'.

Suddenly Leech spotted a tall man standing by the bar. 'Special Branch!' she hissed to Roberts. He replied that she was 'talking nonsense'. Leech explained she was occasionally overcome with guilt at working with him, and asked him if it would be possible for her to become a German citizen after the war, so as to ease her conscience. 'I suggested that if she felt qualms over what she was doing that she ought to offer her resignation. Mrs Leech said that it was not so much the awareness of doing wrong as the fear of being found out and exposed that worried her. She was certain that the information she had given us warranted the death penalty.'

The man at the bar wasn't one of MI5's Watchers, but Leech was quite right that her post was being opened and her calls listened to. This meant Rothschild and Clay knew a huge amount about her personal life, including that she had gone to see a solicitor a few months earlier, complaining that her husband was withholding his affections. 'I am writing to your husband informing him that your instructions show that his conduct appears to amount to cruelty,' the lawyer replied, before going on to explain that 'there can be no proceedings for restitution of conjugal rights for, strange as it may seem, there is no machinery for enforcing marital rights by the court'.

But whatever precautions Leech had taken in contacting Roberts, MI5 would have been bound to hear the call she'd made to him that day. The previous month, when Roberts decided he needed to give a phone number to the Fifth Column, the solution had been straightforward: they were given the number of B1C, Rothschild's department. After all, it wasn't as if anyone who picked up the phone announced to the caller that they had reached MI5. The Fifth Column were told to follow a special procedure when calling, both allowing the B1C switchboard to know how to handle them, and at the same time reinforcing the group's belief that 'Jack King' was merely one part of a much larger machine.

The Fifth Column continued to provide information that would have been unavailable elsewhere. An exchange of interned citizens had been proposed with Germany. One of those listed to go home from a British internment camp saw an opportunity to do a little espionage in the process. 'Some Austrian woman in one of the camps is collecting information from visitors which she intends to take out,' Liddell noted. This fact had been passed to Marita, possibly on the grounds that she and Jack King might be grateful for a way to get secrets out of the country.

Not all the information the Fifth Column provided was reliable. Sometimes people lied to its members, not because they suspected them of working for MI5, but simply to impress them. One of the women that Perigoe was keeping tabs on when she visited the Isle of Man was an Austrian woman in her early thirties called Mirjam Gallagher. Gallagher had spent the years before the war living in London in what might best be described as an open marriage to a half-German actor, with both of them supported by an allowance she received from a former lover in Holland. It was hardly surprising that, at the outbreak of the war, an Austrian living off hard-to-explain sums from a foreigner was suspected of being a spy, and she was swiftly interned.

Her husband Tommy had managed to avoid detention on the grounds that though he was probably a rogue and a swindler, he didn't seem to be working for Germany. But his efforts to secure his wife's release were undermined by her habit of telling people, including one of Marita Perigoe's informants, that she was a German agent. MI5 were never able to completely rule this out, but concluded that she probably just enjoyed telling 'fantastic stories about herself'.

But much of the information was solid, especially about internees' attitudes. One, Ann Sokl, knew about Perigoe's 'Gestapo' connection, and saw in it an opportunity for vengeance. She named an Austrian whom she believed had supplied information to British intelligence and asked for him to be placed on the Gestapo 'Black List'.

'Sokl said that whatever the outcome of the war, the renegades and spies who had helped Britain must be dealt with and taught that betrayal of their own countrymen was not a paying game,' Roberts reported. 'It was odd to think that the preliminary steps to ensure his death were being taken under the noses of the British internment camp authorities.'

In February 1944, Rothschild was summoned to Northampton to examine a crate of onions brought off a ship from Spain, in which something suspicious had been spotted. Before he got there, he had a pretty good idea what the crate would contain.

Decrypted German messages had told MI5 that five bombs had been planted inside shipments of food sent from Spain to Britain. Useful though that information was, it didn't help them locate the devices among the vast amount of cargo travelling this route. The only way to do that was to wait. Sure enough, the steamship *Stan-hope*, which was carrying oranges, had reported three explosions in its hold. Another ship, the *Haywood*, reported one. That left one bomb unaccounted for.

The crate had been placed in an open area for Rothschild to examine it. He had a field telephone, and at the other end of the long wire, one of his assistants, Cynthia Shaw, who sat waiting to record how he disarmed the bomb. Or, if things went badly, how the third Baron Rothschild had met his end.

This wasn't vanity. If Rothschild was killed, it would be important for his successor to understand what he'd got wrong. So he described everything he could see, and everything he did.

'It is a crate in three compartments,' he began. 'The right-hand compartment has onions in it. The middle compartment also appears to have onions in it. The left-hand compartment has already had most of the onions taken out but I can see right at the bottom in the left-hand corner of the left-hand compartment one characteristic block of German TNT.'

German sabotage operations focused on destroying ships and their cargoes while they were in transit. So Rothschild knew this bomb was supposed to have gone off by now. Probably its clockwork timer had malfunctioned, but that didn't mean he was safe. It could well be ticking down as he stood next to it, and all he really knew was that this crate was already overdue to explode.

'I am now going to stop talking and start taking the onions out.'

It was a wooden crate, less than waist high, and someone had started to crowbar it open to get the onions out. They'd stopped when they'd seen the explosive, but Rothschild didn't know how much they'd disturbed the bomb.

'I can now see one block of TNT in the middle compartment, top left-hand side. I can now see another block of TNT in the middle compartment, top right-hand side.'

The onions had swelled and started to sprout during their journey, making it difficult to get them out.

'I am now going to go to the right-hand compartment because I am looking for the delay mechanism or initiating device. There does not seem to be room for it in the middle compartment.'

The TNT was shaped into bricks, three inches wide and five inches long. It was ideal for the purpose of naval sabotage, because it wasn't damaged by water, and it wouldn't accidentally detonate if the crate was dropped or knocked. To set it off, it needed another explosive, and that was what Rothschild was looking for.

'I have come to a block of TNT in the right-hand compartment, furthest away from me to the left of the right-hand compartment. There is a sort of putty-like thing next to it. I am not sure what that is. I am going back to the extreme left-hand compartment because I want to try and get as much TNT out as I can.'

The work was dangerous, but it was mentally absorbing, and Rothschild hated boredom.

'I am now going very gently to take out the cast brick of high explosive.'

There was a block of putty in this compartment as well, and some of it came away when he lifted out the TNT. It was about the same size and shape as the high-explosive brick. He lifted it out and put it on one side.

'I am now going to start doing the same in the centre compartment.'

There were two blocks in there. Rothschild reached out and probed them with great care. 'I shall start with the left-hand one. It seems to be a little loose.'

Both blocks came out. Rothschild assessed his situation. 'I am now going back to the right-hand compartment. The delay mechanism and the starter must be in that compartment, and I am going to start slowly taking the onions away again.'

He could see another block of TNT, and the block of putty he'd noticed earlier, similar to the one he'd just removed. He was increasingly sure that it was plastic explosive.

'I cannot see any delay. I am having difficulty because the onions are jammed right in and I do not want to pull hard.'

The German fuses were beautiful bits of engineering, which allowed their operators to set how many days they wanted to delay detonation. They were wound up, and then ticked down until the moment came to complete an electrical circuit that would start a small detonation. Small, but enough to set off a much larger one if they were connected to the right explosive.

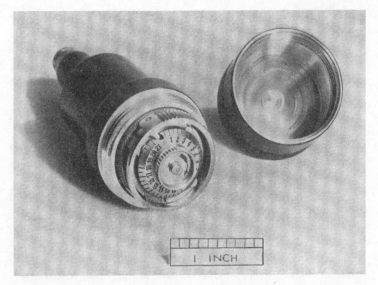

A German 21-day timer

'This is the last block of TNT that I can see and I am going to try very gently to move it away from the plastic with which it is in contact. I do not see the delay or time clock. It must be inside the plastic or possibly buried underneath it.'

Rothschild peeled back a little of the plastic block, to see if he could see a detonator sticking into the TNT. Nothing.

'I have taken out the last block of TNT and I am now going to start looking at the plastic explosive.'

He lifted the putty block out. 'It feels rather heavy.'

One thing at a time. Rothschild carried the blocks of TNT away from the crate. Without a detonator, they were harmless. He returned to the two pieces of putty.

'I am now going to start trying to take this plastic explosive to pieces.'

The first thing he saw was a small cylinder, about the size of a cotton reel. This he recognised as high explosive, designed to set off the TNT when it was itself set off by a smaller detonator.

'I see a primer inside one of them. I am going to try to take that out.'

He was nearly there now, but a slip while handling the detonator would still be fatal.

'I have taken the primer out and I can now see the detonator buried in the middle of the plastic.'

At last, something familiar.

'It is a twenty-one-day Mark II German time clock. I have unscrewed the electric detonator from the Mark II delay, so that one is safe.'

He was confident now, but he mustn't rush. There was a strong chance that the Germans had included a second detonator in the bomb. And there it was.

'I can just see the other Mark II delay inside the other piece of plastic.

'I have taken the other primer off.

'The other detonator is off.

'All over, all safe now.'

When he checked the timers, he found that one had stopped. The other, presumably due to a bump in its unloading and transit, had restarted, and had been due to go off in seven days.

If Rothschild exuded calm at moments such as this, he wasn't always so controlled. Two weeks later, at a drunken MI5 dinner in Liddell's honour at the Hyde Park Hotel, he found himself on the receiving end of pointed remarks from Robin 'Tin Eye' Stephens, the monocled commander of MI5's interrogation centre. Stephens had served for many years with the elite Gurkha regiment, and objected to Rothschild wearing a military uniform without ever having heard a shot fired in battle.

Rothschild, on the other hand, felt that taking live German bombs apart by hand was rather more dangerous than running a prison camp for German spies – or a 'nursing home' for 'miserable seamen', as Rothschild disparagingly called it.

'At one moment it looked as if there might be a stand-up fight,' Liddell recorded. The pair had to be eased apart by David Petrie, the director-general.

Stephens wasn't the only MI5 officer to take against the young aristocrat. While Liddell liked Rothschild, others suspected his advancement was down to his connections, particularly with the prime minister. Although the pair weren't close, few if any other MI5 staff had hosted the Churchills to dinner.

There was also Rothschild's often haughty manner, a product both of his background and his intellect. He knew this was a problem, and proposed a new family motto: 'Quick to give – and to take – offence'.

These things combined when Churchill got word of the exploit with the onion crate. He demanded to know whether the officer concerned was getting any kind of award. Rothschild was offered Membership of the Order of the British Empire, a junior honour that he sneered 'is almost always interpreted as meaning that you have loyally served Paddington Station in a subordinate capacity for over thirty years'. The prime minister, meanwhile, had demanded more information about the operation, and insisted that Rothschild got the far superior George Medal. While gratifying for him, it only fuelled the belief among some colleagues that he was getting special treatment.

Despite the efforts of Robertson and his double agents to suggest to Germany that D-Day might not even come in 1944, it was clear the direction in which the war was currently going. But that didn't stop the Fifth Column from gaining new recruits. In January of that year, Roberts had dinner with a woman who had been recruited by Kohout, Serafina Donko, and her friend Alwina Thies.

Thies was German, but had moved to Britain a decade earlier, when she was in her twenties. She'd come as a clerk, but was now working as a housekeeper for an elderly gentleman in Richmond. She knew that Serafina – Fini to her friends – had a contact who could get information to Germany, and she'd heard something that she wanted to be passed on.

'She had heard from a friend who worked at an important secret factory at Waltham Cross,' Roberts recorded. 'The friend had to work all through the Christmas period, and although Alwina was not enlightened as to what was being made at the factory, she was advised that there were two factories and that their production was essential to the smooth operation of the Second Front.' Thies told Roberts that 'a concentrated bombing of the Waltham Cross area might have excellent results'.

As the conversation continued, Roberts found he was impressed by 'Thies's method of conveying information in an apparently artless sentence. She would mention place X, say something in its praise or to its detriment and then add details of every factory and aerodrome in the vicinity. To me there was no mistaking her intentions but to any listener the conversation would have appeared completely harmless. She permitted herself to express strongly anti-Semitic sentiments but did not refer to or praise the German National Socialist regime.'

As they talked further, he concluded that Thies 'was not Nazi but she wished to help her country'. She hadn't really taken much interest in German politics as a young woman, and had lived in Britain since 1935, but now she was wishing she'd paid more attention.

The outbreak of war had meant she was suddenly subject to considerable suspicion and hostility. In those early days, several people told her that she should be locked up. (Though she didn't know it, she had in fact been considered for internment by MI5 at the start of 1940, but exempted as they had no grounds to suspect her.)

Thies had decided that she must win the trust of her neighbours. The Blitz had presented her with a chance. She helped out the people dealing with incendiary bombs, and cooked and made hot drinks for defence workers. This, it turned out, was enough to prove that she was, in the words of one neighbour, 'a decent German'. Thies treated this condescension with contempt. She explained to Roberts that the British were 'detestable people owing to their insularity and conceit, yet they were soft-hearted and often soft-headed'.

But Thies also told Roberts that all the time she'd been helping her neighbours, she'd been hoping she would one day have the opportunity of doing something for the Fatherland. What the English couldn't understand, she said, was that 'whatever political opinions were held by a German, there was only one loyalty and that was to Germany.'

Her opinions of her neighbours weren't uniformly hostile. At times, she said she liked the British, and when Roberts challenged her on the contradiction, she conceded that, in any event, she preferred the British to the Dutch, 'who were much too hard and exacting'. She was fond of her employer, Mr Martin. 'She laughed and asked me if any German aged 73 would get up early enough to lay the fires and make the morning tea when there was a woman in the house,' Roberts wrote. 'If he knew that she had passed on his Civil Defence secrets to the German SS, it would break his heart.'

But she refused to feel guilty about this. 'Thies told me that Mr Martin was a typical Englishman. He had visited Germany countless times, knew German and German customs but he didn't know the Germans. If he had taken the trouble to get to know them, Thies thought that he would never have left anything of a confidential nature about the house.'

Thies said she had a number of English friends, and they hadn't shown her hostility. 'The trusting nature of the British was a matter of constant amazement to her. She had to admit that she had received many kindnesses.'

Roberts thought highly of his latest recruit. 'I formed the opinion that Alwina Thies is a person who could be a grave danger to this country if in contact with the enemy. Her intelligence is above average.'

Rothschild drew Thies to the attention of his colleague J. G. Denniston, who was in charge of monitoring Germans and Austrians living in the UK. Seeking supporters for the Fifth Column, the peer asked Denniston to send him a note back if he thought the case was a useful one. Denniston obliged.

'This, like many of your cases, is interesting and also disturbing to any feelings of complacency which we may be tempted to harbour,' he wrote. 'Here is a woman who has lived in England since 1935, and has been shown by you to be a strongly patriotic German, ready to do anything for her country without thought of personal gain. Yet for nearly nine years, not a breath of suspicion has touched her.'

Denniston offered a considered assessment of the value of the Fifth Column. 'Your investigations are highly alarming, in that they reveal the presence of violently and actively patriotic Germans in our midst, for the most part unsuspected hitherto; but consoling in that they support the . . . thesis that the Germans are not making use of their resident nationals over here.'

And had he known about Thies, Nevile Bland, the British ambassador whose melodramatic report in 1940 on the fall of Holland had done so much to fuel the Fifth Column panic, might well have been delighted to learn that his suspicions of German servants had, at least in one case, been proved right.

As D-Day approached, the Fifth Column considered drastic action: could they kill General Eisenhower? They knew that the commander of Allied ground forces, Britain's General Montgomery, had set up his headquarters at his old school, St Paul's in Hammersmith, west London. Eisenhower, the Supreme Commander of the invasion, would be going there for meetings. They knew how to get weapons, as Kohout's purchase of the gun the previous year showed. Surely it was worth an attempt?

Though Roberts turned the plan down flat, this was a particularly anxious time for him. Perigoe and Gleave were quite capable of attempting something on their own initiative, and if they did, it would be his fault for failing to stop them. But on the other hand, his refusal to let them act risked raising their already-present suspicions about him. Roberts was increasingly anxious about exposure. He had been playing this role for more than two years now, a long time to avoid a mistake. What if Kohout or Perigoe took it into their heads to follow him one evening? He knew how to spot a tail, but it wasn't easy in the blackout. 'I was close as damn it to exposure and hung on by a hair,' he recalled later.

Meanwhile Rothschild's anti-sabotage duties had increased. 'We spend most of our time preparing people for the Second Front – an endless series of lectures to baboon-like Field Security non-commissioned officers,' he wrote to Duff Cooper at the end of March. 'I have done it for six weeks now, and I'm bored to distraction.'

On 6 June 1944, Allied forces landed at Normandy, successfully establishing a toehold in France. Within MI5, there was pride that Tar Robertson and his Double Cross team, along with the First US Army Group and its occasionally airborne tank landing craft, had successfully convinced Germany that this was merely a diversion from the real attack.

For Rothschild, it was a chance for a change of scene and some fresh excitement. As the Germans retreated, they left surprises behind them for the advancing allies, including booby traps disguised as horse dung on the roads. Rothschild was seconded to the US Army to teach its officers the art of sabotage and counter-sabotage.

After a trip to Rome to view the tricks of the retreating German army, Rothschild arrived in Paris soon after its liberation in August 1944. He took Tess Mayor with him. Officially, she was his assistant, but she like Clay was taking on duties far beyond the secretarial. She was awarded an MBE – the honour Rothschild had rejected – for 'dangerous work in hazardous circumstances' clearing booby-traps around Rocquemont, near Rouen. She filled another role as well. Barbara was still Rothschild's wife, but their marriage had been over for years: Tess and Victor dined out as a couple in Paris.

Victor Rothschild and Tess Mayor, centre, on bomb-disposal duties in France

Alwina Thies's patriotism didn't blind her to the predicament her country was in. As D-Day approached, she had asked Roberts what he thought would happen if Germany lost the war. She was pessimistic. 'The English will not allow us to prepare for the third war as we did for this one,' she observed. 'They will therefore be forced to be harsh, because they know as we know that this result will not be final.'

She told Roberts that she wanted to carry on working for him after the war. 'If she was not allowed to do so, she intended to visit Germany in order to see if she could contact anybody carrying on the struggle. She was certain she could be of help.'

Roberts thought her response 'appalling' for its assessment that force was the only way questions could be resolved. But the question of the future was a live one. When Perigoe and Roberts had begun recruiting, the idea of a German invasion of Britain had still been a possibility that its members could cling to. By the summer of 1944, the question was how long it would take the Allies to reach Berlin.

Within MI5, the success of D-Day saw the return of the argument that the Fifth Column operation should be wound up. Not only had the danger of a German invasion disappeared, there was no longer any risk that one of the members would leak something about the invasion of France.

Liddell requested a 'comprehensive' summary of the operation, and just after D-Day, Rothschild sent it to him. It was largely Clay's work. As well as a brief memorandum, Rothschild and Clay included a series of charts to explain the breadth of the Fifth Column network and its interrelated nature.

Rothschild was now sufficiently concerned about the safety of the operation that he included an extraordinary comment in his covering note to Liddell and his deputy, Dick White: 'You will I think both appreciate that this memorandum and the charts are not entirely suitable for reading on normal office days.' Instead, he proposed that they study them 'at leisure' when no one else was around – at the weekend, or in the evenings.

What kind of document might have been so sensitive that the director of MI5's espionage division couldn't read it at his desk on a normal working day? This must have been a reference to the charts. Rothschild had taken a further precaution with those. They were, he explained, incomprehensible without the unique card index that his department maintained of Roberts's network. When they wanted to look at the charts, Liddell and White would need to ask Clay if they could see the index.

Clay's memorandum was partly a defence of the operation to date, and partly a case for continuing it.

To demonstrate the reliability of Roberts's reporting, his four-page summary of his April 1943 conversation with Brown in which she celebrated the bombing of Brighton was included. Down the margin, sections were marked and numbered in red. Next were thirteen pages of transcript, taken from the recording of the meeting, with more marks in the margin, showing what Roberts had been referring to.

Clay mentioned in passing that Roberts had dissuaded his operatives from sabotage, but the main justification she offered for the operation was intelligence-gathering. 'Its function is to provide the Security Service with records of disloyal and subversive persons and to prevent such persons from carrying out disloyal acts in times of emergency,' she wrote. 'The case is operating so well at the moment that numbers of disloyal persons are coming to light every week.' She cited ten 'subversive or potentially subversive organisations' on which the Fifth Column was supplying information.

Liddell continued his role as the operation's main internal supporter. 'This case is serving a very useful purpose,' he wrote to White and Hollis. 'I would strongly recommend that for the time being it should continue.'

In July, Clay went to see Liddell. With Rothschild's attention focused on Normandy and sabotage, the Fifth Column case was now hers to run alone, and she had a problem on which she hoped for Liddell's advice. 'Jack is rather beginning to get into difficulties,' Liddell recorded afterwards. 'A stage of the war has been reached where he has got to express some rather definite views about the future.'

This was, of course, a live subject within MI5 as well, and one on which there was little agreement. As they came to terms with the idea that things were going badly for Hitler, the natural inclination of the Fifth Column's members was to blame the generals for letting the Führer down. In this, Clay and Liddell decided to encourage them, pointing to the recent replacement of Field Marshal Gerd von Rundstedt, who had been commanding German forces in France. 'We decided that he should quote the instance of Rundstedt's departure, explain that of course the generals are not party men and that although loyal to their country they have not got the same fanaticism as party members,' Liddell wrote.

As Jack King was supposed to be a Gestapo man, he would advocate a Gestapo solution, explaining that his ultimate boss, Heinrich Himmler, was extending his control in an effort to recover the situation.

And Roberts was to continue to urge the Fifth Column against any kind of sabotage. 'He is further to say that defeat, although not yet a fait accompli, must be regarded as a possibility, and that it is therefore important that his followers should take no overt action which would spoil their chances of reforming and playing their part in the preparation for the next war.'

Elsewhere within MI5, Clay had been calling in support. In September 1944, Thomas Shelford, now running F3, the MI5 section that monitored fascist groups, sent a three-page memo setting out his section's view of the operation. He asked his officers to suggest their own examples of where it had helped them. A department that had initially been sceptical about the Fifth Column operation's value was now offering full-throated support.

'I need hardly say that I fully agree with Lord Rothschild's opinion about the importance of being fully informed about these people,' Shelford wrote. 'With the example of Hitler before us, I think that it is dangerous to disregard extremists merely because they can be dubbed neurotics.'

Which was just as well, because two months earlier Kohout had stumbled across a clue to Britain's greatest intelligence secret. One of his recruits was Maria Lanzl, a 32-year-old servant working in Hendon. She had a friend who worked in the household of Superintendent George Hatherill, one of the star detectives of Scotland Yard. This woman reported, correctly, that the headquarters of the Special Operations Executive, Churchill's army of commandos, was in Baker Street. She also offered another nugget: apparently, there was some kind of allied intelligence operation being run out of a country house north-west of London. Kohout passed the information up: surely this was worth investigating? The name of the place was Bletchley Park.

Liddell was horrified. Bletchley was Britain's code-breaking headquarters, the place where some of the world's greatest minds had been assembled in an astonishingly successful effort to read the messages that German and Japanese forces were sending. It was thanks to this work that the Security Service had been confident that its Double Cross operation was believed, and that the Fifth Column wasn't in contact with Berlin. The idea of the resourceful Austrian pottering out to Buckinghamshire on his motorbike to nose around was appalling. It was unlikely that the staff of Bletchley Park were strolling into the local pubs and announcing their success in cracking Germany's supposedly uncrackable Enigma code, but Kohout had already demonstrated his knack for uncovering secrets. It was best to keep him well away. Liddell ordered Roberts to tell Kohout that 'headquarters which are in the country are of no real interest' to the Gestapo.

Kohout's focus, in any case, was elsewhere. 'The group are now concentrating very much on establishing connection with the underground movement in Germany with a view to preparation for the third world war,' Liddell wrote in his diary. Even after fifteen years in MI5, and five years of war, Liddell retained his capacity to be surprised by his fellow man: 'The sentiments of these people are really astonishing.'

And even then, with Germany in retreat, Roberts was still recruiting. In October, Liddell recorded that Joe Bates, an East Ender whose German father had been interned in the previous war, had joined: 'He is about as highly pro-Nazi as anyone we have come across.'

Liddell's desire to restrict knowledge of the Fifth Column operation even within government created its own problems. In December 1944, he received a disturbing report. It was more than eighteen months since he'd been told that the senior diplomat Sir William Strang was among the people who were talking, unconsciously, to the Fifth Column. Strang had now been promoted to the role of British Ambassador to the European Advisory Commission, which was planning the post-war shape of the continent.

Roberts had reported Strang's anti-Semitic views the previous year. But opinions, however unpleasant, were one thing. Now it seemed he was confiding more. Perigoe reported on a conversation Strang had had with Tamara Wilson Crowe, an unmarried teacher who at the start of the war had been vice-principal of a school near Hastings, and was now in touch with Perigoe. 'It looks a little as if he may be having an affair with her,' Liddell wrote in his diary. 'He has told her about his visit to Moscow, about Stalin's refusal to join in the Tripartite Conference, and about a secret mission which he is now to undertake in Brazil.'

This was a conundrum. On the face of it, Strang was a security risk. Whether or not the married 51-year-old diplomat was indeed sleeping with Wilson Crowe, he was certainly telling her more than he ought to be. He had stopped short of divulging the purpose of his mission to Brazil, but he had been rude about conditions in Russia. And he was privy to a lot of secrets. Earlier in the war, Liddell had worked closely with Strang on issues around foreign embassies in London. Even if he hadn't been informed about the Triplex operation, it was probable that he had guessed what was happening. Strang's superiors ought to be informed, and Strang himself ought to be warned to break things off with Wilson Crowe.

But to do so carried risks: Strang might reveal to Wilson Crowe that their conversation had been reported, thus exposing Roberts. And it would be difficult to reveal the issue without revealing internally where the information had come from. An embarrassed Strang might be tempted to seek revenge by attacking the operation as a whole. In these circumstances, the Home Office would be unlikely to defend a controversial exercise run without its knowledge.

'I do not see what I can do with this information without jeopardising the sources,' concluded Liddell.

Besides, what was the benefit? Strang's indiscretions had hit a dead end: that was one of the purposes of the Fifth Column. He could tell Wilson Crowe what he liked, and she could tell Perigoe, but nothing would get closer to Berlin than the Office in St James's.

In Suffolk, the Creasys continued to flourish. They were 'making money hand over fist', Roberts reported after a conversation with Herzig. Ronald's black market operation had expanded beyond agricultural goods and into spirits. He was selling whisky to the American troops at four pounds ten shillings a bottle – more than twice the average weekly wage of a British man. Asked if he was worried about the police, he 'replied vaguely that there were ways and means'. A clue to what those might be came later in the conversation, when he explained that the lower ranks of the police force 'appreciated business initiative'. They had appreciated it enough to warn him that Special Branch were going to pay him a visit just before D-Day, and he had taken a trunkful of fascist memorabilia, including his prized recording of the 'Horst Wessel Song' to his father's house.

But if business was good, there was a new source of strain in the Creasy marriage.

On 15 April 1945, John Randall, a 24-year-old lieutenant in the Special Air Service, was on a reconnaissance mission near Lüneburg in northern Germany when he and his driver noticed large iron gates standing open at the start of a track leading into the woods to their left. Curious to see what this signified, they drove through them. Thirty yards down the road, they found themselves surrounded by prisoners in striped uniforms. Looking at them, Randall realised these were no ordinary prisoners. They were skeletal, starving. Further on he could see others, almost naked, trying to salvage clothes off corpses on the ground. They were so emaciated it was impossible to tell if they were men or women. The memories would never leave him, but what he found it hardest to escape was the smell: a mixture of rotting flesh and excrement. This was Belsen concentration camp.

There were 60,000 mainly Jewish prisoners alive when the British Army found the camp, and another 13,000 corpses unburied. Liberation didn't mean rescue: such were the conditions in the camp, with typhus, dysentery and tuberculosis rampant, that the former inmates continued dying at the rate of hundreds every day. Many were so starved that their bodies were unable to cope with food even when they were given it. In the following month, nearly 14,000 more would die.

The British brought cameras in with them, and the footage, of skeletal corpses lying scattered on the ground, or in mass graves, of prisoners staring about them, apparently in a daze, or weeping as they kissed the hands of their liberators, had a deep effect when it was shown in British newsreels.

Not on everyone: Ronald Creasy told Herzig that, while obviously conditions in the camp had been hard, most of the people there were the 'sweepings of the Polish ghettos' and that it was 'sentimental nonsense' to suggest that these 'Asiatic sub-men' deserved any better. But for Rita, it was the final straw. She told her husband that the Nazi regime was 'rotten through and through', and that she hoped they would never come to power in Britain.

For one member of the Fifth Column, at least, enough was enough.

18

'The Gestapo department'

In June 1945, Liddell took a fortnight's holiday. The war against Germany was over. Victory had changed his workload, but not diminished it. British intelligence officers were now spread across Europe, interrogating their defeated counterparts, trying to understand why operations had succeeded or failed, and what the Germans had been doing without the Allies' knowledge. One young MI6 man, Hugh Trevor-Roper, was attempting to definitively answer the question on everyone's minds: what had been the fate of the Führer? While the US and Britain were confident he was dead, by his own hand, the Russians refused to publicly accept this.

Peacetime brought with it a large administrative burden. Many MI5 staff now wished to return to civilian life. Their exits needed to be managed, their caseloads transferred. For some, demobilisation was complicated by their inability to discuss what they had been doing for the past five years. Liddell was concerned to see them all properly settled.

Others, including Rothschild and Clay, wished to stay in the secret world. Rothschild, perhaps realising that peacetime spying would be less exciting, didn't intend to work full-time. Rather, he sought some kind of consultative role on the scientific side that would allow him to keep his security clearance, and his membership of this most elite of clubs, without the tedium of day-to-day office work. Clay was turning her mind back to her research at the Natural History Museum, but also wished to stay inside MI5.

And then there was the Fifth Column. How should they be demobilised? For months, the question of what should be done with them had been allowed to drift, a reflection of the general unease that senior MI5 officers felt about the case.

Roberts was now monitoring around 500 people, though only a small number of these believed themselves to be working for

Germany. The defeat of fascism in Germany didn't mean that British fascists were ready to give up. Roberts was estimated to be filing a side of foolscap paper in reports every day.

The question of what was to be done with all these people fell into two parts. The unconscious agents needed to be monitored, but this was straightforward. They could be watched in the way that MI5 had watched suspicious people throughout its history. For most, this would be passive, adding the occasional note to their files when they cropped up in a report on someone else, or touched the official world in some capacity. These records would sit waiting against the possibility that they once again became people of interest. A few would be the subject of more intense surveillance, ranging from periodic checks by Special Branch up to the labour-intensive interception of their post and telephone calls.

All this was the ordinary peacetime work of the Security Service, the monitoring of subversive groups. But what of the conscious agents? These people were traitors. They had spent the war years gathering intelligence for the enemy, with great energy and ingenuity. The precedents from similar cases were clear: Irma Stapleton had been jailed on the basis of three meetings, and one act. Gunner Philip Jackson had been sentenced to death for a letter and one evening's conversation. The leading Fifth Column members were on another scale. The files on Marita Perigoe ran across multiple volumes, hundreds of pages. There were recordings of Nancy Brown delighting in the bombing of women and children. Hans Kohout had passed piles of top secret intelligence to a man he thought was sending it to Germany. Surely the prosecution of these people was not simply an option, but a moral duty?

The first argument against prosecution, that it would expose a valuable agent, no longer carried the weight it had in 1941, during the row about the Leeds fascists. The war was over, Germany was defeated. There never had been a ring of German spies to uncover, and there certainly wasn't one now.

Bound up in this was the question of Roberts's own future. Unlike Rothschild's ponderings about what he might find most interesting, this was of urgent practical importance to Roberts: he had a family to support. The Westminster Bank had kept his job open for him during the war, but this offer was expiring.

Petrie, the director-general, seemed to think Roberts could go back to his pre-war relationship with the service: working at the bank by day, doing what else he could in the evenings. 'This may be rather difficult,' Liddell observed.

It certainly would. Roberts wanted to stay inside MI5. He'd worked at the Westminster Bank for fifteen years, bored and unappreciated. War had given him a chance to test himself, to deal in secrets and deception. And he had proved to be exceptionally good at it. That had been what the sacrifices had been for, the weeks away from home, the humiliation of his children being teased for having a father who was a coward. Had he done all that just to go back to where he started?

Added to this was a question of safety. There was good reason to think that the internees on the Isle of Man had worked out that the British Union man Eric Roberts had been a mole. The Leeds group had been held alongside some of those he'd known before the war. Bernard Porter, the Epsom District Leader, lived less than three miles from Roberts's home at Tattenham Corner. During the war, it had been possible to control the movements of these men, but now there was good reason for Roberts to think that his family was in danger of reprisals. Whatever his future, protecting them was his first priority, and he took it seriously. On visits to London, he would tell Audrey and the children to walk at a distance behind him, in case he was spotted by someone he knew. He was reluctant to go and visit Audrey's mother in Wembley, home of many of the Fifth Column members.

Kohout, too, was worrying about his family. When the war had ended, the town of St Pölten, Austria, where his wife Auguste and their son Ernest had spent the previous six years, was captured by the Russians. It seemed that getting home would be little easier than it had been before the peace. Auguste persuaded a Frenchman to smuggle a letter out when he was repatriated, and asked him to post it to her husband. It arrived in July. Uncertain how to get a reply to her, Kohout met Roberts, and asked if the German SS could pass his wife a message, urging her to come to Britain as soon as possible.

He had another favour to ask, too. 'Kohout said that it would be terribly difficult for him to persuade his wife and son that he had played a decent part on behalf of Germany in this war without some visible evidence to that effect,' Roberts reported. 'It was a matter of the utmost importance to him personally that his wife and in later years his son should believe in him.' Would he be able to get some mark of his services?

Roberts, once again finding himself in a similar position to that of the man he was deceiving, was noncommittal, but sympathetic.

There was another area of agreement between the two men. Like Roberts, Kohout didn't want to leave his espionage career behind him. He now proposed to join the Communist Party, and see if he could get himself recruited by Soviet intelligence, as an industrial spy. In reality, he explained, he would be working for the Gestapo. In reality, Roberts considered, Kohout would be working for British intelligence, under the impression he was a double agent when in fact he was, what, a triple agent?

'On the face of it, Kohout's tentative proposals seemed genuine enough,' Roberts told his superiors. 'Kohout worships money, however, and I believe that if he succeeded in contacting Soviet intelligence and he was offered a substantial sum for British Admiralty or other secrets it would be doubtful if the matter would be submitted to us. Kohout would argue in his own mind that by selling the British to the Russians, he would be doing no harm to Germany. I think that he would probably give a faithful report of everything except offers of money.'

The idea appealed to some of MI5's communist-watchers. While questioning Kohout's chances of being successfully recruited by the Soviets, one noted that if he was, 'he will in effect become a very satisfactory type of double agent, as there will be very little risk of his becoming compromised'.

The idea made its way up the chain of command, to Roger Hollis, the head of F section, and a long-time critic of the Fifth Column. He might not have been able to stop Roberts's wartime efforts, but he could certainly nip this idea in the bud. 'I do not think it desirable or necessary,' he wrote.

Three weeks after Liddell returned from his break, there was a meeting to discuss the future of both the Fifth Column and Eric Roberts.

Far from launching a prosecution, Clay and Rothschild were still arguing that the operation should keep running. Their case was bolstered by a note from Graham Mitchell of F3, MI5's fascist department. A section that had treated the Fifth Column with suspicion when Rothschild launched the operation, had now become dependent on it. Referring to Roberts by his codename 'SR', the note explained he was now supplying information on 'almost all the persons of major F3 interest who have their residence, employment or associations in London'. There were cases of 'major interest' that they would have been unaware of but for his work. 'Of those British subjects in or near London who from other sources have been known to harbour pro-German sentiments or a fascist political outlook, there is almost none on whom SR has not supplied something relevant, detailed and vivid,' it said. His reports contained 'no excess verbiage: it is all condensed and it is all immediately relevant'.

There was more praise to come. 'If SR's services were to be lost, F3 would be deprived of its most valuable single source of information.' It named thirteen different cases on which he was the main source, from Oswald Mosley down.

And there was a final point. Germany had been defeated, but for how long? A country that had started two world wars in the space of a single lifetime couldn't be trusted not to start a third. It might look unlikely in 1945, with the country in ruins and divided, but hadn't that been the case in 1918?

'The loss of SR's services would jeopardise future security, not only in respect of a native fascist revival, but also in respect of the growth of a long-term German underground movement preparatory to a third attempt at world domination,' Mitchell's note concluded.

This chimed with Liddell's own instincts. As early as 1943, he had confided to his diary his worries about prosecuting the case. It would mean revealing the operation to the public. Worse, it would mean revealing it to the Home Office. To both these audiences, Liddell feared it would create a 'bad impression'.

'I am quite sure that defending counsel would make a great song and dance about the whole case and that we should be dubbed as the "Gestapo Department",' he wrote, showing a good eye for a headline.

Rothschild meanwhile had sought advice on the feasibility of prosecution. B5, the investigative branch of MI5 with which he'd worked on his sabotage cases, was headed by Leonard Burt, a policeman that the Security Service had borrowed from Scotland Yard.

From his perspective as a criminal investigator, Burt thought a prosecution of the Fifth Column would be difficult on practical grounds: the recordings from the Park West flat wouldn't be admissible in court, so the only evidence MI5 had was the word of Roberts. Defence lawyers would set out to show that he had provoked their clients into active disloyalty, and there was a strong chance that a judge and jury might suspect this was true.

'A prosecution is out of the question,' a note for the meeting written by Clay and Rothschild concluded. So too was any kind of public or private embarrassment of the Fifth Column. 'Exposure, though humiliating to perhaps a hundred fascists, would not destroy the fascist movement in the UK; it would drive them underground.'

Liddell agreed. Rothschild and Clay would get to continue their operation. F3 would get to keep its source. Roberts would get to keep his job. Sir Edward Reid, MI5's banking expert, visited the Westminster Bank, and secured for Roberts another year's leave, giving both him and MI5 the chance to see whether peacetime work suited him.

There was some discussion of rewarding Roberts. At one stage the sum of twenty thousand pounds – more than three-quarters of a million in today's money – was suggested, but rejected by Liddell as 'too much'. Rothschild wrote to Harker suggesting a year's salary, and an official honour, an MBE. The honour never came, and there's no record that the money did either.

And the Fifth Columnists were to carry on, blissfully unaware of the vast amount of evidence MI5 had of their guilt, and the fact that they had been protected by official embarrassment about the way that evidence had been collected.

But not everyone on the Fifth Column operation went unrecognised. For much of 1945, Cynthia Shaw, Rothschild's stenographer on his bomb-defusing runs, was engaged with a particularly tricky task: obtaining German medals for their star recruits. Examples were sourced from the still-raging battlefront. Rothschild's staff at the Royal Mint Refinery were asked if they could make copies. And in January 1946, Marita Perigoe and Hans Kohout were each presented with a bronze *Kriegsverdienstkreuz 2. Klass* – War Merit Cross, Second Class – the German medal for non-combat gallantry. They were, Liddell recorded, 'extremely gratified'. Perigoe announced she would hide hers in the stuffing of her armchair.

Although some German medals were issued after the surrender, it seems probable that the last Nazi medals of the Second World War were awarded, in secret, by the British Security Service, to two people the German government had never heard of. It is also possible that they were manufactured by a subsidiary of the world's most famous Jewish bank.

The files don't record exactly what Roberts told his recruits about who, with the Third Reich in ruins and Hitler dead, had issued these decorations. They don't record the explanation he gave for why in these circumstances they were still needed to collect intelligence for the Gestapo. They don't record who Perigoe thought was still paying her four pounds a week, or her response when whoever it was cut that to two pounds a week.

They do record the meeting that made that decision, on a Monday at the end of November 1946. The subject, once again, was the future of the Fifth Column. Unlike similar meetings that took place during the war, Roberts – now a permanent fixture at MI5 – was present. There were seven names under discussion apart from Perigoe's. Eileen Gleave was still on the list, providing information on resurgent fascist groups. So was Joe Bates, the enthusiastic recruit from October 1944 – 'in touch with a wide circle of pro-Nazi Germans and dual-nationals in the East End'. For most of the list, including Hans Kohout, the assessment given to Nancy Brown was typical: 'Of little interest at the moment but contact should be maintained.'

The meeting closed with instructions to Roberts to make 'every effort' to find new recruits. He was to tell these that 'the remnants of the German Secret Service have amalgamated with the Soviet Secret Service'. The files don't record whether this unlikely story yielded results. In truth, MI5's focus was shifting back to its more traditional enemy. Communism, not fascism, became their primary focus.

Still, if anyone could have convinced someone that he was an English Gestapo recruiter now working with the Russians, it was Eric Roberts. Rothschild and Clay were hardly unbiased, but their description of his work on the Fifth Column as a 'staggering tour de force' seems fair.

Among the many subjects upon which Maxwell Knight had firm views was the capacity of an individual intelligence officer. 'It must be clearly understood that there is a very definite limitation to the number of agents who can be successfully operated by one officer,' he wrote. 'It is my personal opinion that no officer can efficiently look after more than eight agents, and six is probably a better number.'

By the end of the war, Jack Curry estimated Roberts was 'directly or indirectly in contact with some five hundred fascist-minded people'. It was a network some six times the size of the Double Cross operation. Of course, many of these were barely active – the vast bulk of Roberts's time was occupied by a small number of his agents. But it still represented a huge feat.

And not just by Roberts: Rothschild's counter-sabotage department, B1C, was collating the intelligence Roberts brought back, transcribing the recordings, maintaining the private card index, chasing up leads and distributing reports on the Fifth Column members. Much of this essentially administrative work was viewed as women's work, which may be why the woman who ran the operation in Rothschild's absence, Theresa Clay, got little acknowledgement.

But the Fifth Column operation was, in the end, one that MI5 was happy to keep quiet about. It hadn't obviously changed the course of the war. The lives most clearly saved were those of traitors who, had they not found their way to Roberts, might have attempted a treachery that would have risked the noose.

Worse, it had revealed something about Britain that few wanted to acknowledge. The country told itself that, while other nations might be willing to goose-step or bend to the will of a dictator, such things were not in the British nature. But Roberts had found ordinary British men and women who didn't just privately wish Hitler well, but were prepared to risk their lives to help him. Behind them were surely many more who would cheerfully have gone along with fascism if it had seemed the safest course.

It's axiomatic that intelligence agencies are secretive. Often, the secrecy is used to protect people who have risked their lives to pass on information. Sometimes, as with Bletchley Park, the secrecy is aimed at preventing enemies from realising the extent of your capabilities. Both of these were partly true of the Fifth Column case. But there was another reason for MI5's secrecy: embarrassment, both at what they had discovered, and the methods they'd used to do it.

So sensitive was the operation that, when Rothschild submitted his internal history of B1C's war, it didn't contain a single mention of the Fifth Column.

In 1947, Clay, still at MI5 and now signing her own name, sent a note to a colleague, explaining that she was trying to 'destroy or replace by scrambled extracts' all references to original Fifth Column reports. A decade after that, when the Security Service was cleaning out its files, many of Roberts's reports were destroyed. With most of its defenders out of MI5, the Fifth Column operation was being wiped from the institutional memory.

And Roberts? He was already on his way to his next adventure. In 1947 he would travel to Vienna, on loan to MI6, with a mission to get himself recruited as a Soviet agent. The boy from Cornwall had come to London to prove that he was as good as anyone. It had taken longer than he'd hoped, and only those closest to him would ever know, but he had made his way to the very heart of the secret establishment.

Epilogue

'A Great Source of Trouble'

At the end of the war, MI5 had plenty of cause for self-congratulation. It had faced two challenges: attempts by Germany to send agents into Britain, and attempts by people already in the country to get information out. Both had been economically dealt with through the artful use of deception.

The Double Cross operation had gone beyond simply capturing spies, and had succeeded in turning them against their masters, saving lives by deceiving the German high command about the location of the D-Day landings.

Meanwhile the Fifth Column operation had absorbed the energies of those, such as Perigoe and Kohout, who were capable of inflicting serious harm on the British war effort. Had Roberts not posed as their Gestapo spymaster, they might have approached Germany directly themselves, perhaps through the Spanish embassy. Had Berlin had access to genuine intelligence about, for instance, the disposition of troops along England's south coast, it would have jeopardised Double Cross. Worse, had Hitler known the Allies were trying to deceive him about the location of the D-Day landings, he might have guessed their real location, and pushed them back.

And there was an elegance to the decision not to reveal the operation. Like Double Cross, like the cracking of the Enigma Code, it was another secret victory. The Fifth Columnists went to their graves thinking they had kept a great secret: that they had spent the war working for Hitler. They would never know the greater one: that they had spent the war working for MI5.

But there was another twist, one which would hang over MI5 and many of its wartime heroes, including Liddell, Rothschild and Roberts: MI5 had itself been, unwittingly, working for someone else.

Roberts returned from Vienna after just over a year, dispirited.

His mission had been a dangerous failure. He had trailed his coat without success. So far as he could tell, the closest he'd come to Soviet intelligence was a moment when he was fairly sure they had tried to kill him. There seemed to have been little interest in recruiting him.* He had a theory as to why.

Before he'd left, Liddell had hinted that he suspected MI6 might have been penetrated by the Soviets. On his return, the pair had a longer conversation. Roberts feared being put behind a desk, and wanted Liddell's help staying in the field. In the past, the two men had got on together. Liddell had been the main senior backer of the Fifth Column operation. Roberts had gone to him when he was having problems with Maxwell Knight. But this time, he got little support. 'He told me that in an agent context, no man could go on indefinitely,' Roberts recalled. 'Sooner or later, he became tired and jaded, if not blown.'

Liddell changed the subject, and asked Roberts if he suspected MI5 had a traitor. Roberts's mind went back to the suspicions he had long held about some of his colleagues. During the war, he'd assumed that such a person would be working for German intelligence. Perhaps that had been his mistake.

Looking at Liddell, he replied that the Soviets seemed so uninterested in learning about the part of Allied operations that he'd been working in that the only explanation could be that they already had better sources of information. And if the communists had placed agents there, they would have tried to place them in MI5, too, as that was the main threat to their espionage operations.

'He asked me how I would penetrate the Office if I were a Soviet spymaster,' Roberts recalled. 'The question both titillated and flattered me. I said the Soviet agent would have to be a man who by ability and social acceptability could reach a command position. He must have attended the same schools and universities as the rest of the people in the Office.' Despite his years in MI5, Roberts still felt his own social inferiority keenly. 'It would be useless for a chap like myself to attempt the assignment. I said that if the Soviet agent became a member of one or two of the

---

* Because this operation was carried out at the behest of MI6, it remains classified.

most exclusive clubs, I doubted if anybody would be willing to entertain doubts of his loyalty.'

'At which stage would our man be recruited?' Liddell asked. Roberts had no reply. Somehow, a change in the other man's manner made him wonder if he'd gone too far. 'Guy seemed lost in thought.' Abruptly, Liddell brought the conversation to a close, and Roberts was sure he'd overreached. 'We never exchanged another word.'

Roberts thought he'd upset Liddell. But it is possible that their conversation prompted him to take another step along the road to pulling together some thoughts that had been nagging him for years.

In 1942, Liddell confided a worry to his diary: 'There is no doubt that the Russians are far better in the matter of espionage than any other country in the world.' He continued, 'I am perfectly certain that they are well bedded down here and that we should be making more active investigations. They will be a great source of trouble to us when the war is over.'

By 1949, when he spoke to Roberts, he knew that cables between the US and the UK had been sent to the Soviets during the war, probably from the British embassy in Washington. At that stage the inquiry was focused on junior members of staff, but it would gradually shift upwards, and identify a much more senior diplomat, Donald Maclean. With his exposure came that of Guy Burgess – Victor Rothschild's former tenant and Tess Mayor's former flatmate – and, in time, Kim Philby.

As well as being a huge professional blow to the reputation of British intelligence, their exposure was a personal blow to Liddell. Burgess and Philby were men he had trusted, that he'd shared confidences with. And he, the master spy-catcher, had never realised they were traitors. At different times in the years that followed both Liddell and Rothschild would also come under suspicion of being Soviet agents. It would blight their careers. Liddell left the Security Service having failed to achieve his ambition of becoming director-general, and died in 1958. 'I find that I miss him a great deal,' Theresa Clay wrote to Roberts a few months later, 'because although I did not see him very often he was one of those people one liked to think were around.'

*

After the failure of his Vienna secondment, Roberts was brought back to work in the Office. He was given a desk job, handling other people's reports. When he noticed he was being tailed by MI5's Watchers, he became convinced that he too was under suspicion. In 1956, deeply unhappy, diabetic – 'a product of years of anxiety', his doctor judged – and drinking more than he knew was healthy, he was pushed out of MI5.

He seized the opportunity and left the country. He had already helped his eldest son, Max, to take a sponsored job on a farm in Canada, and Peter had followed. Aged nineteen and twenty, they were now living in Toronto. Eric, Audrey and Crista joined them. After poring over atlases in the library, he decided to head on west. When they ran out of continent at Vancouver, they carried on to Vancouver Island, where Roberts was shocked to run into a former MI5 colleague in a restaurant – a chance encounter, he acknowledged, as she seemed as horrified as he was. Sensing he needed to go still further, he took his family to Salt Spring, an island off Vancouver Island.

Eric Roberts on Salt Spring Island

Here, at last, the man who had grown up next to one ocean found peace next to another. It was probably not a coincidence that he settled in a place where any strangers would be noticed, nor that his house overlooked the bay, allowing him to watch the ferries and sea planes arriving – 'an ideal refuge', he called it. His diabetes prevented him from working and so it was Audrey's turn to lie about her age, pretending to be younger to get a job in a bank and support them both. They gardened and, like so many other British spies, Eric took to writing. He researched and published a history of the island, but it was his short stories based on his time in Vienna that came closest to the work that had dominated his life. Each was vivid, darkly humorous and ended with a grisly death.

The Roberts house was a welcoming one, often crowded with their children and their friends, and in time their grandchildren, who adored their grandfather's obsession with playing pranks on them.

But Eric Roberts had one more secret to share. In 1968, a car pulled up outside his house. Inside was an MI5 officer, Barry Russell Jones, accompanied by a Canadian police officer. The Security Service was trawling through its history, searching for clues to traitors that it might have missed. The journey to Canada to interview Roberts was part of that. In the days that followed, Roberts would suffer a physical collapse, as long-suppressed memories flooded to the surface. But on the day itself, he was expecting his visitors. When Jones arrived, he handed him an envelope.

Inside was the name of one of the men Roberts had told Dick Brooman-White that he suspected of being a German agent in 1941. The response had embarrassed Roberts into silence, but his doubts had never left him. He now believed he had got the country for whom the man was spying wrong, but not the identity of the agent.

When Jones opened the envelope, he was able to give the retired spy a final classified briefing. The man whom Roberts had named had confessed to being a Soviet spy four years earlier, in return for a guarantee of anonymity and immunity from prosecution.

The name in the envelope was that of Guy Liddell's assistant, the young recruit who had so entertained his masters on his first day at work with his sardonic assessments of the warnings from anxious citizens about poisoned ice creams and people with German ancestry: Anthony Blunt.

Blunt's confession that he had been working for the Soviet Union throughout the war had been 'devastating' to Rothschild: 'I lost confidence in my ability to judge people.' The pair had been close since their university days, and Blunt had been another of Rothschild's wartime tenants, which of course meant he had also been Tess's flatmate. Worse, Rothschild had introduced Blunt to Liddell, so that he could be assessed for recruitment to MI5.

In his interrogation, Blunt had already revealed some of the missed moments when MI5 might have caught the Cambridge Spies. One of the earliest turned out to have been provided by Roberts, with his 1935 report of an 'excited and urgent' woman wiring money to a Hungarian in Zurich. The Security Service was, as Knight observed at the time, already interested in the woman in question, Edith Tudor-Hart, but it had not been interested enough. The previous year, Tudor-Hart had taken a young Kim Philby to a bench in Regent's Park, where he met a man named 'Otto', who was there to recruit him for Soviet intelligence. Tudor-Hart was, Blunt observed decades later, 'the grandmother of us all'. Roberts's nine-line report on her activities told of one of the few incriminating things MI5 ever caught her doing. When they did eventually put a tail on her in the 1950s, the most they managed to catch her doing was dodging a bus fare.

Eric Roberts died in 1972, aged 65. The *Salt Spring Driftwood* newspaper noted his work as a local historian, his three children, and three grandchildren, and that he was a freeman of the City of London. It didn't mention his membership of seventeen sub-versive organisations, the countless aliases and codenames, his fifteen years as an agent of Maxwell Knight, his sixteen years as an officer of MI5, and his five years masquerading as the Gestapo man Jack King.

But then he'd never wanted recognition, as he explained in 1969, in a letter to an MI5 colleague: 'I regarded my role to be that of success in the cold.'

*

Audrey survived Eric by sixteen years, living to the age of 88. She had been central to her husband's success as an agent, not simply because of the way she ran the family during his long absences, but because of the support she gave him, enabling him to keep his secret and public lives in balance. Through it all, she had remained cheerful, optimistic and devoted to Eric.

Rothschild married Tess Mayor. She proved a much better match for him than Barbara, sharing his tastes and managing his eccentricities, and they went on to have three children. Perhaps the marriage succeeded because they had worked closely in moments of real danger, or perhaps the war had changed some of Victor's expectations of a woman's role. He continued his driven existence, working in research at Cambridge University and for Shell, consulting for the government, and trying, not entirely successfully, to keep his distance from the family bank. If his children sometimes found him difficult or distant, his friends found him relentlessly generous. Dogged by rumours that he too was a traitor, he finally wrote a letter to newspapers in 1986: 'I am not, and never have been, a Soviet agent.' He died in 1990. His memorial was attended by three prime ministers, and featured a recording of jazz piano as well as the more usual sacred music. Tess died in 1996.

Theresa Clay stayed on at MI5 until 1948. As a woman, she was still only ranked as an 'assistant officer'. But there are signs that her role running the Fifth Column operation was formally acknowledged: by 1946, there was a new note at the bottom of Roberts's reports, still typed in red and underlined: 'NO ACTION TO BE TAKEN WITHOUT REFERENCE TO MISS CLAY.'

In 1949, Theresa joined the staff of the Natural History Museum, returning to her study of bird lice, on which she became a world expert, and rising to the rank of deputy keeper in 1970. She was the author of a number of authoritative works, and often cooperated with Miriam Rothschild, Victor's sister. She seems to have been as silent about her wartime work as she was about her private life, but she stayed in touch with her wartime colleagues, attending Victor and Tess's annual New Year party in Cambridge and corresponding with Roberts in Canada, encouraging him to write fiction. 'I always thought you would be able to do this well,' she told him. 'You were always good at expressing yourself.'

Theresa Clay

Richard Meinertzhagen, her . . . well, whatever he was . . . died in 1967, and she defended his reputation for the rest of her life. After her death in 1995, the extent of his ornithological frauds became clear, and it is hard to see how she could have been unaware of them. But not all the birds Meinertzhagen discovered were fakes. The Afghan Snowfinch, which he found in the Shibar Pass in 1937, was genuine. He named it for Clay: *Montifringilla theresae*.

John Bingham, the Maxwell Knight agent who caught Irma Stapleton, among others, stayed on in MI5, working in the counter-subversion section. On the side, he became a crime writer. In 1958, he began mentoring a young recruit, David Cornwell, and encouraging him as an author. Cornwell was a less successful spy, but, under the pen name John le Carré, a much more successful novelist. His greatest character, George Smiley, was based in part on the diffident Bingham. In 2014, Bingham was initially identified as the man behind Jack King, before MI5, in a highly unusual move, revealed the real identity of one of their agents, to ensure that Eric Roberts got the credit he deserved.

*

Cornwell also worked with Maxwell Knight, but was unimpressed. He recalled him as 'part charlatan, part fantasist, but above all, a very cunning control freak. He possessed power of a sort over men and women, especially those he had groomed and manipulated, and that was his kick.' Knight's great days as a spymaster ended with the war, but he stayed on in MI5 until 1961. By then he had developed a second career as a TV naturalist, and would encourage children to get outdoors and be a 'nature detective'. In 1944 he had got married, for the third time, to Susi Barnes, a woman who had worked in the MI5 registry, and shared his distaste for sex. They and his menagerie lived in relative contentment in Camberley, Surrey, for the rest of their lives. In 1965, he was invited to fill a vacancy on the council of the Zoological Society of London, where he found himself working alongside Ivor Montagu, the Soviet agent whom he had set Roberts to tail around London four decades earlier. When Knight died in 1968, his funeral was attended by the great and the good of the world of natural history, and 'lots of men in brown felt hats who didn't really identify themselves'.

Roger Fulford, who had wanted the Fifth Column closed down in its infancy, clung to his dream of a seat in Parliament, but the Liberal Party's fortunes weren't strong enough to deliver it. He stood for election and was defeated twice more. But he found literary success after the war with a series of histories, including several on the Royal Family. To the end of his life, he continued to be argumentative, as fellow members of the committee of the London Library attested.

Laurence Fish went on to become one of the most versatile illustrators of the following decades, known for his magazine covers and his 'Go By Train' posters, which advertised the glamour of towns such as Ayr and Whitley Bay. Away from his commercial work, he was an accomplished fine artist. He died in 2009.

Roberts often wondered what became of Edward Blanshard Stamp after the war. 'My guess is that either he was loaded with honours or was subsequently sentenced to a lengthy stretch in Dartmoor. I hope it was the latter,' he wrote in 1969. It was in fact the former. He had returned to the law and became a Lord Justice of Appeal in 1971.

Sir William Strang, who had spoken so foolishly to a member of the Fifth Column, was protected from the consequences of his mistakes for the same reasons they were. He helped to negotiate the partition of post-war Germany, securing the industrial north-west zone for British occupation, and advising on its reconstruction. In 1949, he was appointed permanent under-secretary in the Foreign Office, the most senior non-political role. His time in the job was to be dominated by the discovery of the Soviet penetration of MI6, something he struggled to comprehend. He was in charge until 1953, and in 1954 took a seat in the House of Lords as Baron Strang of Stonesfield.

Rothschild never caught him, but there had been a spy inside Siemens all along, and an important one. In 1939, just after the start of the war, the British legation in Oslo received a parcel, containing a few pages of typescript and a cardboard box. The box held a trigger tube, for German anti-aircraft shells. The pages covered a huge range of German scientific research, from radar to torpedoes. Because some of its anonymous claims were demonstrably wrong, most in MI6 were inclined to discount the whole. But not the Secret Service's scientific adviser, Reginald Jones. He was to use it as a crib sheet through the war, finding it proved right again and again.

But it would be another decade before he discovered the source. Hans Ferdinand Mayer was a 45-year-old scientist working for Siemens in Germany. In the inter-war years he developed a close friendship with an Englishman, Cobden Turner, who helped him get a Jewish schoolgirl out of Germany. Feeling that Turner's behaviour was representative of English decency, he decided to help Britain. His offer of further information was never taken up, and in 1943 he was arrested by the Gestapo for listening to the BBC, and sent to Dachau, where he was lucky to survive the war. In 1953, a chance meeting between Jones and Turner led the MI6 scientist to realise that Mayer must have been his secret helper. The two men met in 1955, but agreed to keep Mayer's secret.

He died in 1980. Jones was clear on the value of his work: 'As the war progressed and one development after another actually appeared, it was obvious that the report was largely correct; and in the few dull moments of the war I used to look up the Oslo report to see what should be coming along next.'

Schmidt's Restaurant, frequented by Walter Wegener in the 1920s as he sought to connect with his late father's German side, stayed in business for several more decades, despite a reputation for some of the grumpiest waiting staff in London. It gained brief notoriety in 1951 when the diplomat Donald Maclean celebrated his 38th birthday with lunch there, before fleeing the country that evening after a tip-off that he was about to be unmasked as a Russian spy.

Dorothy and Walter Wegener lived out the rest of their lives in Whitstable. By late 1944, when Walter was released from internment, Theresa Clay noted that Dorothy's case file had reached ten volumes. But she did find a man, marrying William Ashmore, a lorry driver, in 1946. She died in 1980, two years after Walter.

Bernard and Marita Perigoe divorced after the war – he'd been in prison most of their married life in any case. He remarried in 1949, and had two daughters. He remained active in politics, getting elected as a councillor in Harrow, but his time behind the wire had at least cured him of his enthusiasm for fascism: he became a communist. He told his friends that he'd been behind enemy lines during the war. Which, in a sense, was true.

Marita carried on reporting to MI5 until at least 1947. In 1949, having apparently accepted that Britain wasn't on the brink of a fascist revolution, she boarded RMS *Strathaird*, bound for Sydney to join her mother, May. A year after arriving there, and still only 36, she married John Gordon McKenzie, a 63-year-old civil servant who was in charge of schools in New South Wales. In November 1952, McKenzie went into his office on a Saturday. When he hadn't returned home in the afternoon, an anxious Marita called the building's caretaker, who went to McKenzie's office and found him dead on the floor from a heart attack. Flags were flown at half mast in schools throughout the state.

There was little call for picture restoring in Australia, so Marita became a costume designer for the theatre, something she turned out to be rather good at. Like Adolf Hitler, she preferred traditional styles of painting, and though pleased that her niece – and namesake – Marita Brahe had decided to become an artist, she was unimpressed that she followed the modern style, and tried, unsuccessfully, to correct her.

She married for the third time in 1958 to Edward Jackson, who was also in the costume business. He died nine years later. Her fourth and final marriage was to David Burney, an actor. Marita sold her business, and the couple returned to England in the late sixties, where they lived in a thatched cottage in the countryside once painted by John Constable, an artist of whom Marita approved. She died in 1984, in a residential park for the elderly outside Ipswich, not far from Ronald Creasy's farm.

Marita Perigoe

Hitler's forces may never have made it to west London, but Eileen Gleave did, at least briefly, hook herself a nice blond SS man. In December 1946 she visited a prisoner-of-war camp near Shepherds Bush, west London, where some Germans were still being held, to ask whether any would be allowed to join her for a Christmas celebration – the camp allowed its inmates out on a day-release basis. The prisoner who showed her into the guard room, and who gladly accepted her invitation, was Joachim Kirmse, a German paratrooper who had been captured in 1943 in North Africa. After a spell in a prisoner-of-war camp in the US, he had been transferred to England after the peace. There the authorities tried to establish his real story – he had boasted to somebody that he'd been a Gestapo lieutenant before blotting his copy book and transferring to the regular army.

Kirmse's Christmas in Gleave's flat had a profound effect on him. There were eight people at the party, including Marita Perigoe, who was living in the flat opposite at the time, but Kirmse said later that he and Gleave 'felt drawn to each other'. Ignoring the others, they talked intently about their lives. 'In Eileen, I found the woman with the perfect heart,' he said. 'She is without blemish.'

If Gleave was delighted with Kirmse, the man she was then living with, a fascist named Oliver Gilbert, was less pleased. There was a 'mutual misunderstanding' between them, Kirmse judged. Or perhaps Gilbert understood too well. In any case, he moved swiftly out.

Driven by love, and a desire to avoid returning to Germany, Kirmse absconded from the camp in April 1947 and moved in with Gleave. For three months he hid out in her flat, staying quiet while she was at work and, by his account, avoiding contact even with Marita.

MI5 knew, or suspected, that Gleave was hiding Kirmse for most of this time. But there seemed no great urgency in retrieving him. Theresa Clay, still running the Fifth Column operation, may have hoped he would lead them to a more interesting subversive group. By July, it was decided it was time to round him up. Just after 7 a.m. on a Monday morning, Detective Inspector George Smith of Special Branch knocked on Gleave's door.

She let the policeman into her kitchen, but denied having seen Kirmse since April. Smith noticed there were two dirty cups on the table and asked if he could have a look around. Eileen hesitated, and then agreed. 'I went to a bedroom situated at the front of the premises and noticed that the large divan bed there had apparently been slept in by two persons,' Smith reported. 'I endeavoured to open the wardrobe door and, after exerting considerable pressure, was successful. I found a man standing inside, naked.'

'Oh you bloody fool,' Gleave said to Kirmse. 'Why didn't you clear out when you had the chance?'

Gleave was prosecuted for harbouring an escaped prisoner, but the magistrate took pity, partly because it was only after Kirmse's capture that she learned another of the reasons for his reluctance to return to Germany: he had a wife and five children there. She was bound over to keep the peace for twelve months.

In March 1950, Gleave followed Perigoe to Australia, and there the records for her end, though Marita's niece recalls a woman named Eileen helping her with the sewing for Marita's costume company.

Hilda Leech and her husband retired to a smallholding in Devon, and then to a small village outside Launceston, Cornwall. After the 1956 Suez Crisis, she wrote to Parliament suggesting that the prime minister, Anthony Eden, should be hanged. The following year, the local police reported to MI5 that 'she has, on occasions, acted in a peculiar manner'.

MI5's director-general wrote back: 'Mrs Leech is known to us and in the past had a number of fascist connections. At present we tend to the view that the balance of her mind is disturbed.'

Ronald Creasy never gave up on fascism. He and Rita had another child, a daughter, and lived out their days in the small town of Eye in Suffolk, with a weathervane over their house in the shape of the British Union's lightning bolt logo. He was unashamed of his beliefs, giving regular interviews about them. He died in 2004. His gravestone describes him as '1939 BU Councillor, District Leader and Prospective Parliamentary Candidate, Eye Division'. It goes on: 'Individual thinker, pantheist and man of spirit'. Rita died in 2008.

The Soviet Union never acknowledged responsibility for the Katyn massacre. After its collapse, the Russian government began to release the papers around both the killings and the subsequent cover-up. There are memorials to the dead around the world.

After a journey in which it looked briefly as though their British papers might not be enough to get them out of Austria's Russian sector, Auguste and Ernest Kohout made it home to England in August 1945, six years after they'd left. The reunion wasn't easy: Ernest didn't know his father, and Hans was unused to having a child in the house. But he was keen to show his wife that he'd been trying to help the German cause. His medal may have helped, and in March 1946, he took her to meet Roberts. Kohout handed over a bundle of reports, apologising for their poor quality but saying that he 'would be proud to do anything in his power to help the German Secret Service'. They discussed Kohout's theories about the future of global politics. 'Mrs Kohout looked impressed by her husband's mental gymnastics,' Roberts reported. 'Both Kohout and Mrs Kohout invited me to spend a weekend with them.'

Hans and Auguste had another son, Martin, in 1947. Putting his days as a fascist behind him, Hans went into business with a Jewish friend, Harry Green. With Green handling the sales while Hans managed the production side, the aluminium foil company they set up together was a great success. In due course Ernest went to work there, stopping in the pub with his father on the way home most days. Perhaps fearing that his wartime activities would catch up with him, Hans would warn his sons that, as an immigrant family, they must take care never to get on the wrong side of the authorities. But he nevertheless stayed in touch with some of his friends from the war, visiting the Creasys in Suffolk with his family. He died in 1979.

Auguste survived her husband by seventeen years, dying in 1996. When Ernest went through his father's things, he found a red box containing a Nazi medal. Auguste assured him it had been given to her father as a mark of his long service on the Austrian railway. Amused, Ernest hung his father's War Merit Cross on the wall of his toilet.

Hans Kohout's Kriegsverdienstkreuz

Note on Sources

It has been possible to tell this story thanks to the decision to open a selection of MI5's historic files. This process, which has been going on for more than a decade, turns out to be like slowly tipping thousands of jigsaw pieces onto the floor. Some pieces belong to a well-known part of the picture, filling in holes with fascinating new details. Some only add mysteries, apparently fitting nowhere at all. And sometimes, a piece lands that suddenly reveals how a previously empty space in the puzzle fits together.

The Marita Perigoe file, opened in February 2014, was such a piece. Before MI5 files are released to the public, they are carefully read, in case they reveal operational details, such as the names of informants: more than seventy years after the last note was made on Perigoe, parts of her file are still classified. The MI5 staff checking this file realised that they were looking at the description of an operation they knew nothing about.

Even at that point, its scale was still unclear. A few months later, several more jigsaw pieces landed, revealing Eric Roberts as the agent at the heart of this discovery. And as with a jigsaw, the sudden understanding of one part of the puzzle led to the re-examination of previously mysterious pieces, many of which it was now possible to fit together. Files that had been open for years were no longer mildly interesting individual events, but part of a greater story.

This book is the result of putting together those pieces. It hasn't been straightforward. I have been able to find no living witnesses to this operation, and most of those involved in it were unaware of its true nature. Except for one extraordinary letter that Eric Roberts wrote to a former colleague at MI5 following Barry Russell Jones's 1968 visit, I can find no evidence that any of those who did understand what was happening ever spoke about it. (Though sometimes this makes things easier. Where I have been able to compare tales told later by MI5 officers with the contemporary records, I have found, perhaps unsurprisingly, some evidence of embellishment and even on one occasion the wholesale borrowing of someone else's adventure. Spies do lie.)

So I have had to rely on the files, the notes that those involved wrote at the time. This presents a series of challenges to the researcher. In the decades after the war, the Security Service destroyed many of its older records. Largely this process of 'weeding' was because the information was considered unimportant, but I have found one hint of a deliberate effort to destroy references to the Fifth Column operation. The files that remain are often incomplete, and there are others that either no longer exist or haven't been opened. Within the available paperwork, there are questions and doubts. MI5 had to rely, in part, on gossip collected and passed on to them, generally by policemen. One can detect a tendency to accept such reports uncritically. In some files, a salacious morsel is repeated in note after note until it has hardened into unquestioned fact.

All this means that writing this book has been a process of trying to describe the picture shown by a jigsaw puzzle for which I do not have all the pieces. There are mysteries. I am hopeful that in the future, files will be opened that solve some of them. I am also conscious that in the future information may be uncovered which reveals that I have mistaken some aspect of this operation.

What we do have are transcripts of conversations in the Park West flat, as well as the notes from shorthand that were taken by Special Branch in the Philip Jackson and Irma Stapleton cases. Every word in the book that appears inside quotation marks was either spoken or written by the person to whom it was attributed.

Acknowledgements

In writing this book, which deals with the worst side of human nature, I have had encounter after encounter with the best side. I've enjoyed warm hospitality on two continents, seen my questions dealt with patiently by archivists and researchers, and been carried along by the endless support of colleagues, friends and family. However, any blunders in the book are my responsibility alone.

My first thanks must go to Eric Roberts's children, Crista McDonald and Max Roberts. Talking about secrets they had kept for decades wasn't easy for either of them, but the conversations we had were invaluable. I'm grateful too for the welcome that they and their spouses, Mick and Rosemary, gave me in Canada, and for the insights and assistance of Eric's grandchildren, Heather, Stephanie, Rosanne and Marilyn. Eric's wider family, Robin, Roger and Richard Kennard, and Eveleen Thorne, offered me their memories of the man, as did John Dickson, son of his friend Jimmy.

If the Roberts family found raking over the details of this story difficult, it was even harder for the relatives of the Fifth Column. I'm particularly grateful to Ernest Kohout for his willingness to give me lunch and talk about his father, when others might have slammed the door in my face. Marita's nephew and nieces in Australia and Britain – David Brahe, Diana Brahe, Marita Ogburn and Sara Morren – bore the shock well, and offered me their memories of their aunt. Leslea Linnett put me in touch with Louise Percival, who went above and beyond in helping me to trace the story.

Much of my time working on this book has been spent reading old pieces of paper, and I'm eternally in the debt of Richard Dunley and all the staff at the National Archives, Melanie Aspey at the Rothschild Archive, Andrew Riley and Heidi Egginton at Churchill College, Cambridge, James Elder at the BT Archives,

Sally Cholewa at the RBS Archives, and the staff at the Weiner Library, the Natural History Museum Archives and the London Metropolitan Archives.

Jean Bray agreed to let us use her late husband Laurence Fish's wonderful bomb diagrams. Michelle Blagg shared her research into Victor Rothschild and the Royal Mint Refinery. Michael Denton confirmed that spies had indeed met in his father's basement. Mark Cocker and Robert Prys-Jones gave insights into the enigmatic Theresa Clay, and their thoughts on Richard Meinertzhagen. Katie Harrison gave me a vital introduction. Robin Lumsden instructed me on German medals. Harry Patel arranged for me to visit 499 Park West. Stephen Dorril and Christopher Andrew both offered their perspectives on the operation, and Jonathan Evans gave a professional view. Grace Hailstone went through the Slade School of Art archives and helped me find the picture of the woman we believe to be the young Marita Brahe. I'm grateful too for the assistance of some people who would prefer not to be named.

This tale started as a piece for Bloomberg News, which was deftly edited, as so much of my work has been over the last fourteen years, by Eddie Buckle. In the course of the subsequent 100,000 words, my colleagues Alex Morales, Tim Ross, Svenja O'Donnell, Kitty Donaldson, Andrew Atkinson, Alan Crawford, Emma Ross-Thomas and Flavia Krause-Jackson put up with my absences and gave useful advice. Reto Gregori managed not to roll his eyes when I mentioned I was writing yet another book, and John Fraher allowed me to disappear for two months in the midst of the chaos of 2016. Ed Johnson cheerfully agreed when I asked him to help me find a document in the State Library of New South Wales.

The best thing about my journalistic career has been that I have spent so much of it in good company. Both the Parliamentary Press Gallery and Honourable Company of Archive Reporters are people who make it a joy to go to work. I'm especially grateful for the encouragement and advice of Ben Macintyre, Tim Shipman, Peter Hennessy, Andrew Sparrow, Rafael Behr and the first person to suggest that I should write this book: Ross Hawkins. Many people covered the Eric Roberts story when the Fifth Column files were opened in 2014. Sanchia Berg's 2016 BBC documentary

'The Spy Who Suffered' went into more detail about his pre- and post-war work, including his time in Austria.

I wouldn't have known how even to begin such a project without the advice and support of my agent, Sally Holloway, who got the idea instantly and held my hand every step of the way. At Weidenfeld & Nicolson, Alan Samson was an enthusiastic and trusting publisher, Simon Wright did a brilliant job on the text, and John English saved me from my own mistakes.

Throughout, Phil Cowley, Thomas Penny and Michael Paterson were good friends, who gave encouragement and advice, and offered vital insights on early drafts, as did Henry Hemming. To discover that someone else is working on a book involving some of the same people as you, as Henry and I did in the summer of 2015, is a tense moment. I am glad that we have become comrades rather than rivals.

My uncle, Chris Squire, has always encouraged me in my writing. For this book, he even visited the archives with me and helped me work my way through the hundreds of files.

My father, David Hutton-Squire, believed in this book from the start. He read archive files and manuscript drafts, catered for me for a week in Yorkshire while I holed up in his dining room hammering out words, and even paid for me to upgrade my seat to one with room for my long legs on a flight to Canada. For these things, but much more for everything else, I will never properly be able to express my gratitude.

My sons, Fraser and Cameron, have put up with absences and lost weekends driven alternately by this book and by Britain's unending political turmoil. They have offered me their thoughts on the title and the cover, as well as leaving drawings of spies on my desk. They have, throughout, been my great joy.

My final thanks go to my wife, Sophie, who despite having to put up with authors all day is prepared to put up with me, too. Without her patience, support, advice and love, I'd never have got past page one.

Bibliography

Andrew, Christopher, *The Defence of the Realm*. Allen Lane, 2009.

Baker, Rob, *Beautiful Idiots and Brilliant Lunatics: A Sideways Look at Twentieth-Century London*. Amberley Publishing, 2015.

BBC, *The Politics of Thinking*, 1984.

Bishop, Patrick, *Battle of Britain*. Quercus, 2009.

Bowen, E. J., rev. K. D. Watson, 'Hartley, Sir Harold Brewer (1878–1972)', *Oxford Dictionary of National Biography*. Oxford University Press, 2004.

Bower, Tom, *The Perfect English Spy: Sir Dick White and the Secret War 1935–90*. William Heinemann, 1995.

Carter, Miranda, *Anthony Blunt: His Lives*. Macmillan, 2001.

Cathcart, Brian, *The News From Waterloo*. Faber & Faber, 2015.

Charnley, John, *Blackshirts and Roses*. Brockingday, 1990.

Colville, John, *The Fringes of Power: Downing Street Diaries 1939–1955*. Hodder & Stoughton, 1985.

Curry, John, *The Security Service, 1908–1945*. Public Record Office, 1999.

Davies, D. Seaborne, 'The Treachery Act, 1940', *Modern Law Review* 4:3 (1941): 217–220. JSTOR. https://www.jstor.org/stable/1090487.

Dorril, Stephen, *Blackshirt: Sir Oswald Mosley and British Fascism*. Viking, 2006.

Duffy, Peter, *Double Agent*. Scribner, 2014.

Fairn, Duncan, 'Maxwell, Sir Alexander (1880–1963)', *Oxford Dictionary of National Biography*. Oxford University Press, 2004.

FBI, 'Spies Caught, Spies Lost, Lessons Learned'. 3 December 2007: https://archives.fbi.gov/archives/news/stories/2007/december/espionage_120307.

Feldenkirchen, Wilfried, *Siemens 1918–1945*. Ohio State University Press, 1999.

Gardiner, Juliet, *Wartime*. Headline, 2004.

Garfield, Brian, *The Meinertzhagen Mystery*. Potomac Books, 2007.

Gillman, Peter and Leni, *Collar the Lot!* London: Quartet, 1980.

Glover, Michael, *Invasion Scare 1940*. Pen and Sword, 1990.

Gottlieb, Julie V., *Feminine Fascism*. IB Tauris, 2003.

Griffiths, Richard, *Patriotism Perverted*. Constable, 1998.

Hastings, Max, *The Secret War*. HarperCollins, 2015.

Hemming, Henry, M. Preface, 2017.

Hodgkin, Alan, *Chance and Design: Reminisecences of Science in Peace and War*. Cambridge University Press, 1994.

Jones, R. V., *Most Secret War*. Hamish Hamilton, 1978.

Koehler, Hansjürgen, *Inside the Gestapo: Hitler's Shadow Over the World*. Palls Publishing Co., 1940.

Macintyre, Ben, *Double Cross*. Bloomsbury, 2012.

Masterman, J. C., *The Double Cross System*. Pimlico, 1995.

Masters, Anthony, *The Man Who Was M*. Basil Blackwell, 1984.

Maugham, W. Somerset, *Strictly Personal*. Doubleday, Doran & Co., 1941.

McKinstry, Leo, *Operation Sealion*. John Murray, 2014.

Mitchell, Andrew Martin, 'Fascism in East Anglia : the British Union of Fascists in Norfolk, Suffolk and Essex, 1933–1940'. PhD thesis, 1999.

Mullally, Frederic, *Fascism Inside England*. Claud Morris Books, 1946.

STV News. 'WWII Spycatchers Revealed After 70 years', 3 September 2009: https://stv.tv/news/tayside/120593-wwii-spycatchers-revealed-after-70-years/

Orwell, George, 'Antisemitism in Britain', *Collected Essays, Journalism and Letters, Vol. III*. Secker & Warburg, 1968.

Pugh, Martin, *Hurrah for the Blackshirts!* Jonathan Cape, 2005.

Roberts family archive, n.d.

Rose, Kenneth, *Elusive Rothschild*. Weidenfeld & Nicolson, 2001.

Rothschild, Hannah, *The Baroness*. Virago, 2012.

Rothschild, Miriam, *Dear Lord Rothschild*. Balaban, 1983.

Rothschild, Victor, *Meditations of a Broomstick*. William Collins & Sons, 1977.

—, *Random Variables*. William Collins Sons & Co., 1984.

—, BBC *Desert Island Discs* interview, 7 July 1984.

Stubley, Peter, *Calendar of Crime*. The History Press, 2014.

'The Red Book: Membership list of Captain Ramsay's Right Club', 1939.

Thurlow, Richard, *Fascism in Britain*. Blackwell, 1987.

US Holocaust Museum, n.d.: https://www.ushmm.org/wlc/en/article.php?ModuleId=10006188

US War Department, *Instructions for American Servicemen in Britain*. Washington DC, 1942.

van Straubenzee, Alexander, 'The Gate of Hell', *Daily Telegraph*. 10 April 2005.

Walton, Calder, *Empire of Secrets*. William Collins, 2013.

West, Nigel and Oleg Tsarev, *Triplex: Secrets from the Cambridge Spies*. Yale University Press, 2009.

West, Nigel, *The A–Z of British Intelligence*. Scarecrow, 2005.

—, *The Guy Liddell Diaries, Volume I: 1939–1942*. Routledge, 2005.

Wilkinson, Dr Oliver, 'Review of Prisoners of Britain: German Civilian and Combatant Internees During the First World War', *Reviews in History*, 2014.

Notes

KV refers to Security Service files, HO to Home Office files, CAB to Cabinet Office files, FO to Foreign Office files and HW to GCHQ files, held at the National Archives in Kew.

3 two months pregnant: KV2/680.
3 'not nursed the people': KV2/680.
4 'like 40,000 others': Martin Pugh, *Hurrah for the Blackshirts!* (2005).
6 'Hitler's invasions of Poland': HO 186/278, 'If the Invader Comes' (1940).
7 'Britain's pocket Fuehrer': *Daily Express*, 24/5/1940.
7 'Precautions that should': *Daily Mirror*, 24/5/1940.
7 'A cheap place': KV 2/680.
9 The enemy planes: *Yorkshire Post*, 5/8/1940.
10 'I am not a copper': KV 2/680.
11 'Although these people': KV 2/680.
11 'They were seized with unparalleled speed': *Chicago Daily News*, 15 April 1940, quoted in Michael Glover, *Invasion Scare 1940* (1980), and Peter and Leni Gillman, *Collar the Lot!* (1990). Also in *Birmingham Mail*, 16/5/1940.
12 On Friday 23 August: The file on the case says Friday 24 August 1940, and carries this error through to subsequent days. I have assumed that MI5 got the days of the week right, and the dates of those days wrong.
12 'It was impressed on him very strongly': KV 2/680.
15 One of those fights: John Charnley, *Blackshirts and Roses* (1990).
18 'I was perpetually hungry': Roberts family archive.
19 'an excellent worker': Roberts family archive.
21 'mannish woman': Julie V. Gottlieb, *Feminine Fascism* (2003).
21 'the saviour of his country': Christopher Andrew, *The Defence of the Realm* (2009).
21 'Bloody Fools': Henry Hemming, *M* (2017).
23 'The family fortune': Anthony Masters, *The Man Who Was M.* (1984).

23 paid work of a patriotic nature: Hemming (2017).

25 'I read Kipling's infernal *Kim*': Roberts family archive.

25 'unscrupulous and dishonest person': KV 4/227 Maxwell Knight, 'History of the operations of MS during the war 1939–45'.

28 Roberts showed promise: Roberts family archive.

28 one even followed Knight's path: Hemming (2017).

29 Roberts would finish his day: Roberts family archive.

29 Knight was now in the position: Hemming (2017).

29 He was far from alone: Pugh (2005).

30 'I grew to hate': Roberts family archive.

32 'Parliamentary government is conducted': *Daily Mail*, January 1934.

33 'I am not very sympathetic': Quoted in Frederic Mullally, *Fascism Inside England* (1946).

33 'A woman who intervened': Quoted in Mullally (1946).

34 'The almost simultaneous occurrence': John Curry, *The Security Service, 1908–1945* (1999).

34 'I am anxious to see you': Roberts family archive.

34 'Get in touch with our friends': Roberts family archive.

34 'a small regular sum': KV 4/227.

35 'retaining fee': Roberts family archive.

35 'The officer should take an interest': KV 4/227.

36 'Nothing is too small': Roberts family archive.

36 'They will obviously regard': Roberts family archive.

36 'Don't utter a single word': Roberts family archive.

37 'One has to tread very warily': Roberts family archive.

37 'She is of interest': Roberts family archive.

39 'Capt. Hick struck me': KV 2/2145.

39 'the most loyal pro-German': KV 5/2.

39 'my best and safest plan': KV 2/1343.

39 'To be an accomplished double-crosser': Roberts family archive.

41 'Roberts is thoroughly familiar': KV 2/3874.

42 'They spent the whole evening': KV 2/680.

42 'where it would lead to British soldiers': KV 2/680.

43 'the other members present': KV 2/680.

43 the bombs had been meant: Patrick Bishop, *Battle of Britain* (2009).

43 'big raid': John Colville, *The Fringes of Power* (1985).

44 'too inept to be much use': KV 2/680.

44 'talked somewhat wildly': KV 2/680.

44 'any act which is designed': D. Seaborne Davies, 'The Treachery Act, 1940' (1941).

45 'He did not like leaving the dirty work': KV 2/680.

45 'pro-German and anti-Jew': KV 2/680.

45 'more stupid than dangerous': KV 2/680.

45 'Because I am a National Socialist': KV2/680.

46 'After thanking him for his offer': KV 2/680.

46 'There is now a definite conspiracy': KV 4/186.

46 'The Leeds group are quite isolated': KV 2/680.

46 'the BU as an organisation': KV 2/680.

47 'the case of Miss Crewe': KV 2/680.

47 'This information is amateurish': KV 2/680.

47 'The organ is working': KV 2/680.

48 'gave me an Xmas sample': KV 2/680.

48 'just to look at': *Yorkshire Post*, 5/11/1940, p. 6.

48 'Fireworks supplied by the RAF': *Daily Mirror*, 6/11/1940, back page.

48 'We've done a job!': This and subsequent quotes from the visit are from KV 2/680.

51 'The attempt had been further wrecked': KV 2/680.

52 A barometer board: *Yorkshire Post*, 14/9/1940.

52 'they kept reiterating': This and subsequent quotes from the visit are from KV 2/680.

58 Sir Alexander Maxwell: Duncan Fairn, 'Maxwell, Sir Alexander (1880–1963)' (2004).

58 'a plump man': Somerset Maugham, quoted in Nigel West, *The Guy Liddell Diaries, Volume I: 1939–1942* (2005).

58 'always beautifully dressed': Stuart Hampshire, quoted in Miranda Carter, *Anthony Blunt* (2001).

59 just thirty-six officers: Andrew (2009).

59 'In the meantime the Germans': KV 4/185.

60 space to intern only 18,000: Gillman (1980).

60 'Farce': KV 4/185.

60 'Large numbers of enemy aliens': KV 4/185.

60 'every person within the fortress': Gillman (1980).

60 'The paltriest kitchen maid': FO 371 25189.

62 One of those men was Eric Roberts: The Red Book: Membership list of Captain Ramsay's Right Club (1939).

63 'Anderson began by saying': KV 4/186.

63 'Collar the lot': Gillman (1980).

63 By July, 753 BUF members: Andrew (2009).

64 'Why this policy was never carried out': KV 4/186.

65 'Unden Order': KV 4/186.

65 'appear to have prepared a kind of Black List': KV 4/186.

65 'Dealt with letter from lady': KV 4/186.

66 'Ostensibly these are said to be let out': KV 6/50.

66 'too far-fetched even for Hitler': CAB 120/468.

66 'the police have found pieces': HW 15/43/59.

67 'I do not think there is a case': KV 2/680.

67 'After their trial, Miss X': Andrew (2009).

68 'down at Windsor': KV 4/187.

68 'I appreciate it may be thought': KV 2/680.

68 'the more disreputable riff-raff': KV 2/680.

72 Wormwood Scrubs . . . was hit: Andrew (2009).

74 'Wasn't it marvellous?': KV 2/899.

75 The supposed German agent: KV 2/898 and Hemming (2017).

75 'He told me all about the Briscoe case': KV 4/187.

75 Nathaniel Mayer Victor Rothschild: Hannah Rothschild, *The Baroness* (2012).

76 When Victor was born: H. Rothschild (2012).

76 She was also considered quite daring: H. Rothschild (2012).

77 a servant was told to walk backwards: H. Rothschild (2012).

77 'simultaneously spoilt and regimented': Victor Rothschild, *Meditations of a Broomstick* (1977).

77 Victor's earliest memory: V. Rothschild (1977).

78 Cambridge-to-London record: Kenneth Rose, *Elusive Rothschild* (2001).

78 'I don't like failing at jobs I do': BBC, 'The Politics of Thinking' (1984).

80 an invitation to the White House: Rose (2001).

80 Sir Harold Hartley: E. J. Bowen, rev. K. D. Watson, 'Hartley, Sir Harold Brewer (1878–1972)', *Oxford Dictionary of National Biography* (2004).

80 Hartley recognised that Rothschild's mind: Rose (2001).

82 'I never thought he cared': Alan Hodgkin, *Chance and Design* (1994).

82 Queen Victoria expressly rejected: Rose (2001).

83 'If I ever have a son': Miriam Rothschild, *Dear Lord Rothschild* (1983).

83 Jewish jokes had disappeared: George Orwell, 'Antisemitism in Britain', *Collected Essays, Journalism and Letters, Vol. III* (1968).

83 'I am Lord Rothschild': Rose (2001).

84 the Waterloo story was a lie: Brian Cathcart, *The News From Waterloo* (2015).

85 'He is quite ruthless': KV 4/186.

86 'I am surprised that somebody': KV4 186.

87 'He thought that we should first try': KV 4/186.

89 'The only problem with this story': Brian Garfield, *The Meinertz-hagen Mystery* (2007).

89 'banned from the British Museum': Garfield (2007).

90 'When one takes a bomb ... to pieces': BBC *Desert Island Discs* interview 7 July 1984.

90 The first bomb Rothschild tackled: Rose (2001).

90 'It was difficult to get hold of': Victor Rothschild, *Random Variables* (1984).

92 'obvious pleasure': V. Rothschild, *Meditations of a Broomstick* (1977).

93 'intricate surgical operation': V. Rothschild, *Meditations of a Broomstick* (1977).

95 'although professedly an English firm': KV2 3313.

95 'obtained direct or indirect access': KV2 3313.

95 'all German subjects': Hansjürgen Koehler, *Inside the Gestapo* (1940).

96 Encouraged by her husband: STV News, 'WWII Spycatchers Revealed After 70 years' (2009).

96 Liddell passed this information: FBI, 'Spies Caught, Spies Lost, Lessons Learned' (2007), and Peter Duffy, *Double Agent* (2014).

97 'In every armament factory in America': Duffy (2014).

97 'The accused showed': KV 2/3313.

97 In 1939, it had 26,000 employees abroad: Wilfried Feldenkirchen, *Siemens 1918–1945* (1999).

98 'far from pro-Nazi': KV 2/3313.

99 a nest of spies: KV 2/2782.

99 'funds beyond his salary': KV 2/2782.

100 'outspokenly anti-British': KV 2/3313.

100 'but the rubber factory': Koehler (1940).

100 'An organisation like Siemens': KV 2/3800.

102 'grossly inaccurate': Roberts family archive.

103 In 1900, at the start of a new century: Carl's story, and Walter and Dorothy's, are in KV 2/540.

104 A month after Britain declared war: Gillman (1980).

104 Along with 25,000 other civilians: Dr Oliver Wilkinson, 'Review of Prisoners of Britain: German Civilian and Combatant Internees During the First World War', *Reviews in History* (2013).

104 'circular arguments': Gillman (1980).

104 'People were still walking around': This and subsequent quotes from the letters are from KV 2/540.

107 The Home Office Warrant system: Andrew (2009), and Calder Walton, *Empire of Secrets* (2013).

107 'The reasons that persons join correspondence clubs': KV 2/3800.

108 'would be keeping extremely quiet': KV 2/3800.

109 'a series of boys': Goronwy Rees, 'A Chapter of Accidents', cited in Rose (2001).

109 'How easily in these darkened streets': Rose (2001).

110 'In the part of London where I work': This and subsequent quotes from the letters are from KV 2/3800.

110 'alarm and despondency': Leo McKinstry, *Operation Sealion* (2014).

117 'pots of jam, syrup, etc': KV 4/123.

120 The first to arrive: McKinstry (2014).

120 'They were singularly badly directed': KV 4/186.

121 'a poor fish': KV 4/187.

121 'Strong has a great regard': KV 4/186.

121 'I began by explaining': KV 4/188.

122 'Good evening, John': HO 45/22382.

124 He fought desperately: KV 4/188.

125 'mighty risks': KV 2/945.

125 'Churchill and his rotten gang': KV 2/3319.

125 'A chap like me': KV 2/3319.

126 'Civilians and military personal': KV 2/3319.

126 At various points during the war: Nigel West and Oleg Tsarev, *Triplex: Secrets from the Cambridge Spies* (2009).

127 'Jock had a habit': KV 4/191.

127 'I cannot afford to take any risks': KV 2/3321.

131 A passing policeman: J. C. Masterman, *The Double Cross System* (1995).

131 'some searching questions': KV 4/188.

132 Carl Brahe: Christened Frederick Charles, but known as Carl to his family.

133 'We didn't think the British public': KV 2/3874.

134 'attractive appearance': KV 2/2677.

134 'composed solely of women': KV 2/2677.

135 'said to have committed himself': KV 2/3800.

136 'A woman of this type': KV 2/3800.

136 'At a convenient moment': KV 4/189.

136 'killed without compunction': McKinstry (2014).

137 'It seems that certain of them already know': KV 4/189.

137 'some innocuous object like the Union Jack': KV 2/3800.

138 'the fools entrusted with the formation': KV 2/540.

138 'Swiss Bank Corporation': KV 4/189.

139 'German Secret Service': KV 2/3800.

140 The line between observer and provocateur: KV 4/188.

140 'took exception to the agent provocateur': KV 4/188.

140 'Intelligence matters were usually of such complexity': KV 4/472.

141 'the PM might speak to the Home Secretary': KV 4/191.

142 'was exactly the technique': KV 2/3800.

144 'the organisation has certain somewhat melodramatic ideas': KV 2/3800.

145 'Gleave would, in time of invasion': KV 2/2677.

145 'a sexual pervert': KV 2/793.

146 'go there and scrub the floors': KV 2/3874 and KV 2/3799.

146 the craft had wing floats: KV 2/3799.

147 'willing to hide German agents': KV 2/3799.

149 'Marita explained': KV 2/3800.

149 In the US, the FBI: Peter Duffy, *Double Agent* (2014).

150 'Look at Marita': This and subsequent quotes are from KV 2/3874.

152 'She feels secure': KV 2/3800.

152 'It has been found impossible': KV 2/3800.

153 'No official or other single individual': KV 4/227 Maxwell Knight, 'History of the operations of MS during the war 1939–45'.

154 'I still pin my faith': Roberts family archive.

155 'remains violently anti-Semitic': KV 2/2677.

155 'There are few, if any': KV 2/3800.

155 'all, without exception, listen in': KV 2/2677.

156 'The papers that day': *Sunday Express* 30/8/42.

156 'The *Daily Mirror* carried a light story': *Daily Mirror* 29/8/42.

157 'We have been having a long discussion': KV 2/3873.

158 'I hear you are more or less': KV 2/3874.

158 'a Jewish war of revenge': Richard Griffiths, *Patriotism Perverted* (1998).

161 'Britain may look a little shop-worn': US War Department, *Instructions for American Servicemen in Britain* (1942).

165 'The whole of the Rothschild family': BBC *Desert Island Discs* interview (1984).

167 The leading initial critic: KV 4/190.

168 Time and again: KV 2/3800.

168 'We certainly do not': KV 2/3799.

168 'I have rarely heard': KV 6/119.

168 'experiments were going on': KV 2/3800.

168 'the whole question in its proper perspective': KV 4/190.

169 'We must I think': This and subsequent quotes from the diary are from KV 4/190.

173 'would be willing to do anything': KV 6/118.

173 'very high up and drawing a huge salary': Garfield (2007).

174 There had been one, Jane Archer: Andrew (2009).

175 'a matter of expediency': KV 6/118.

185 'a washout': KV 2/3874.

186 As raids over Germany increased: http://www.rafinfo.org.uk/bcww2losses/.

187 'the man who broke the bloody beam': R. V. Jones, *Most Secret War* (1978).

188 'I told Kohout that he was not to consider': KV 2/3873.

189 'Kohout has hit upon something': KV 6/118.

193 'Roberts gave his reply: "Yes"': KV 4/190.

194 'Robbie, you have the art': Roberts family archive.

196 'necessary or desirable': KV 4/191.

197 He proposed blackmailing the organisation: KV 2/3873. The file doesn't specify the exact nature of Bernard's blackmail demand, but it is clear that he had threatened exposure of the Fifth Column.

198 'showed an excellent capacity': KV 2/3873.

200 'She keeps on telling me how funny it is': KV 2/3874.

201 'They were watching the RAF': KV 2/3874.

202 'I looked in vain': KV 2/3873.

203 'It was a very successful raid': KV 2/3874.

204 'very simple advice': and following quotes are from KV 2/2487.

205 'She swore that Britain would get it back': and following quotes are from KV 2/2487.

205 'is now working wholeheartedly': KV 2/3800.

205 'Herzig looks honest and decent': KV 2/3800.

206 'she's very keen': KV 2/3874.

206 'more or less backed out': KV 2/3800.

206 'dirty traitor': KV 2/3874.

207 'Marita remarked that she sometimes wondered': KV 2/3873.

207 'I'm compelled to be quite frank': KV 2/3874.

207 'Kohout proudly produced a revolver': KV 2/3800.

209 'anything for a litre of wine': (Macintyre).

210 'She really ought to be locked up': KV 4/191.

213 Men had been forced out of work: Andrew Martin Mitchell, 'Fascism in East Anglia' (1999).

214 'I could see our privileges': Mitchell (1999).

215 'The fascist idea': (Mitchell).

215 Creasy persuaded Mosley: Stephen Dorril, *Blackshirt* (2006).

216 A local journalist wrote confidentially: KV 2/4021.

218 Hitler was 'a good man': KV 2/4021.

218 'The happiness, the contentment': Mitchell (1999).

218 'National Socialist atmosphere': KV 2/4021.

218 Perigoe mentioned the Creasys: KV 2/4021.

219 'pretty immoral': KV 2/4022.

221 'I fear that this report does not': KV 2/4022.

221 Kohout visited the Creasys again: KV 2/4022.

221 'HIS MAJESTY WLADYSLAW THE FIFTH': KV2/4022.

223 she'd been 'rather silly': KV 2/4022.

224 'It should be considered': KV 2/4022.

224 'I call upon God': Peter Stubley, *Calendar of Crime* (2014).

225 In 1941, the US Army Air Force: Juliet Gardiner, *Wartime* (2004).

226 viewed as 'dangerous people': KV 2/4022.

228 'The recent Allied successes': and following quotes are from KV 2/3800.

231 'Careless Talk Costs Lives': KV 2/3874.

231 In May 1943, Sir David Petrie: KV 2/3873.

232 'exact experimental results': KV 2/3873.

232 'whose genius at this type of work': KV 2/3800.

233 'there is nothing to which exception': KV 4/192.

234 'On a Tuesday evening': KV 4/193.

234 'We do not consider that Jack': KV 2/3800.

235 'proved to be an egg shell of a man': Roberts family archive.

236 'When looking at the devastation': KV 2/3800.

239 Hilda Leech meanwhile: KV 6/119.

240 'Some Austrian woman': KV 4/193.

241 'Sokl said that whatever the outcome': KV 2/3800.

242 That left one bomb unaccounted for: KV 4/193.

242 'It is a crate in three compartments': V. Rothschild, *Meditations of a Broomstick* (1977).

245 a 'nursing home' for 'miserable seamen': Rothschild letter to Duff Cooper, quoted in Rose (2001).

245 'At one moment it looked': KV 4/193.

245 The pair had to be eased apart: Rose (2001).

246 'is almost always interpreted': Rothschild letter to Duff Cooper, quoted in Rose (2001).

246 'She had heard from a friend': KV 2/3801.

247 'whatever political opinions were held': KV 2/3801.

249 'I was close as damn it': Boberts family archive.
    'We spend most of our time': Rothschild letter to Duff Cooper, quoted in Rose (2001).

254 'headquarters which are in the country': KV 4/195.

254 'It looks a little': KV 4/195 Dec. 20, 1944.

256 On 15 April 1945: Alexander van Straubenzee, 'The Gate of Hell', *Daily Telegraph* (2005).

256 In the following month: US Holocaust Museum.

260 'This may be rather difficult': KV 4/466.

261 'On the face of it, Kohout's tentative proposals': KV 6/118.

263 'A prosecution is out of the question': KV 2/3800.

265 'staggering tour de force': KV 2/3800.

265 'It must be clearly understood': KV 4/227.

265 'directly or indirectly in contact': Curry (1999).

266 'destroy or replace by scrambled extracts': KV 6/67.

269 'There is no doubt': KV 4/190.

269 By 1949, when he spoke to Roberts: KV 4/471.

269 At that stage the inquiry: Tom Bower, *The Perfect English Spy* (1995).

272 'devastating': V. Rothschild, *Random Variables* (1984).

272 'I lost confidence': BBC, 'The Politics of Thinking' (1984).

275 'part charlatan, part fantasist': Letter to the author.

275 'lots of men in brown felt hats': Hemming (2017).

277 It gained brief notoriety: Rob Baker, *Beautiful Idiots and Brilliant Lunatics* (2015).

Index